TORAH:
LAW OR GRACE?

SIMCHAT TORAH BEIT MIDRASH®

TORAH: LAW OR GRACE?

Kingdom PRINCIPLES for Kingdom LIVING

RABBI RALPH MESSER

SIMCHAT TORAH BEIT MIDRASH PUBLISHING™
PARKER, COLORADO

Published by Simchat Torah Beit Midrash Publishing
Post Office Box 4810
Parker, Colorado 80134

Simchat Torah Beit Midrash Publishing is a division of
Simchat Torah Beit Midrash International Center, Parker, Colorado

Printed in the United States.

ISBN: 978-0-983-36568-6
ISBN: 978-0-615-44467-3

DEDICATION

To each of my students and to all those I desire to assist in discovering their true potential, by walking in the Principles of God, led by the Holy Spirit.

To all the individuals who have ever quietly dreamt of becoming or doing something significant with their lives, yet they never believed it was possible... and now you are facilitating Torah classes worldwide.

To the millions of people negatively influenced by the misconceptions of many misguided doctrines, teachings, and even spiritual leaders, resulting in a continuing blindness to your true abilities found only in the Torah Principles, led of the Holy Spirit.

To the aspiring and developing Torah teacher within each of us—may we all discover the original meaning and intention of our Creator.

To my Simchat Torah Beit Midrash family and the International Center for Torah Studies...thank you for believing in me when no one else did.

ACKNOWLEDGEMENTS

This book is a product of a lifetime of personal learning and development, as well as the collective contribution of many mentors, teachers, supporters, advisors, friends, and family. I am continually cognizant that each of us are the sum total of our own learning and the contributions made by so many people to our lives as we journey towards our ultimate destiny.

No achievement in life is without the help of many known and unknown individuals who have impacted us. We owe every measure of our success to the vast array of input from so many who make this work possible:

- To my beloved wife of 32 years, Maureen, for your unwavering support.
- To my parents: Ralph Sr. and Beatrice Messer.

To my daughter Nicole and son-in-law Will Martin and their daughter Shaina...

To my son Russell Messer and his wife Dina and their children Naomi and Asher...

To my son Brandon Messer and his wife Heidi and their daughter Tori...

To my son Grant Gabriel Messer.

To my son Aaron John Messer...

To my daughter Moriah Sharon Messer...

...For allowing your dad to pursue his passion and purpose in taking Torah to the Nations. The Lord has called this family for the divine assignment of teaching the Torah, led of the Holy Spirit, to all Nations.

To my lead Board Members, John and Anne Nanton, John and Nancy Shuffle, Judy Murphy, Jan and Linda Jensen, and the balance of the Board Team.

To Pastor Mark Byrne, Deborah Schermerhorn, Safronia White, Rosie Brinkman and Stephanie Bevins. Your relentless pursuit of and patience with me during the inception, development, and delivery of this work was a tremendous source of motivation and encouragement. You are a writer's dream and a gift to the literary arts.

To my Pastoral Staff: Pastor Dick Beck, Pastor Michael Schaefer, Pastor Will Martin, Pastor Nicole Martin, Pastor Mark Byrne, Minister Russell Messer, Minister Jeremy Thompson, and Minister Dee Marcanno.

To the Project Management Team that facilitated this book: Pastor Nicole Martin, Pastor Mark Byrne, Minister Russell Messer, Principal Brandon and Heidi Messer, Rosie Brinkman, Safronia White, Kenny and Carla Teague, Karen Beck, Hope Medina, and Carol Williams.

To my Simchat Torah Beit Midrash family and the International Center for Torah Studies family, who allowed me the privilege to develop, share, and test the Hebrew concepts and Principles presented in this book during our relationship over the past thirty-two years. Without you, my vision for this book would have remained just a dream. I am forever grateful.

Finally, I acknowledge and thank the ultimate Torah Teacher above all teachers, Yeshua, who Himself established the standard for all true teachers to measure up to. I am forever indebted and grateful to You for Your eternal gift of life and for igniting within me the Spirit of Messiah.

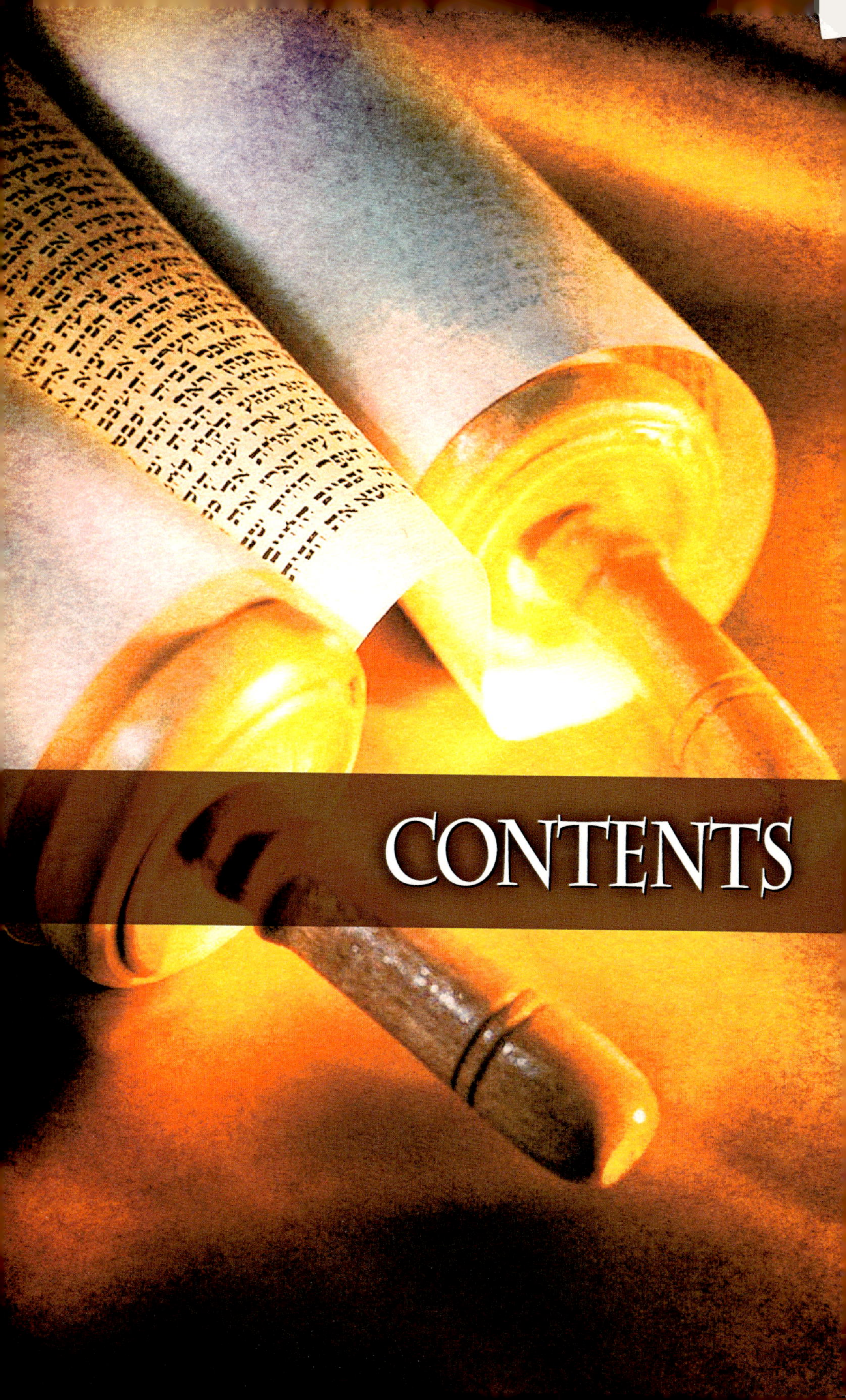
CONTENTS

At the beginning of each chapter in this book you will find a QR (Quick Response) code. Each code can be scanned by the QR reader or camera on your smartphone to link to additional teaching material on STBM's website: www.Torah.tv. (For those who do not currently have access to smartphone technology, please visit www.Torah.tv and click on "Articles" to access printed teachings of the QR code content) By simply scanning the QR codes, the reader has access to more than 18 hours of related teaching at no additional cost!

FOREWORD

FOREWORD

In the Bible there is a prophecy, and that prophecy states that in the end times a great multitude of people will rise up suddenly from among the nations and return to Israel. The prophecy tells us that this movement of people will start happening simultaneously across the world, from the four corners of the earth, as if these people are responding to some kind of Biblical post-hypnotic suggestion.

The Bible records that after the historic Exodus from Egypt, the Israelites turned away from the God of their deliverance to serve the pagan gods of the civilizations around them. For their disobedience and disregard of the Word of God, the prophets correctly predicted that the tribes of Israel would be conquered and exiled until the end of time, when they would be found and redeemed.

So let me ask you a question...What if it were actually happening? I'm talking about millions of people fulfilling a nearly 3,000 year old prophecy. And today we can match the prophecies with real world events. And the reason it should matter is because once these people do what the Bible predicts they will do—they trigger the Apocalypse!

Armageddon, a name synonymous with the Apocalypse is in fact, Mount Megiddo (*Har Megiddo* in Hebrew), a fortress city in northern Israel. Armageddon is the location for one of the bloodiest future conflicts on the earth. But it won't happen before the Israelite tribes who once lived on this land return. According to prophecy, the countdown to the Apocalypse and final redemption begins when these tribes "awaken" one-by-one and return.[1]

The message contained in this book has huge spiritual ramifications, the effects of which can be felt across the globe. I have taught throughout the world, and no teaching has provoked more controversy or been met with such tension and resistance as this one. The spirit realm, principalities, powers, and rulers of darkness oppose this message like no other. At times, the very mention of the word *Torah* (God's Teaching and Instruction) provokes this intense opposition because the enemy knows his days are numbered. This message and the understanding of this truth are a fulfillment of the prophetic move of God at the end of the age. The restoration and re-gathering of God's people has begun—the great end-times harvest (Matthew 13) and the final **Greater Exodus** (Jeremiah 16).

Torah: Law or Grace? is the chronicle of a journey and I invite you to go on this journey with me. Your true identity as a believer, that undiscovered "something" that you've been searching for, and a greater understanding of the living God of prophecy dwelling within you is about to be revealed!

—*Rabbi Ralph Messer*

PREFACE

Detroit Tribal Revival, Part 1

To view a video segment of this resource, scan the QR code using your mobile device.

There are two parallel components to the Gospel message: the Person Yeshua (Jesus) and the Principles of Yeshua.

THE PERSON YESHUA	THE PRINCIPLES OF YESHUA
Yeshua is the Son of God.	The Principles are the System of God.
Yeshua is the Life of God within you.	The Principles are the Instructions of God around you.
Yeshua creates your peace.	The Principles create your prosperity.
Yeshua is the King.	The Principles are the Kingdom.
Yeshua is the Experience of God.	The Principles are the Expertise of God.
Yeshua (Salvation) is always experienced instantaneously.	The Principles (Redemption) are learned progressively.

Webster's Dictionary defines a 'principle' as:

a: a comprehensive and fundamental law, doctrine, or assumption.
b: a rule or code of conduct
c: habitual devotion to right *principles*; e.g. "a man of *principle*."

Yeshua defines and *develops* His Principles within you! His Principles produce the abundant life that will exceed your greatest dreams. Your dreams require a Torah Principle! There are 613 Torah Principles found in Genesis, Exodus, Leviticus, Numbers, and Deuteronomy *(See Appendices A and B).*

A Torah Principle applied accurately will cause you to prosper financially, physically, emotionally, and spiritually!

Wisdom is seeing what God sees. Understanding is doing what God does.

A Torah Principle produces self-confidence which is magnetic.

Strength is the product of focus and focus is the product of a Torah Principle.

Rejecting a Torah Principle makes you undecided, unlearned, unfocused, and unenthusiastic.

Rejecting a Torah Principle is like having faith in your adversary.

Ignoring a Torah Principle produces failure and delays Divine success.

Obeying a Torah Principle multiplies productivity and schedules success.

A Torah Principle in action influences the atmosphere around you.

A Torah Principle contains God's Divine Presence.

The Divine Presence is experienced by walking in the Torah Principles.

A Torah Principle applied accurately will always produce the desired result.

When you pursue a man-made principle that God did not instruct, it will not sustain you emotionally, physically, or financially.

A Torah Principle is defined as self-imposed standards and restrictions motivated by a desire that is greater than the alternatives.

A Torah Principle is defined as the nature of discipline which causes self-management, regulated by a code of conduct or a specific set of goals and commitments, dictated by an intended result.

Torah Principles are a series of decisions prescribed by a determined destiny.

The Torah is the Spirit of Discipline that is rooted in self-control, and self-control is a fruit of the Spirit.

A Torah Principle develops the understanding that he who cannot rule himself will never control life.

A Torah Principle develops the understanding that self-discipline is the manifestation of the highest form of government—self-government.

The words 'disciple' and 'discipline' come from the Hebrew root word *talmid* meaning 'student' or 'pupil.' A disciple or *talmid* is therefore, a "student of the Torah!"

A disciple—a student of the Torah—is a learner dedicated to concentrated and focused instruction, and committed to learning to think like his Teacher (Yeshua) thinks.

A Torah Principle cultivates an attitude of persistence and a spirit of leadership that never gives up until it achieves its goal—it is a spirit that never quits.

Your Faith attached to a Torah Principle generates the power to hold on in spite of everything, the power to endure, and the ability to face defeat again and again and never give up.

Your Faith attached to a Torah Principle produces the endurance to believe, and the ability to keep pushing forward, even in the face of difficulty, knowing that victory is yours.

Torah Principles produce leaders who persist because they have a firm grasp of their purpose, who know where they are going, and who are confident they will arrive there.

INTRODUCTION

Detroit Tribal Revival, Part 2
To view a video segment of this resource, scan the QR code using your mobile device.

"In the beginning
God created the heavens
and the earth.
The earth was without form,
and void;
and darkness was
on the face of
the deep. And the
Spirit of God
was hovering over the
face of the waters.
Then God said..."[1]
(Genesis 1:1-3)

"In the beginning
was the Word, and the
Word was with God, and
the Word was God. He
was in the beginning with
God...In Him was life, and
the life was the light of men.
And the light shines in the
darkness, and the darkness
did not comprehend it."[2]
(John 1:1-4)

Most believers today have not been taught the distinction between **Salvation** and **Redemption.** These two components of the Gospel message are summed up in the Person Jesus Christ—*Yeshua* in Hebrew. Salvation is *only* found in the Person Yeshua while Redemption is manifested through the Principles of Yeshua—the *Torah,* simply defined as **God's Teaching and Instruction.**

Salvation secures your eternal standing in Heaven and Redemption relates to your temporal walk on the Earth. It is the grace of God that draws you to Salvation (Yeshua), and it is the grace of God that leads you to Redemption (Torah).

The Person Yeshua is
the Grace of Salvation!

The Principles of Yeshua are
the Grace of Redemption!

The Principles of Yeshua govern the universe, affecting you and everything around you. Yeshua is the King and the Torah is His government in the earth. Yeshua and the Torah are not a religion, but rather a visible manifestation of the invisible God, the King and His Kingdom, Salvation and Redemption—*the Kingdom of Heaven.*

God rules His Kingdom by His Word. Everything He does, He does using the Principles of the Torah. When you operate in the Torah, you assume your legal position and standing as a child of the King. God's purpose for your life becomes clearer and His Voice is heard as you follow His *Teaching and Instruction.*

When you return to the Principles of the Torah, you are returning to your source. When you return to your source, you encounter your Creator. In the Presence of your Creator, change occurs, and His purpose becomes established within you. As you honor and follow the Person and the Principles of Yeshua, you discover that you are not keeping the Torah, but rather the Torah is keeping you! You didn't choose to follow Jesus, Jesus chose you (John 15)! Likewise, you didn't find the Torah, the Torah found you. God is the One who is motivating you and causing you to obey His Voice, in order to establish His purpose through you, and in the earth.

"Thus the heavens and the earth were finished,
and all their array. By the seventh day God completed
His work which He had done, and He abstained on the
seventh day from all His work which He had done.
God blessed the seventh day and sanctified it
because on it He abstained from all His work which
God created to make." [3]

(Genesis 2: 1-3)

As the Creator of all things, God established the order of the universe, the luminaries in the heavens, and a paradise on the earth called Eden. However, there was a problem! The Garden of Eden concealed a formidable enemy determined to sabotage the plan of God by deceiving His preeminent creation—Man. God created Man, both male and female, in His image and likeness. God blessed Man with dominion and authority, and destined Man to rule and reign over all creation. God's kingdom was to be established on the earth and His government was to be the code of conduct for mankind.

However, from the Garden, Man has been lured away from following God's ways, as other, un-godly forms of dominion and conduct began to develop. Man's attempts to perfect his own ways became rituals and religions trying to appease God. Man even desired to become his own god and to establish his own form of government. The tragic results have been a loss of Man's original dominion and authority, causing mankind to weaken and decrease in strength. Man's fallen nature soon became a *mockery* of God rather than the human nature *revealing* God, as originally intended.

God's purpose and redemptive plan for mankind is given in His Word. It is instilled within our hearts and minds according to the New Covenant. God and Man were meant to dwell together! God desires to manifest His holiness within Man and for Man to display this holiness on the earth. God's Kingdom is being established on the earth in our days! As a believer, the dominion and authority of the King dwell within you. You are part of His royal family, His covenant, His constitution and government called, the *Kingdom of Heaven*—God's movement upon the earth!

In order to move forward in this revelation of God's Kingdom, we must look back into the Hebrew roots of the Christian faith. From there we can begin to recover a proper understanding of the Torah, the history of Judaism and the early Church, and the changes that estranged Christianity from its Hebrew heritage—ancient misunderstandings which, in many cases, still permeate the teachings and doctrines of Christianity today.

CHAPTER 1

TORAH: THE HISTORICAL UNDERSTANDING

Detroit Tribal Revival, Part 3
To view a video segment of this resource, scan the QR code using your mobile device.

As we begin, ask yourself this question: Did Jesus have a King James Version of the Bible? Did He have a Catholic Bible? What Scriptures did Jesus use? He had the Torah!

So just what is *Torah?* Traditionally, the word Torah refers to the first five Books of the Bible: Genesis, Exodus, Leviticus, Numbers, and Deuteronomy (also known by the Greek word, *Pentateuch*). The Torah was given to Moses and the Israelites at Mount Sinai, *after* God had delivered them from the bondage of Egyptian slavery. In other words, the Torah was given to a **redeemed** people to teach them how to live a **redeemed** lifestyle.

The Hebrew word "Torah" is derived from two other Hebrew words: *"or"* (Strong's #216) meaning "light" and *"yarah" (Strong's #3384)* which means to "shoot an arrow."

"In the beginning God created the heavens and the earth.
The earth was without form, and void;
and darkness was on the face of the deep.
And the Spirit of God was hovering over the face of the
waters. Then God said, "Let there be light (or):"
and there was light (or)." [1]

(Genesis 1:1-3, emphasis added)

The light *(or)* of Creation is a fitting root word for Torah. The ancient sages have long taught that God created everything with the 22 letters of the Hebrew alphabet and the Torah. The very first words of the Bible portray the utter nothingness into which God spoke and created all things. In Hebrew, the account in Genesis calls this environment *"Tohu v'bohu"* meaning *"chaos and emptiness."* It was this oppressive darkness, devoid of life, that was forever pierced by the Divine "light" of God. This primordial light *(or)* was the very first utterance of Creation, even "days" before the formation of the sun, the moon, and the stars. God spoke, and light was the manifestation of His Word. By His light *(or),* God drove back the darkness, and brought order to chaos.

"By the Word of the LORD the heavens
were made, and all the host of them
by the breath of His mouth...
Let all the inhabitants of the world
stand in awe of Him." [2]

(Psalms 33:6-8)

Torah is the blueprint and its study is the soul of Creation. God's ineffable word took physical form. Heaven and earth and all their fullness became the clothing for the word of God which infuses creation, and without which the world could not continue to exist. The fire of Torah became garbed in ink and parchment, and God's wisdom, which is the essence of Torah, was embedded in its words and letters.[3]

A second root word of Torah is *yarah,* meaning to shoot an arrow.[4] Picture an archer releasing an arrow from his bow. If the arrow hits the target, in other words, the arrow was properly directed and guided, and it reached the goal to which the archer had pointed it—in Hebrew, the arrow is *Torah*—it hit the mark. If the arrow misses, however, it is called by the Hebrew word *"chatah"* or *"sin"* in English, which simply means to miss the mark.

> *The Hebrew word Torah has been translated into English as "Law." Strictly speaking, Torah refers to the first five books of the Bible, including the instructions they contain. In the wider sense of the word, Torah is often used to refer to the whole of Hebrew Scriptures, what many call the Old Testament. The more proper name for the Hebrew Scriptures is the word TANAKH.* [5]

The Hebrew word *Tanakh* is an acronym for the three major sections of the Scriptures:

- TORAH: *Genesis, Exodus, Leviticus, Numbers, & Deuteronomy*
- NEVI'IM: *The Major and Minor Prophets*
- KETUVIM: *The Writings—Psalms, Proverbs, Ecclesiastes, etc.*

Combined, these three sections comprise the Old Testament or *Tanakh*. While the *Nevi'im* (Prophets) and the *Ketuvim* (Psalms, Proverbs, etc.) are the subject of many teachings and study today, ironically, the Torah (Genesis—Deuteronomy) is one of the least studied, and therefore most misunderstood sections of the average Christian's Bible. Frequently, the familiar *through-the-Bible-in-a-year* reading attempt stalls out quickly after the fascinating stories in Genesis and Exodus give way to the detailed instructions for offerings, the priests, and the Sanctuary given in Leviticus, Numbers, and Deuteronomy. Not surprisingly, this generally results in a limited understanding of these foundational Scriptures. Combined with a prevailing undercurrent of teaching which states that the Torah no longer applies to believers, most non-Jewish members of the Body of Christ have a profoundly distorted view of the Torah.

Surprising to many, the Hebrew word *Torah* does not mean "Law." In its simplest definition, "Torah" means "Teaching" and "Instruction" therefore, the **Torah** is **God's Teaching and Instruction!** If Jesus, our Lord and Savior, lived according to the Torah, and taught from the Torah, how did His followers come to be so distanced from these Scriptures of Jesus? How is it that many believers today even question whether or not the Torah has been done away with?

Just where did we get the idea that Judaism is a religion of law and works, while Christianity is a religion of grace and faith? When did we separate the Creator into a wrathful God of the Old Testament and a merciful God of the New Testament? How did we get to the point where we hold Synagogue services on Saturday and Church services on Sunday? How did we come to view the Torah as an oppressive "Law" of God, and "Grace" as freedom in Christ Jesus?

When and how were these seeds of division and confusion planted? How did our current beliefs and understandings begin, and where did all the confusion originate? By uncovering the history surrounding the Scriptures, the Jewish people, and the Church, we can understand what the Torah is and what it is not, and we'll be better positioned to answer the question: "What is the Torah: Law or Grace?"

THE JEWISH MINDSET OF TORAH

Early in the 12th century, the now famous Rabbi Moshe ben Maimon (Rambam) developed a comprehensive list of the Principles found within the Five Books of Moses—the Torah. Rambam listed 613 separate Commands—248 Positive (e.g. *"You shall…*) and 365 Negative (e.g. *"You shall not…*). He further compared the 248 positive Commands to the 248 bones and organs in the human body, and the 365 negative Commands to the 365 days in a solar year.[6] Rambam's work was so foundational that his numbering system is still widely in use today. *(For a complete list of the 613 Principles please see Appendix A and B in the back of this book.)*

When studying the 613 Principles of the Torah, it quickly becomes apparent that there are various types of Commands. Rambam and others further divide these 613 Principles into separate categories. There are Commands for men, women, kings, priests, and offerings; Commands that can only be observed within the Land of Israel, and only within the Sanctuary or Temple in Jerusalem.

Moses recorded all of the 613 Commands or Principles given by God, yet the Scriptures relate that only the first ten were heard by the entire congregation of Israel gathered at Mount Sinai (Exodus 20). These "Ten Commandments" provide the best system for categorizing all of the 613 Principles of the Torah. On two tablets, God inscribed the Ten Commandments. The first five commandments teach us about our relationship with God. The last five commandments instruct us about our relationship with one another.

> *God created the world from a plan and for a purpose. His plan was the Torah, which preceded the world, and His purpose was that human beings find the meaning and the goal of creation in the Torah. "He looked into the Torah and created the world," and He designed the universe to make it possible for human beings to carry out the commandments.*[7]

When questioned by the experts in the Law of Moses, Jesus was asked which of the Commands was the greatest in all of the Torah. His response is beautiful and elegant, returning simplicity to an otherwise complex codification of God's Law. Jesus summarized all of the Torah and the Prophets in one word!

613 Commands of the Torah—God's Teaching and Instruction. 613 Principles which govern our relationship with God, and with each other; Instructions from God for men, women, kings, and priests; Teachings for Feasts and Festivals, Offerings, and the Sanctuary. 613 Commands in the five Books of God's Law; Ten Commandments written on two Tablets; one Great Command—Jesus' summary of the Law—one unifying Word.

"Jesus said to him,
'You shall **love** the LORD your God
with all your heart, with all your soul,
and with all your mind.'
This is the first and great commandment.
And the second is like it:
'You shall **love** your neighbor as yourself.'
On these two commandments
hang all the Law and the Prophets." [8]
(Matthew 22:35-40, emphasis added)

JUST SOMETHING ABOUT THAT NAME

"This is the history of the heavens
and the earth when they were created,
in the day that the **LORD God**
made the earth and the heavens..." [9]
(Genesis 2:3-4, emphasis added)

The Creation account in Genesis begins by using the Hebrew term *Elohim,* translated into English as "God." After the creation of Man, Genesis Chapter 2 expands the revelation of the Creator, with the first mention of the four-letter Name for God—*YHWH.* This Name, considered by many to be too holy to utter, is called the *Tetragrammaton* (four letters), and is most often translated into English as 'Lord' or 'LORD' using all capitals.

Because ancient Hebrew contains no actual vowels, the correct pronunciation of *YHWH* is uncertain. Even with the inclusion of vowels used in modern Hebrew, there remain hundreds of possible pronunciations of the Name *YHWH.*

The Ten Commandments clearly prohibit taking the Name of God in vain—perhaps best understood as "to not use the Name of God in a common manner." While discussion and debate still surround the actual intent and wording of this Command, a safeguard against transgressing the instruction developed very early in Judaism. To protect against inadvertently—or even intentionally—speaking God's Name in vain, tradition soon evolved towards avoiding the use of the Name *YHWH* at all. In honor and respect, God's Name soon became 'ineffable' or unspeakable, and other terms were developed to refer to God without speaking the four-letter Name of *YHWH.*

The lone exception to this practice was the *Kohen Gadol* (High Priest) of Israel, who once a year pronounced God's holy Name on *Yom Kippur* (Day of Atonement)—the second of the Biblical Fall Feasts (Leviticus 23). Carrying basins containing the blood of a sacrificial goat, the prepared incense for the Golden Altar, and bearing the names of the tribes of Israel upon his breastplate, the High Priest would enter the holiest place in the Sanctuary—the Holy of Holies. After placing the incense on the altar, and anointing the cover of the Ark of the Covenant (also called the Mercy Seat) with the blood, the High Priest would then declare the ineffable Name of YHWH in witness of the yearly atonement and forgiveness for the sins of the people (Leviticus 16).[10]

Most Synagogues today, as well as the vast majority of Jewish Biblical texts and literature, use a substitute term for the Tetragrammaton—*Hashem*, a Hebrew term meaning "the Name." In Hebrew understanding, the term "*Hashem*" has taken on two complementary meanings:

1. The ineffable Name—YHWH
2. Lifestyle—Torah

It's important to understand that the Hebrew language is verb-based as opposed to a noun-based language such as English. In other words, Hebrew is a language that is centrally focused on action and movement (verbs), rather than objects and places (nouns). This contrast between Hebrew and most Western languages becomes all the more clear when considering not just the holy Name of God, but all names in general. From the Hebrew perspective, names identify the nature and character, the activity and lifestyle of an individual. One of the reasons the Scriptures contain multiple "Names" for God is to progressively reveal more and more of His infinite nature and character. God's Name is synonymous with His action and activity on the earth—God's movement called, the Kingdom of Heaven.

A clear example of this Hebrew understanding is found in the Torah as Moses receives a revelation of God's Name that was unknown to the earlier generations.

"God spoke to Moses and said to him:
'I am the Lord. I appeared to Abraham,
to Isaac, and to Jacob,
as God Almighty, but by
My Name **Lord** I was not known to them.'" [11]

(Exodus 6:2-3, emphasis added)

Contextually, God is not telling Moses that He neglected to reveal Himself to the Patriarchs—to Abraham, Isaac, and Jacob. In fact, God is telling Moses that He had indeed *appeared* to each of them, but that the revelation of the Name YHWH—LORD was given to Moses. As previously discussed, the Tetragrammaton appears first in Genesis Chapter 2. Yet Exodus 6 tells us that the LORD is revealing Himself to Moses by a Name that was not known to the patriarchs. The Bible may be implying that by the time of Abraham—born approximately 1948 years after Creation—the correct pronunciation of the Tetragrammaton (YHWH) had gone from respectfully 'unspeakable' to entirely 'unknown.' The exchange between God and Moses can be thought of as a restoration of the Name of YHWH. This was not a restoration of a title or a specific name that God prefers His people to use, but rather, this is an increased revelation of God's nature, character, and actions (lifestyle). This revelation is given just as God is about to manifest Himself to Moses and the Israelites in their deliverance from Egyptian slavery and the oppressive bondage of Pharaoh. The LORD later expounds upon His nature and character contained within this Name:

"Now the Lord descended in the cloud
and stood with him there, and proclaimed
the Name of the Lord. And the Lord passed
before him and proclaimed,
"The Lord, the Lord God,
merciful and gracious, longsuffering, and
abounding in goodness and truth,
keeping mercy for thousands,
forgiving iniquity and transgression and sin,
by no means clearing the guilty,
visiting the iniquity of the fathers
upon the children and the children's children
to the third and the fourth generation." [12]

(Exodus 34:5-7)

Remember that when your Bible uses the term "LORD" this is a translation of the four-letter Hebrew Name of God—YHWH. It is this Name, not the title "God" (*Elohim* In Hebrew) which appears nearly 7,000 times in the Torah and the *Tanakh.* The revelation of this Name is profound and progressive throughout the Bible, describing God's nature and character, *and* declaring the lineage and the lifestyle of the King of kings and LORD of lords in His Incarnation—YHWH in the flesh.

King David, in one of his many Messianic prophecies declared that the Messiah would come in the Name of YHWH.

"The stone which the builders
rejected Has become the chief cornerstone.
This was the LORD's doing;
it is marvelous in our eyes.
This is the day the LORD has made;
We will rejoice and be glad in it.
Save now, I pray, O LORD; O LORD,
I pray, send now prosperity.
Blessed is he who comes in the
name of the LORD!" [13]

(Psalms 118:22-26)

Jesus (Yeshua) came in the Name YHWH and the lifestyle of Torah. A significant aspect of Yeshua's ministry on earth was to manifest the Name of God to His people. YHWH's nature and character are fully expressed in His Salvation—Yeshua, Jesus Christ. And the lifestyle and activity of YHWH are eternally proclaimed in His Redemption—the Torah, God's Teaching and Instruction.

" I have manifested Your Name
to the men whom
You have given Me out of the world.
They were Yours, You gave them to Me,
and they have kept Your word.
"Now they have known that all things
which You have given Me are from You." [14]

(John 17:6-7)

THE KINGDOM OF HEAVEN

Another common practice in Jewish writing is to hyphenate all references to God's Name, for example G-d or L-rd. While the Bible does not make use of hyphenations, there are four prominent "substitute" terms used in the Bible to refer to YHWH, without actually using the four-letter Name of YHWH. These terms are:

- Kingdom of Heaven
- Kingdom of God
- Son of Man
- Son of God

"The people who sat in darkness
have seen a great light,
And upon those who sat
in the region and shadow of death
Light has dawned."
From that time Jesus began
to preach and to say,
'Repent, for the kingdom of
heaven is at hand.'" [15]
(Matthew 4:16-17, emphasis added)

As the Gospels relate the accounts of Jesus' earthly ministry, one particular phrase stands out above most others—*the Kingdom of Heaven.* In fact, Jesus *(Yeshua)* taught more on this one topic than any other, including salvation! As defined earlier, the Kingdom of Heaven is God's movement and activity on the earth. However, from the Hebrew perspective, the term "Kingdom of Heaven" refers not only to the activity of YHWH, it also refers to YHWH Himself!

When Jesus states that the *Kingdom of Heaven* is at hand, He is declaring that the power and Presence of YHWH is standing in our midst! Jesus is putting into motion the great move of God called the *Kingdom of Heaven,* which revealed both the **Salvation** of God (the Person Yeshua), *and* His **Redemption** (the Principles of Yeshua).

> *The Kingdom of Heaven—God's movement on the earth—is led by Jesus Christ (Yeshua HaMashiach in Hebrew) and walking in the Torah. Paul had this exact idea in mind when he wrote to the believers in Galatia to "walk in the spirit…" (Galatians 5:25). The walk (halachah in Hebrew) refers to the Torah. The Spirit is, of course, Jesus, Himself. Paul meant that believers should allow the Holy Spirit to control their*

lives so that they could live a life that pleased God. The Holy Spirit would live out the Torah which was written on their hearts and minds (Jeremiah 31:31-33; Hebrews 8:8-12)—this is the New Covenant! God is taking what's already written on your heart and manifesting it by His Spirit to produce purpose, obedience, and abundant blessings in your life. The Torah was not abolished; it has been placed within us! [16]

When your confession (Jesus) matches your conduct (Torah), it is called *Ha Kavod*—the Glory of God. When the Scriptures refer to the glory, the related Hebrew words are temple, tabernacle, place, and lineage. Therefore, when you *walk in the Spirit* today, your lineage to the thousandth generation is blessed by the power of the Holy Spirit, and blessed in your obedience to the Torah. The "weakness" of the covenant at Mount Sinai was human disobedience (Hebrews 8). Under the New Covenant, this weakness is overcome by the obedience and righteousness of Jesus in you. His Holy Spirit inspires and enables you to follow His Teaching and Instruction, not written on Tablets of stone, but placed upon tablets of flesh (2 Corinthians 3). This is the New Covenant, first given in Jeremiah Chapter 31, and repeated in Hebrews Chapter 8.

"Behold, the days are coming,
says the Lord,
when I will make a new covenant
with the house of Israel and
with the house of Judah—
"not like the covenant that I made
with their fathers in the day
that I took them by the hand
to lead them out of the land of Egypt,

My covenant which they broke,
though I was a husband to them,
says the Lord." But this is the covenant
that I will make with the
house of Israel after those days,
says the Lord:
I will put My law in their minds,
and I will write it on their hearts;
and I will be their God,
and they shall be My people." [17]

(Jeremiah 31:31-33; Hebrews 8:8-12)

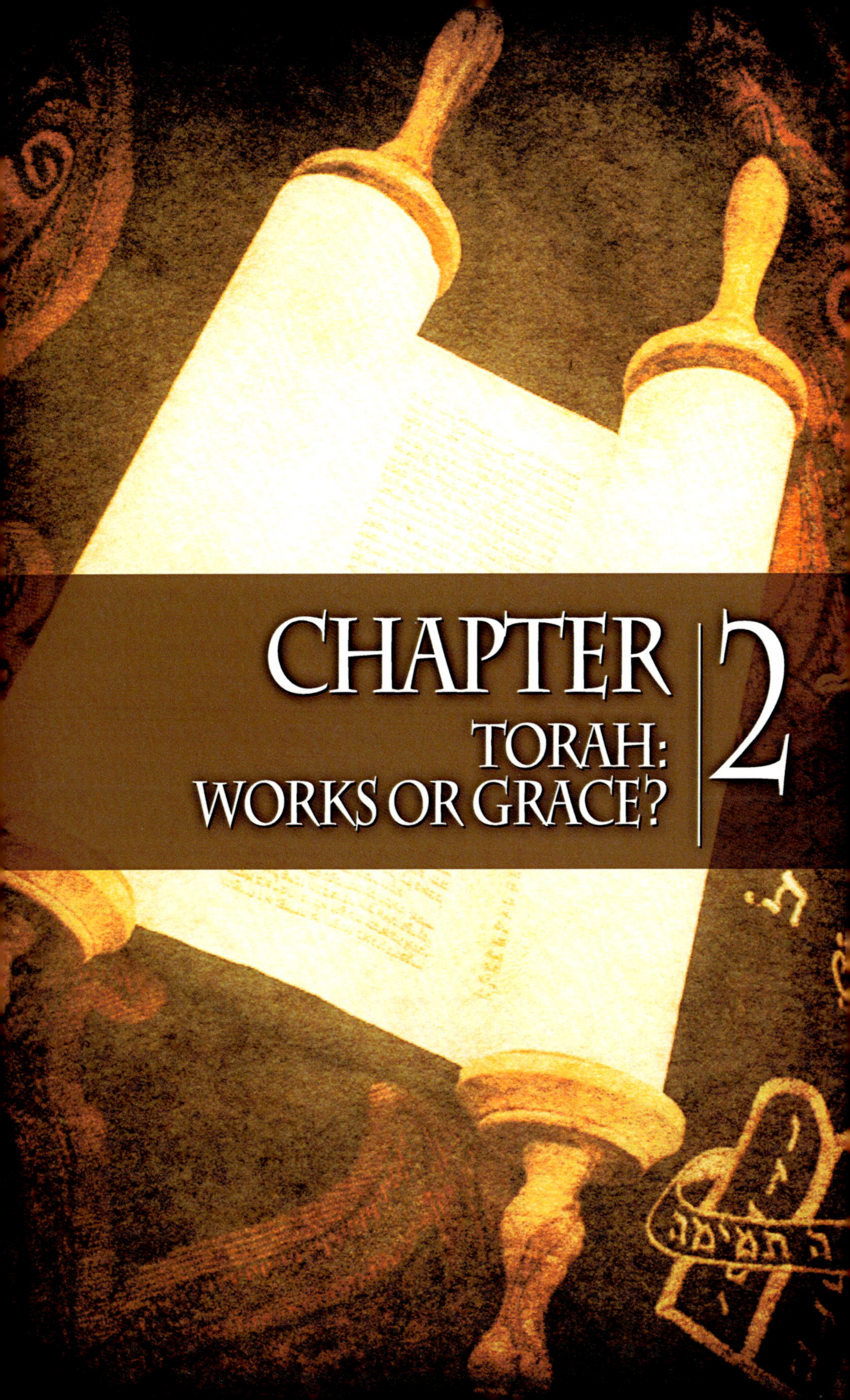

CHAPTER 2

TORAH: WORKS OR GRACE?

One God, Part 1
To view a video segment of this resource, scan the QR code using your smartphone.

The church has taught that Judaism is a religion of law and works while Christianity is a religion of grace and faith. When Christians speak today about the Jewish or Hebrew roots of their faith, they often state that the Hebrew roots teaching is trying to put Christians ***"under the Law."*** [1]

The cornerstone of our faith is the Biblical truth that Salvation is by grace and NOT works! In fact, the Bible does not make an issue out of 'Law or Grace,' man made it that way. The Hebraic understanding of Torah and grace is much different from the popular Western understanding. As a Christian, you have no doubt heard multiple sermons contrasting the "Law of Judaism" with the "Grace of Christianity."[2] Now think about that for a moment. If I say the *"Law"* of Judaism versus the *"Grace"* of Christianity, which sounds more appealing: Grace or Law?

> *The thought often presented is that in the Old Covenant the Jews were saved by the Law, which is bad, but in the New Testament, Jesus did away with the Law so that we are now saved by grace and faith—which is good. The clear teaching of this mindset is that there is* ***no Grace*** *and faith in the Old Covenant Law and* ***no Law*** *in the New Testament grace and faith. For centuries, law and works and grace and faith have been contrasted as if they are two opposing means of salvation.*[3]

In Romans Chapter 3, the Apostle Paul addresses the very question still being asked today: *"Has the Torah been abolished?"* Paul's answer leaves no room for doubt stating, *"Heaven forbid!"* Paul not only confirms the validity of the Torah for believers, he also says that as believers we are supposed to confirm or fulfill the Torah.

"Therefore, we hold the view
that a person comes to be
considered righteous by God on the
ground of trusting, which has nothing
to do with legalistic observance
of Torah commands.
Or is God the God of the Jews only?
Isn't he also the God of the Gentiles?
Yes, He is indeed the God of the Gentiles,
because, as you will admit, God is one.
Therefore He will consider righteous
the circumcised on the ground
of trusting and the uncircumcised
through that same trusting.
Does it follow that we abolish
Torah by this trusting?
Heaven forbid! On the contrary,
we confirm Torah." [4]

(Romans 3:28-31 CJB)

Paul's clear teaching in the Book of Romans is that salvation is based solely on faith in Jesus (Yeshua), and not in the least based on works. However, Paul continues by challenging the mindset that the Torah has therefore been made void or somehow replaced by faith in Jesus. In fact, much of Paul's ministry was devoted to teaching the proper understanding and *application* of the Torah to the Gentile believers in Yeshua!

The first century "Church" consisted predominantly of Jewish believers in Yeshua meeting together with the growing number of non-Jewish believers (referred to then as Gentiles). The majority of Jewish believers would have been taught the Torah from birth and therefore would have understood the *"ritual application of law"* which included:

- Circumcision
- Laws of *Kashrut* (Dietary Laws)
- The Sabbath

This *ritual application of law* defined the distinct identity of the Jewish people prior to the coming of the Messiah. The "Christians" of that time were the believing Gentiles who had come to know the God of Abraham, Isaac, and Jacob, through Jesus, and subsequently through His disciples' ministry. Although the term "Christian" would not be associated with the followers of Jesus for some time, the distinct cultural and historical difference between the Jewish and Gentile believers was already at issue. Even the term "Gentile" becomes problematic in understanding the relationship between the Torah and Christians today.

"Remember that you, once Gentiles in the flesh—
who are called Uncircumcision by what is called
Circumcision made in the flesh by hands—
that at that time you were without Christ, being aliens
from the commonwealth of Israel and strangers from
the Covenants of Promise, having no Hope
and without God in the world. But now in Christ Jesus
you who were once far off have been brought near
by the blood of Christ." [5]

(Ephesians 2:11-13, emphasis added)

According to the Bible (Ephesians 2:12), before your salvation in Jesus you were:

1. Without Christ
2. An alien from the Commonwealth of Israel
3. A stranger to the Covenants of Promise
4. Without hope
5. Without God

After your salvation in Yeshua (Ephesians 2:19) you are:

1. WITH Christ
2. NO LONGER a stranger and foreigner (Gentile)
3. A CITIZEN of the Commonwealth of Israel

The term *Gentile* is actually identifying believers by their former state—*before* salvation in Christ. A much better term for believers in Jesus who were not raised in the Torah and traditions of the Jewish people is "Nations" or "Believing Nations." This brings to light the challenges Paul and many others faced in the first century Church. Just how were the believing Jews to teach and apply the New Covenant—a covenant based on the Torah (Jeremiah 31; Hebrews 8)—to the believing Nations (former Gentiles), who had little or no familiarity with the Torah and its 613 Principles? What relationship to the Torah did all believers, both Jew and Gentile, have *after* they had received salvation in Yeshua (Jesus)?

When Paul exhorts believers regarding *"putting on the full counsel of the LORD"* (Acts 20:27), he is referring to the counsel and understanding found in the Torah. The early Church did not teach what we have been commonly taught in Christianity today. Believers in the first and second centuries were taught the Torah! After all, the New Covenant is not *really* a new walk, it is a *re-newed* walk of Torah, fulfilled by the righteousness and sinless life of our Jewish Lord, Yeshua, Jesus Christ!

As previously stated, the Bible of Jesus was the Torah. Jesus did not have a King James Version of the Bible. He didn't have the NIV, and He did not have the Living Bible. Jesus taught from the scroll of the Torah.

This was life to Him, and it was life to the early Church witnesses of the Gospel, to the Apostles, to Paul, to Matthew, Mark, Luke, and to John.

So let me ask you a question: How did we get to the point today that we can view the Torah as an oppressive law, or as something negative? To the Jewish people the Torah is guidance, teaching, and instruction. The Commands in the Torah are given to teach and disciple you; to discipline your daily habits. Remember, you don't decide your future, you decide your habits, and your habits decide your future! Jewish people today continue to observe the instructions of the Torah. However this is coupled with their belief and faith in God, and not replaced by it. The idea that God has somehow nullified the eternal Principles of His Word is a completely foreign concept to the Jewish mind.

ONE GOD - THREE THEORIES

- Trinitarianism
- Modalism
- Monotheism

1. TRINITARIANISM

Trinitarianism, or the concept of the Trinity, is a Christian doctrine that attempts to explain the multi-faceted nature of God. The doctrine asserts the following:

- There is one and only one God.
- God eternally exists in three distinct persons.
- The Father is God, the Son is God, and the Holy Spirit is God.
- The Father is not the Son, the Son is not the Father, the Father is not the Spirit, etc.[6]

The term "Trinity" does not appear in the Bible. Theophilus of Antioch (c. 180 A.D.) first used the Greek term *trias* (a set of three) in reference to God, His Word, and His Wisdom. Tertullian, an early Church

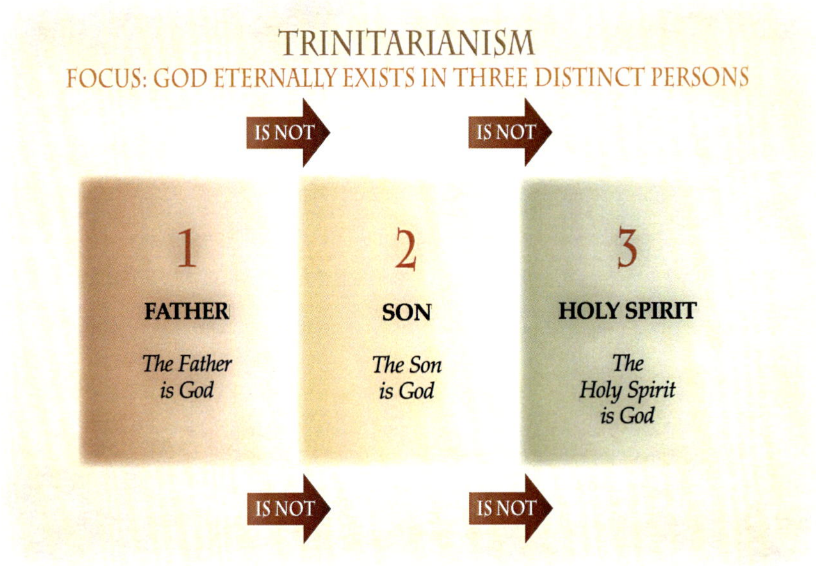

father (c. 215 A.D.), was the first one to state this doctrine using the Latin term, *Trinitas* (Trinity), referring to the Father, Son, and Holy Spirit. The doctrine of the Trinity evolved in the early Church in reaction to the heretical teachings of Arianism regarding Jesus. Arianism attempted to reconcile the belief in one God by denying the full Divinity of Jesus. Arianism taught that Jesus was divine, but that He was a lesser deity, created by the Father.

2. MODALISM

Modalism is the belief that God is one Person who has revealed Himself in three forms or modes. According to Modalism, Jesus is God acting in one mode or role, and the Holy Spirit is God acting in a different mode. While Trinitarianism teaches that God exists as three Persons: Father, Son, and Holy Spirit, Modalism teaches that God is one Person who has manifested Himself in three mutually exclusive modes at various times. For example, when God appeared in the "mode" of Jesus, the "mode" of God the Father no longer existed. Modalism denies the basic

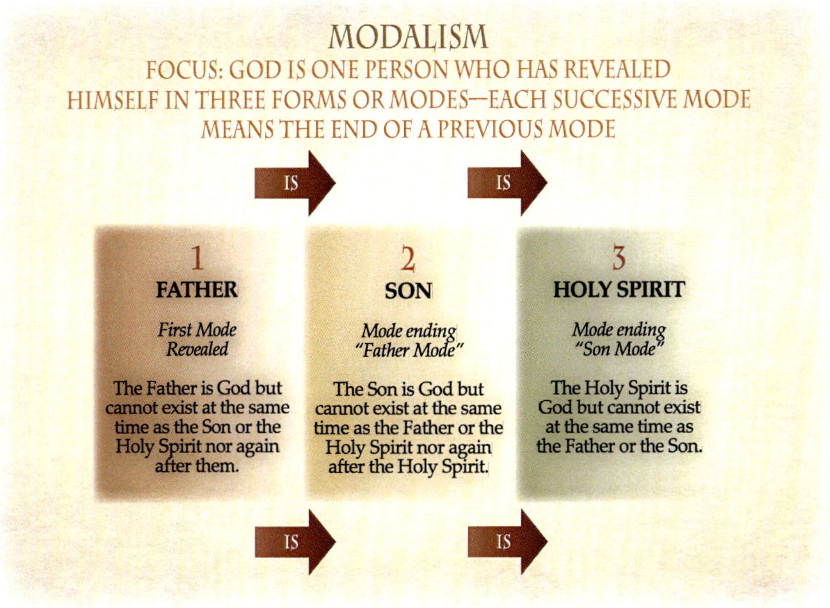
MODALISM
FOCUS: GOD IS ONE PERSON WHO HAS REVEALED HIMSELF IN THREE FORMS OR MODES—EACH SUCCESSIVE MODE MEANS THE END OF A PREVIOUS MODE
IS
IS
1
FATHER
First Mode Revealed
The Father is God but cannot exist at the same time as the Son or the Holy Spirit nor again after them.
2
SON
Mode ending "Father Mode"
The Son is God but cannot exist at the same time as the Father or the Holy Spirit nor again after the Holy Spirit.
3
HOLY SPIRIT
Mode ending "Son Mode"
The Holy Spirit is God but cannot exist at the same time as the Father or the Son.
IS
IS

distinctiveness and coexistence of the Trinity—God in three eternal, co-existent Persons: the Father, the Son, and the Holy Spirit.

3. MONOTHEISM

Monotheism, or the belief in One God, affirms the Biblical truth of God's One-ness. Unlike Trinitarianism, Modalism, and Arianism, Monotheism upholds the Scriptural tenet without attempting to explain God in His numerous manifestations. Monotheism is the foundation through which the finite human mind can even begin to grasp and understand our infinite God. Monotheism does not separate God the Father, Son, and Holy Spirit into eternally separate and distinct Persons, Modes, or Manifestations. Monotheism expresses the fundamental Scriptural truth that God is One, and this One and only God is:

- Omnipresent: Existing everywhere at all times. YHWH has no spacial boundaries. He fills the universe and beyond…and He is always near.

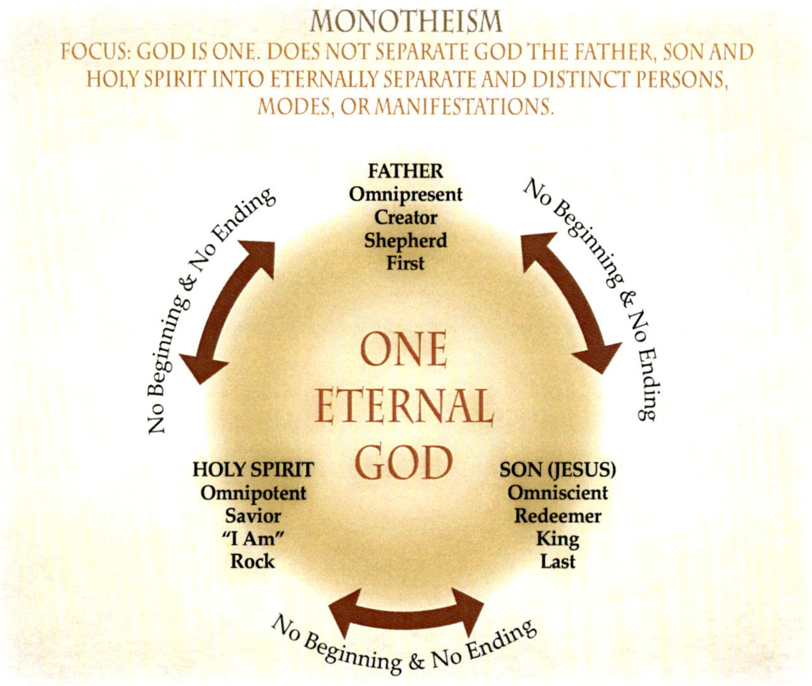

- Omniscient: Knowing all things. YHWH knows all our thoughts and deeds, in the past, present, and future.
- Omnipotent: YHWH is all-powerful.
- Eternal: Without beginning and without end. YHWH transcends time.

Trinitarianism and Modalism are clearly western or Greek in thought and orientation. The concepts related to both of these theories are decidedly linear. When attempting to explain the infinite God using western terms such as Trinity or even "Modes" of God, this Greek thought results in a linear timeline of God's revelation and manifestation. By contrast, eastern or Hebrew thought is consistenly circular and eternal. From the Hebrew perspective God transcends time and space. God exists everywhere and at all times. The numerous manifestations of YHWH throughout the Bible, are simply progressive revelations of the same One God.

"Hear O Israel! The Lord our God the Lord is One." [7]

(Deuteronomy 6:4)

The Jews profess and believe in One God. This Biblical cornerstone of the Jewish faith is called the *Shema.* As far as the Jews are concerned, the God of the Old Testament **could not** be a different God in the time of the New Testament. When the Jewish people see the typical Church portrayal of Jesus, they wonder if Christians believe that Jesus is somehow a different God than the God of Abraham, Isaac, and Jacob? This causes more than a little confusion as to the validity of Christianity and those who are followers of Jesus as the Messiah. It's confusing, because if you believe in the Scriptural tenet of One God, then you must also believe that Jesus *is* God. Logically then, if you believe that Jesus is the God of the Old Testament, then you believe in the Ten Commandments, after all, where do the Ten Commandments come from? They come from God! And as recorded in the Torah, the Ten Commandments state:

"You shall have no other gods before Me." [8]

(Exodus 20:3, emphasis added)

Therefore, if the God of Abraham, Isaac, and Jacob is the God of the *Tanakh* (Old Testament), and God is One *(Shema),* then the God of the New Testament **must be** this same God. So then, why does Christianity appear to be introducing a new Jesus, with new commands, and a new covenant, distinctly inconsistent and even contrary to earlier Biblical Principles? The truth is, He's not a new Jesus, He is the Word of YHWH Who appeared to Abraham (Genesis 15). He is *Elohim* our Creator and He is *Adonai* our Lord. He is the salvation of the Living God (Isaiah 12), and He is the visible manifestation of the invisible God (Colossians 1:15).

Do you believe that Jesus created the universe or do you believe that Jesus is a separate God from the One Who created it? Do you believe that the God of the Old Testament is different than Jesus, or are God the Father and Jesus One and the same? Is God the Father a different God than Jesus the Son? Is the Holy Spirit a different God than God the Father? How can we believe in three separate and distinct Persons within the "God-head" and still assert that "YHWH is One!"?

Whatever natural explanations or illustrations people use to describe the multiple manifestations of YHWH, including His Incarnation as Jesus (Yeshua), you cannot nullify the foundational truth that God is One and there is no other! The clear message of the Gospel—the "Good News"—is that Jesus is YHWH, and YHWH desires to dwell within His people.

- Jesus in His Divinity is YHWH...
  and in His humanity is Man.
- Jesus in His Divinity is the Father...
  and in His humanity is the Son.
- Jesus in His Divinity is Spirit...
  and in His humanity is Flesh.
- Jesus in His Divinity came to save us...
  and in His humanity He died to redeem us.

The following side-by-side Scriptures help to clarify Biblically, the "One-ness" of God and the Divinity of Jesus.

"Hear, O Israel:
The Lord our God,
the Lord is one!" [9]
(Deuteronomy 6:4)

"I and My Father
are one." [10]
(John 10:30)

"And God said to Moses,
'I AM WHO I AM.'
And He said, "Thus you
shall say to the children
of Israel, 'I AM has
sent me to you.'" [11]
(Exodus 3:14)

"Jesus said to them,
'Most assuredly, I say
to you, before Abraham
was, I AM.'" [12]
(John 8:58)

"Now see that I,
even I, am He, and
there is no God besides Me;
I kill and I make alive;
I wound and I heal." [13]
(Deuteronomy 32:39)

"Therefore I said to you
that you will die in
your sins; for if you
do not believe that
I am He, you will die in
your sins." [14]
(John 8:24)

"The Lord Himself is
God in heaven above and
on the earth beneath; there
is no other." [15]
(Deuteronomy 4:39)

"No one has ascended
to heaven but He who came
down from heaven, that is,
the Son of Man who is in
heaven." [16]
(John 3:13)

"a just God and a Savior;
there is none besides
Me. "Look to Me, and
be saved, all you ends of the
earth! For I am God, and
there is no other." [17]
(Isaiah 45:21-22)

"Thus says the Lord,
the King of Israel,
and his Redeemer,
the Lord of hosts:
'I am the First and I am
the Last; Besides Me
there is no God." [19]
(Isaiah 44:6)

"For unto us a Child
is born, unto us a Son is
given; and the government
will be upon His shoulder.
and His name will be
called Wonderful,
Counselor, Mighty God,
Everlasting Father,
Prince of Peace." [21]
(Isaiah 9:6)

"...looking for the
blessed hope and
glorious appearing of
our great God and Savior
Jesus Christ" [18]
(Titus 2:13)

"I am the Alpha and
the Omega, the Beginning
and the End," says the Lord,
"who is and who
was and who is to come,
the Almighty." [20]
(Revelation 1:8)

"He who has seen Me
has seen the Father;
so how can you say,
'Show us the Father?'
Do you not believe that
I am in the Father,
and the Father in Me?" [22]
(John 14:9-10)

"The Lord is my shepherd;" [23]
(Psalms 23:1)

"The grass withers, the flower fades, but the word of our God stands forever." [25]
(Isaiah 40:8)

"The Lord came from Sinai, and dawned on them from Seir; He shone forth from Mount Paran, and He came with ten thousands of saints; from His right hand came a fiery law for them." [27]
(Deuteronomy 33:2)

"I am the good shepherd." [24]
(John 10:13)

"Heaven and earth will pass away, but My words will by no means pass away." [26]
(Matthew 24:35)

"Behold, the Lord comes with ten thousands of His saints," [28]
(Jude 1:14)

CHAPTER 3

THE HEBREW ROOTS OF THE CHRISTIAN FAITH

Torah: Law or Grace?, Part 1
To view a video segment of this resource, scan the QR code using your smartphone.

"Do you not know that you are the temple of God and that the Spirit of God dwells in you?" [1]

(1 Corinthians 3:16)

When the LORD says that you are the temple of the Living God, He is imparting His desire to dwell within you. He says that you and your lineage are a house of YHWH. Your Commonwealth inheritance wasn't only to be born again. It also meant that you would continue to walk into what God has already prepared for you—the Torah. And when you are following the Torah in a systematic, Spirit-filled way, it is called the Realm of Life. When you step into this realm you will maximize your productivity, you will multiply, and the LORD will make fruitful all of the things that you put your hands to. You will prosper spiritually, physically, financially, and emotionally.

It now becomes abundantly clear why the enemy has propagated so much deception and debate about the Word of God, and why the Torah been presented as "legalism" rather than lifestyle. Remember, these are not salvation issues! The Torah can never save you. Salvation is not of works, but ONLY in Jesus Christ, *Yeshua HaMashiach.*

Just as Jesus did not carry a King James Version of the Bible, He also did not celebrate Christmas and Easter, or instruct any of His followers to do so. These "holidays" were incorporated into Christianity some 300 years after the resurrection of Yeshua. The Biblical Holy Days have not changed since they were given and recorded in Leviticus Chapter 23. They are the Feasts and Festivals of the LORD called *Moadim* in Hebrew—Feasts that include Passover, the Day of Atonement, and the weekly Sabbath.

Most churches today do not even teach about the Biblical Feast Days. Many believers consider these Feasts to be 'Jewish' only, and have absolutely no familiarity with the Biblical Feasts and the specific blessings they contain. As I've stated, when your confession matches your conduct, it's called the glory of God. The Church wants to experience the glory, yet we're trying to obtain it without any regard to God's Teaching and Instruction (Torah), and faith requires an instruction.

So how did we get here? How did we come to believe that the "Church" began in Acts Chapter 2, when in fact, the Church *and* Acts 2 come right out of the Torah? The great outpouring of the Spirit was a perfectly timed fulfillment of the Feast of *Shavuot* (Pentecost)—the fourth Biblical Spring Feast (Leviticus 23). The Apostles and those gathered with them were keeping the Command of God. Three times a year, on the Feasts of *Pesach* (Passover), *Shavuot* (Pentecost), and *Sukkot* (Tabernacles), the men of Israel were instructed to come up to Jerusalem. They were following this exact instruction of the Torah, at exactly the right time, in exactly the right place—and God met their obedience with a miracle!

THE EARLY CHURCH

Rabbi Stanley Wagner holds a PhD in Jewish history and is recognized as one of the foremost authorities on the history of Israel. Rabbi Wagner, speaking at a National conference, stated his five-point rule regarding Israel:

1. You can say you love Israel
2. You can say you love the People of Israel

3. You can say you love the God of Israel
4. You can say you love the Land of Israel
5. BUT, if you don't love the Torah (God's teaching and instruction) and you teach against it, you will be anti-Semitic and history has shown you will eventually turn your back on the Jewish People! [2]

In the 2nd century A.D., an influential and charismatic individual named Marcion taught that the God of Abraham, Isaac, and Jacob—the God of the Torah—was a ***"law-giving"*** *God, and that Jesus came down to set us free from this law, and Jesus came to bring us Grace! Marcion taught a two-Deity principle which identified two separate Gods—a wrathful God of the Old Testament and a forgiving God of the New Testament. Even though Marcion's writings were later condemned as heresy, and Marcion himself was excommunicated from the Church, his teachings contrasting Law and Grace heavily influenced the early church fathers.*[3]

In the 4th century there was a man by the name of John Chrysostom (344-407 AD) who was a Bishop of the Church of Antioch…However, John Chrysostom hated Jews. He blamed the entire Jewish people for the death of Jesus and sought to separate Christianity from its Hebrew Roots. John Chrysostom gave a series of eight sermons in which he spoke violently against the Jews. These sermons were put into a written format and widely circulated. Although many early church fathers spoke harshly against the Jews, John Chrysostom was the most vicious. His sermons fanned the flames of anti-Semitism and would become the teaching and practice of the church for the next 1,600 years.[4]

Sixteen hundred years, just think about that. Nearly two millennia of time and Chrysostom's sermons still permeate Church doctrine and teaching today!

From Marcion and Chrysostom, continuing with Origen, Eusebius, Constantine, St. Augustine, and St. Thomas Aquinas, from century to century, differing philosophies, theologies, and events influenced the early Church fathers to view and teach the Torah as something negative. Because they themselves had become disconnected from the Hebraic background of the Scriptures, they actively sought to sever Christianity from its Jewish roots—especially the Torah.

Origen, as still taught in many seminaries today, is considered to be a preeminent Greek scholar and theologian. Origen was merely a man, but looked upon himself as a god, even castrating himself based on this misconception. Origen's primary student, Eusebius, propagated Origen's flawed teachings about the Torah, further distancing believers and primary Church doctrines from the Hebrew roots of the Christian faith.

> *Because of their background and education, the early church fathers of the second, third, and fourth centuries, misunderstood and misinterpreted many of Paul's sayings, which they used to establish differences between Christianity and Judaism that cannot be supported in the Bible. These Greek-Christian scholars became leaders of the emerging Gentile dominated church and their false theology contrasting law and grace as opposing means of salvation became official church doctrine.*[5]

After Origen and Eusebius, Church history would again dramatically shift under the Roman Emperor Constantine who "legitimized" Christianity as the official state religion of Rome. As Emperor, Constantine faced the complex problems of indoctrinating a predominantly pagan and polytheistic (multiple gods) Rome into the still emerging tenets of Christianity. To make Rome's "new" religion more palatable to the people of his empire, Constantine changed the Sabbath Day to Sunday at the Council of Nicea, c. 325 A.D., and enacted other sweeping changes which combined pagan idolatry worship with the Torah—a process called *syncretism.*

Constantine replaced the Biblical Feast of Passover with a formalized celebration of Easter—a day *syncretized* from a pagan festival at the Spring Equinox honoring the Babylonian fertility goddess *Ishtar.* December 25th, a long-standing pagan celebration of Saturnalia (Winter Solstice, also believed to be the birthdate of the pagan god *Mithra*), became Christmas and a commemoration of the birth of Jesus.

Born a Roman citizen, Constantine was immersed in a pagan society and entirely estranged from the Hebrew roots of the Gospel he professed. His efforts to incorporate or syncretize pagan worship, and therefore worshippers, into Rome's new religion at last divorced Christianity from its Hebrew roots. Syncretism changed the face of Christianity, as well as the Church's understanding of, and relationship to the Torah, throughout the centuries—even to this very day.

> *Augustine, another early church father, was a great scholar. In the 5th century, he wrote a monumental work, which is still taught in seminaries today, called "The City of God." Like Marcion, Augustine taught that God came down to give us the "Law" and then Jesus Christ came down to give us "Grace." Augustine promoted Marcion's ideas concerning Law and Grace as opposites. His writings influenced the church for centuries and were, unfortunately, carried forward at the time of the Protestant Reformation. Marcion's false teaching on law and grace would become the core doctrine of much of Western Christianity that is taught today.*[6]
>
> *Marcion rejected the Hebrew Scriptures. He believed that Paul's teachings about grace were in total opposition to the Law. Yet, Paul said that he always kept the Law and the traditions of his people.*[7]

"But this I confess to you,
that according to the Way which they call a sect,

so I worship the God of my fathers,
believing all things which are
written in the Law (Torah) and in the Prophets." [8]

(Acts 24:14)

"Take them and be purified with them,
and pay their expenses so that they may
shave their heads, and that all may know
that those things of which they were informed
concerning you are nothing, but that you
yourself also walk orderly and keep the law." [9]

(Acts 21:24)

"Paul called the leaders of the Jews together,
so when they had come together,
he said to them: 'Men and brethren,
though I have done nothing against
our people or the customs of our fathers,
yet I was delivered as a prisoner from
Jerusalem into the hands of the Romans.'" [10]

(Acts 28:17)

When the Bible was translated into English, Torah was interpreted using the Western (Greek) concept of Law, and not as Instruction (Hebrew) for righteous living...This misunderstanding of the true meaning of the word "Torah" combined with the anti-Semitism of the early church fathers resulted in a misinterpretation of some of the sayings of Jesus, the Gospel writers, and especially Paul, when they spoke about the Law. The Greek-speaking church fathers erroneously concluded that the Jews were saved by keeping the Law but now through Jesus we are saved by grace, so there is no longer a need for the Law, and it has been done away with.[11]

HEBREW ROOTS OF SCRIPTURAL INTERPRETATION

The Hebrew roots of the Christian faith encompass the walk of Torah. The Hebrew roots of the Christian faith characterized the walk of Isaiah, Jeremiah, and Ezekiel. The Hebrew roots of the Christian faith manifest the Spirit that was upon Elijah, King David, and King Solomon. The Hebrew roots of the Christian faith provide the foundation for the Gospels and New Testament writings, including the prophecy of Revelation given to John on the island of Patmos. The Hebrew roots of the Christian faith—the Torah—described and determined the walk of Jesus Christ!

If you want to know God's *purpose* in your life, the Hebrew word is *"Torah."* It's the greatest gift you could ever receive as a born again Christian. The God of Abraham, Isaac, and Jacob loves you so much that you were fully saved at Calvary and you are fully redeemed. Now as a redeemed person, you receive your Commonwealth inheritance—the Torah, the ***Teaching and Instruction of God!***

"There are seventy faces to the Torah: Turn it around and around, for everything is in it." [12]

The Jewish sages teach that there are 70 varied interpretations of any Scriptural passage in the Torah. In Hebrew this is called, *"Shiv'im Panim laTorah"—"The Torah has 70 faces."* This phrase is used to indicate the different levels of Torah interpretation. In other words, the Torah is like a diamond with each facet reflecting part of the intricate brilliance of the "light" of truth. If you view the Torah from any particular vantage point or perspective, the light will be uniquely different from any other point of view. The seventy facets or faces of the Torah range from the surface level of meaning to the deeper levels which must be discovered by searching within the words and context, or by referring to other Scripture passages. There are four primary categories of Hebraic Scriptural interpretation. The Hebrew methodology used to study the Bible is known by the acronym *pardes:*

Peshat = Literal; Simple

Remez = Hint; Refer

Drash = Discussion; Allegory

Sod = Secret; Hidden

PESHAT

The *peshat,* or simple level of interpretation recognizes the literal meaning of each word and verse without delving deeper into any spiritual application or moral implications of the Biblical text. The sages teach that this primary level includes the historical and grammatical understanding, and can never be entirely replaced by any additional interpretation. Therefore any deeper exegesis (Scriptural interpretation) or alternative facet that annuls the literal meaning of the verse is considered invalid.

REMEZ

Remez, meaning to refer or hint, digs slightly deeper to uncover meanings which are only *hinted* at by the Torah. The practical application of this level utilizes other Scripture passages or references to help explain the primary text. Passages related by key words, definitions, and contextual similarities are particularly useful in the *remez* level of interpretation.

DRASH

The *drash* level of interpretation moves deeper into the allegorical meaning derived by a discussion—called *midrash* in Hebrew. *Drash* relates the application of any particular principle or concept that can be extracted from the literal or surface text. Differing from the *sod* or deepest level of interpretation, the *drash* understanding holds that the persons or events detailed in the primary text reflect actual occurrences designed and recorded to teach a Biblical truth.

SOD

Sod (pronounced "sûd"), meaning secret or hidden, is the deepest level of Hebraic Scriptural interpretation. For believers, the most familiar Biblical examples of *sod* teaching are the parables of Yeshua. The purpose of *sod* interpretation is to reveal that which is not at all obvious to the casual reader. *Sod* utilizes people and events as types and shadows of future revelations. As indicated above, while the *sod* level can never dismiss or nullify the literal interpretation of the text, *sod* is seeking understanding on a significantly deeper level. For example, when Yeshua teaches the parable of the "treasure hidden in a field" (Matthew 13), the purpose of the parable is not to identify the buyer or the field specifically, but rather to teach the greater lesson and priceless value of finding such treasure, here representing **the Kingdom of Heaven.**

As I continue to travel all over the world today, standing before congregation after congregation, I have to remind people what the Word of God says, because, in essence, they've been taught that much of the Word doesn't pertain to them anymore.

"I say unto this mountain,
be removed and cast into the sea." [13]

(Mark 11:23-24)

Without hearing and understanding the Scriptures in their original language, it becomes nearly impossible to grasp the fullness of the meaning and context of the Bible. Take for example, Yeshua's words in Mark Chapter 11. This passage is frequently used within the context of faith, and seen as an exhortation to possess "faith that moves mountains!" But when you take these words back to their Hebrew roots, an entirely different interpretation is revealed.

The word "sea" in Mark 11 is alluding to people groupings or groups of people (see also Revelation 17:15). Jesus makes this famous statement while standing amidst the tombstones on the summit of the Mount of Olives. He is looking across the Kidron Valley towards the second Temple, standing on what is today called, the Temple Mount. The first two Temples (and the future Third Temple) stood on this exact same spot, a mountain in Jerusalem named Mount Moriah (*Moriah* means "God's Teaching" in Hebrew). Jesus says, "I say unto *this* mountain (God's Teaching—Torah), be removed and cast into the sea (people groupings and groups of people)." Surrounded by the graves of thousands, Jesus is speaking prophetically of the coming day when the Torah would again be revealed to the multitudes of people, and become not only an active faith to them, but literally life from death. I've got news for you: the mountain has, in our lifetime, been removed and cast into the sea!

This facet of the Scriptures remains hidden until you begin to understand the Bible from the Hebrew perspective. After all, Yeshua spoke Hebrew! That's why people, wherever I go and when I simply mention the word Torah and teach them even the first little bit of truth about Hebrew roots, they nearly fall out of their chairs thinking, "Where has this been?"

The modern-day view from the Mount of Olives looking across the Kidron Valley towards Mount Moriah.

CHAPTER 4
THE LANGUAGE OF EXILE

The Voice of the Principles, Volume 1, Part 1

To view a video segment of this resource, scan the QR code using your smartphone.

When your Bible uses the term "House of Jacob," it is specifically speaking of both the Northern and Southern Kingdoms of Israel (also called the "House of Israel" and the "House of Judah" respectively) joined together as one. Since the Bible clearly differentiates between these two kingdoms, it will be helpful to briefly explore their Biblical history from the Hebrew point of view.

"Now the sons of Jacob
were twelve:
the sons of Leah were Reuben,
Jacob's firstborn, and Simeon,
Levi, Judah, Issachar, and Zebulun;
the sons of Rachel were
Joseph and Benjamin;
the sons of Bilhah, Rachel's maidservant
were Dan and Naphtali;
and the sons of Zilpah, Leah's maidservant,
were Gad and Asher.
These were the sons of Jacob
who were born to him
in Padan Aram." [1]

(Genesis 35:22-26)

The descendants of these twelve sons of Jacob (Israel) formed the Twelve Tribes of Israel. As sons of Jacob, each tribe originally walked in the Torah—God's Teaching and Instruction. The Twelve Tribes are often referred to as the House of Jacob because all the tribes originated from the patriarch, Jacob. More than forty years after the historic Exodus from the bondage of Egypt, the Twelve Tribes of Israel began to settle again in the Promised Land. Each tribe was given a portion of the Land on which to dwell—with the exception of the tribe of Levi. God had specifically instructed that the Levitical Priests were not to have an inheritance related to the physical Land of Israel (Numbers 18).

Throughout the Bible there is animosity between the Twelve Tribes. Just as Jacob's sons Judah and Joseph were rivals, the later tribes of Judah and Joseph (Ephraim) became rivals. Even under King David this animosity was evident after his son Absalom's revolt (2 Samuel 20:1). After the death of King Solomon, this rivalry, combined with a foolish decision by Solomon's son, Rehoboam (1 Kings 12:16), sparked civil war. The result was a divided kingdom and the Twelve Tribes of Israel became two distinct groups. For two hundred years, until the fall of the Northern Kingdom in 722 B.C.E., there were two kingdoms of Israel dwelling side by side: a larger one in the north and the east, called *Israel* (the "Ten Tribes" of 1 Kings 11:35), and a smaller one in the south called *Judah.* These two groups are often referred to as the Northern Kingdom and the Southern Kingdom.

The Southern Kingdom consisted of three tribes: Benjamin, Judah, and half of the tribe of Levi. Of these three, Judah was the most numerous; therefore, this group is commonly called the *House of Judah.* The Northern Kingdom consisted of the other ten tribes: Reuben, Simeon, Issachar, Zebulun, Dan, Naphtali, Gad, Asher, Joseph (also known as Ephraim and Manasseh), and the other half of the tribe of Levi. These ten tribes are often referred to as the "Lost Ten Tribes" of Israel. The largest and most dominant of these tribes was Ephraim; therefore, they are also called the *House of Ephraim* or the *House of Israel.*

- **The House of Judah = the Southern Kingdom (the Jewish people)**
- **The House of Israel = the Northern Kingdom (the "Lost Ten Tribes"—also called the House of Ephraim)**
- **The Whole House of Jacob = the House of Judah and the House of Israel**

Jerusalem remained the capital of the Southern Kingdom of Judah, while the Northern Kingdom of Israel established three capitals of its own: Shechem, Tirzah, and Samaria. As prophesied in Scripture, due to their disobedience and disregard of the Torah, both the Northern and Southern Kingdoms were eventually conquered and exiled to foreign lands.

"Behold, the eyes of the Lord GOD
are on the sinful kingdom,
and I will destroy it
from the face of the earth;
Yet I will not utterly destroy
the house of Jacob," says the LORD."
For surely I will command,
and will sift the house of Israel
among all nations,
as grain is sifted in a sieve;
yet not the smallest grain
shall fall to the ground." [2]

(Amos 9:8-9)

The Southern Tribes of Judah were exiled to Babylon for a period of 70 years, after which, many of the House of Judah returned to Israel with Nehemiah to reclaim their Land and their ways (Nehemiah 1). Despite repeated hostilities and occupations, Judah still remained as a district (Judea) in New Testament times (Luke 3:1). Because they returned quickly to the Land and maintained their relationship to the Torah and their traditions, the House of Judah can still be clearly recognized as the Jewish people today.

The Northern Tribes of Israel were conquered by the Assyrians and sent into exile, eventually being dispersed to Europe, Africa, Asia, and America—*the ends of the earth.* In exile, the tribes would ultimately forget even their own history and heritage, losing the connection with the Torah and their Hebrew identity. Biblically significant, this phrase "the ends of the earth" is consistently used in reference to the House of Israel being sown or scattered into the nations. The Bible also frequently uses the term "afar" in reference to this same concept:

"Fear not, for I am with you;
I will bring your descendants from the east,
and gather you from the west.
"I will say to the north, 'Give them up!'
and to the south, 'Do not keep them back!'
Bring My sons from afar,
and My daughters from
the ends of the earth" [3]

(Isaiah 43:5-6, emphasis added)

The Northern Tribes—*the Lost Ten Tribes*—have yet to fully return to the Land of Israel or the Torah. When we refer to the House of Judah (the Southern Kingdom), we can readily recognize the Jewish people because they have maintained their identity, traditions, and heritage. But we have no similar way of identifying these Lost Ten Tribes—the House of Israel still scattered throughout the Nations.

How many reading this book have European, Asian, or Russian background? How many of you have ancestors who fled the pogroms of Russia, or the political/economic oppression of Europe and Asia, traveled through Ellis Island, and are today further scattered across America?

During the Spanish Inquisition—a holocaust in its own right—Jews were horribly persecuted and eventually forced by edict out of Spain. Historians believe that Christopher Columbus may very well have been Jewish, fleeing the persecution. Regardless of whether Columbus was a Jew himself, he was partially financed by the Jewish people seeking refuge from the Inquisition.[4]

The connection between Africa and Israel is well documented, even within the pages of the Bible. Many African Jews were dispersed to North, Central, and South America through the Slave Trade from 1,502–1,860. Again, they were scattered to the *"ends of the earth"*—in this case, America. The movement of slaves flourished along the established trade routes in the Atlantic Triangle: Europe to Africa, Africa to North and South America, and back to Europe. Trading terminology used within the Triangle, such as manufacturing and merchandise, were in reality, shiploads of slaves being traded on the world market.[5]

As a result of exile and the continuing and widespread dispersion of Israel, the Jewish people were compelled to translate the Torah from Hebrew into the foreign languages of their host countries, including Greek, and ultimately English. Several problems arose in this process of translation because the Hebrew language cannot be transmitted accurately across linguistic lines. You have to more than double the amount of words utilized when translating from Hebrew to Greek, and almost triple the amount of words translating from Greek to English. The result is that the original language and meaning become diluted. At times, we have difficulty hearing the original message of our Bible because we are reading from a obscured translation, rather than from the original.

A good example of this confusion resulting from translation is the word 'faith.' "Faith" in Christianity is often defined as "belief." However, "faith" in Hebrew is the word *"emunah." Emunah* did not originally mean belief, it meant steadiness and steadfastness in the commands of God. It's an action word, continuous and ongoing; faith is obedience in action. *Emunah—Faith* requires an instruction. Remember, when your conduct matches your confession, it is called the glory of God. Many believers have been discouraged because they put their faith in their Jesus (confession), yet they had no persistence because they were never given the Instructions of the Torah (conduct). When the things they confessed over and over again didn't come to pass, they became discouraged wondering, "God, why aren't You moving on my behalf?"

When you look up the word "faith" in a Thesaurus (dictionary of synonyms) you will find these synonyms or similar words: "confidence; belief."

Faith = Confidence; Belief

Now let's take each of these words separately to understand this concept of faith more fully.

A synonym for "confidence" in the Thesaurus is "certainty" or "absolute certainty."

Confidence = Certainty; Absolute Certainty

A synonym for "belief" in the Thesaurus is "principle" or "principles."

Belief = Principle; Principles

Therefore, if faith is confidence, and belief is principles, then faith can also be defined as "confidence in the principles."

Faith = Confidence (Absolute Certainty) in the Principles (Belief)

Faith = Confidence in the Principles

"For we walk by faith (confidence in the Principles),
not by sight." [6]
(2 Corinthians 5:7, emphasis added)

"So then faith (confidence in the Principles) comes by hearing, and hearing by the Torah (Principles) of God." [7]
(Romans 10:17, emphasis added)

Faith (confidence in the Principles) resides within the 613 Principles of the Torah, and faith comes by hearing. From the Hebrew perspective, hearing *(shema)* is not simply the passive act of listening, hearing involves listening *and* obeying. In fact, the familiar phrase in Judaism is: "Study to do; do to listen." To the Hebrew mind, the reality of *"working out your salvation"* (Philippians 2) is the understanding that the Voice of God is "heard" when you are actively participating in His Principles—the Torah.

According to the New Covenant, your obedience is empowered by the Holy Spirit, and this Spirit-led obedience is the gateway to your next instruction. Picture the ripple effect of a rock skipping across the surface of a body of water. The initial impact produces a number of expanding currents that reach far beyond the original action. Each resulting ripple has the potential to further the momentum of the next ripple and so on. Participating in the Torah Principles produces a very similar "ripple effect" in your life. In the midst of your initial act of obedience, the Voice of God gives you a future directive. Your obedience, led of the Spirit, is the energy that generates your next instruction from God. Simply hearing the Principles, or even studying the Principles of God is not sufficient and no further direction will be issued. This is why, in part, the Bible asserts that *"faith without works is dead"* (James 2).

"For we are His (YHWH's) workmanship,
created in Messiah Yeshua for the principles,
which God prepared beforehand
that we should walk in the principles." [8]

(Ephesians 2:10 HNV, emphasis added)

Biblical faith (obedience in action), an active faith, and a faith that moves mountains, is absolute certainty in the Principles of the Torah. Faith is activated by needs and desires. Your worship in the Holy Spirit combined with the Torah gives you an exact instruction at exactly the right moment for every need and each desire. So as believers today, knowing that faith means *obedience in action,* what instructions are we to obey?

"As the Father loved Me, I also have loved you;
abide in My love. If you keep My commandments,
you will abide in My love, just as I have kept
My Father's commandments and abide in His love.
These things I have spoken to you,
that My joy may remain in you,
and that your joy may be full." [9]

(John 15:9-11)

We become obedient to the Principles of God, by the grace of Yeshua, Jesus Christ. In other words, Yeshua activates His faith *within us,* manifesting purpose and determination to walk in our God-given dominion on the earth, fulfilling our potential, and becoming a kingdom of priests and a holy nation after the Order of Melchizedek (Hebrews 6).

"For I will take you from among the nations,
gather you out of all countries, and bring you into
your own land. Then I will sprinkle clean water on you,
and you shall be clean; I will cleanse you from all your
filthiness and from all your idols. I will give you a new heart
and put a new spirit within you; I will take the heart of stone
out of your flesh and give you a heart of flesh.
I will put My Spirit within you and cause you
to walk in My statutes, and you will keep My judgments
and do them. Then you shall dwell in the land
that I gave to your fathers; you shall be My people,
and I will be your God."[10]

(Ezekiel 36:24-28)

If the Torah is legalism, or if Jesus truly came to do away with the Law, as so many have been led to believe, why would God want to write it on our hearts according to the New Covenant (Jeremiah 31; Hebrews 8)? Just think about this for a moment. God has written the Principles of the Torah on our hearts, and given us the Holy Spirit to live out these Principles ***through*** *us so that our lives reflect His Holy character! While the law is forever the same, the administration of it has changed from external tablets of stone—a stony heart—to the fleshly tablets of our heart.*[11]

Contained within the Commands or Principles of God is the Voice of YHWH. The Voice Who spoke all things into existence (Genesis 1); the Voice that thundered forth the impartation of the Torah from Mount Sinai (Exodus 19); the Voice of the Good Shepherd—Yeshua, Jesus Christ (John 10); and the Voice of the Holy Spirit that fell upon the Apostles (Acts 2)—YHWH alone is the Voice speaking from Genesis to Revelation and YHWH is the Voice of the Principles.

"And when they had prayed,
the place where they were
assembled together was shaken;
and they were all filled with the Holy Spirit
(Voice of the Principles), and they spoke
the word (Torah) of God with boldness." [12]

(Acts 4:31, emphasis added)

"However, when He,
the Spirit of truth (Voice of the Principles),
has come, He will guide you into all truth
(the 613 Principles of God);
for He will not speak on His own authority,
but whatever He hears He will speak
(the Principles of God);
and He will tell you things to come." [13]

(John 16:13, emphasis added)

"The earth was without form, and void;
and darkness was on the face of the deep.
And the Spirit of God (Voice of the Principles)
was hovering over the face of the waters." [14]

(Genesis 1:2, emphasis added)

"You also gave Your good Spirit (Voice of the Principles) to instruct them, And did not withhold Your manna from their mouth, And gave them water for their thirst." [15]

(Nehemiah 9:20, emphasis added)

"Yet for many years You had patience with them, and testified against them by Your Spirit (Voice of the Principles) in Your prophets. Yet they would not listen; Therefore You gave them into the hand of the peoples of the lands. Nevertheless in Your great mercy You did not utterly consume them nor forsake them; For You are God, gracious and merciful." [16]

(Nehemiah 9:30-31, emphasis added)

"Behold! My Servant whom I uphold, My Elect One in whom My soul delights! I have put My Spirit (Voice of the Principles) upon Him; He will bring forth deliverance to the Nations. [17]

(Isaiah 42:1, emphasis added)

"I will pour water on him who is thirsty, And floods on the dry ground; I will pour My Spirit (Voice of the Principles) on your descendants, And My blessing on your offspring;" [18]

(Isaiah 44:3, emphasis added)

"The Spirit of the Lord God (Voice of the Principles) is
upon Me, because the Lord has anointed Me to preach
good tidings to the poor; He has sent Me to heal the
brokenhearted, To proclaim liberty to the captives,
And the opening of the prison tothose who are bound;" [19]

(Isaiah 61:1; Luke 4:18, emphasis added)

"Behold, O My people, I will open your graves
and cause you to come up from your graves, and bring you
into the land of Israel. Then you shall know that I am the
Lord, when I have opened your graves, O My people, and
brought you up from your graves. I will put My Spirit
(Voice of the Principles) in you, and you shall live, and I will
place you in your own land. Then you shall know that I,
the Lord, have spoken it and performed it," says the Lord.'" [20]

(Ezekiel 37:12-14, emphasis added)

"Then you shall know that I am in the midst of Israel:
I am the Lord your God and there is no other. My people
shall never be put to shame. "And it shall come to pass
afterward That I will pour out My Spirit (Voice of the
Principles) on all flesh; Your sons and your daughters
shall prophesy, Your old men shall dream dreams,
Your young men shall see visions." [21]

(Joel 2:27-28, emphasis added)

"'Not by might nor by power,
but by My Spirit (Voice of the Principles),'
says the Lord of hosts." [22]

(Zechariah 4:6, emphasis added)

"Do not cast me away from Your presence,
And do not take Your Holy Spirit
(Voice of the Principles) from me." [23]

(Psalms 51:11, emphasis added)

"What You give them they gather in;
You open Your hand, they are filled with good.
You hide Your face, they are troubled;
You take away their breath, they die and return to their dust.
You send forth Your Spirit (Voice of the Principles),
they are created; And You renew the face of the earth." [24]

(Psalms 104:28-30, emphasis added)

"Behold! My Servant whom I have chosen,
My Beloved in whom My soul is well pleased!
I will put My Spirit (Voice of the Principles) upon Him,
and He will declare justice to the Gentiles." [25]

(Matthew 12:18, emphasis added)

"And I will pray the Father, and He will give you another Helper, that He may abide with you forever—the Spirit of truth (Voice of the Principles), whom the world cannot receive, because it neither sees Him nor knows Him; but you know Him, for He dwells with you and will be in you." [26]

(John 14:16-17)

"...all that Jesus began both to do and teach, until the day in which He was taken up, after He through the Holy Spirit (Voice of the Principles) had given commandments to the apostles whom He had chosen," [27]

(Acts 1:2, emphasis added)

"Therefore take heed to yourselves and to all the flock, among which the Holy Spirit (Voice of the Principles) has made you overseers, to shepherd the church of God which He purchased with His own blood." [28]

(Acts 20:28, emphasis added)

But if the Spirit of Him who raised Jesus from the dead dwells in you, He who raised Christ from the dead will also give life to your mortal bodies through His Spirit (Voice of the Principles) who dwells in you. [29]

(Romans 8:11, emphasis added)

"For as many as are led by the Spirit of God
(Voice of the Principles), these are sons of God." [30]

(Romans 8:14, emphasis added)

"...that the God of our Lord Jesus Christ, the Father of glory, may give to you the Spirit of wisdom and revelation (Voice of the Principles) in the knowledge of Him," [31]

(Ephesians 1:17, emphasis added)

"Now we have received, not the spirit of the world, but the Spirit (Voice of the Principles) who is from God, that we might know the things that have been freely given to us by God." [32]

(1 Corinthians 2:12, emphasis added)

"Do you not know that you are the Temple of God and that the Spirit of God (Voice of the Principles) dwells in you?" [33]

(1 Corinthians 3:16, emphasis added)

"Now the Lord is the Spirit; and where the Spirit of the Lord (Voice of the Principles) is, there is liberty." [34]

(2 Corinthians 3:17, emphasis added)

"Hold fast the pattern of sound words
which you have heard from me,
in faith and love which are in
Christ Jesus. That good thing which
was committed to you, keep by the Holy Spirit
(Voice of the Principles) who dwells in us." [35]

(2 Timothy 1:13-14, emphasis added)

"And the Spirit (Voice of the Principles)
and the bride say, "Come!"
And let him who hears say, "Come!"
And let him who thirsts come.
Whoever desires,
let him take the water of life freely." [36]

(Revelation 22:17, emphasis added)

When you are participating in the Principles of the Torah, you will begin to hear the Voice of the Principles. The Holy Spirit (Voice of the Principles) continuously talks to you about your needs and desires. The Holy Spirit is interceding for you continuously. Your life is constantly covered with this prayer and intercession. You may feel alone, you may feel isolated, you may even have tormenting thoughts that nobody really cares for you at all. But in reality, the opposite is occurring! While you are asleep, Yeshua watches over you. While you work, Yeshua prays for you. When you feel doubtful, alone, or discouraged, Yeshua speaks to you. You truly are His "special treasure" (Exodus 19), the "redeemed of the LORD" (Psalms 107), and the "apple of His eye" (Zechariah 2).

"For the LORD's portion is His people; Jacob is the place of His inheritance. He found him in a desert land and in the wasteland, a howling wilderness; He encircled him, He instructed him, He kept him as the apple of His eye." [37]

(Deuteronomy 32:9-10)

"Happy is the man who finds wisdom (Torah),
and the man who gains understanding;
for her proceeds are better than the profits of silver,
and her gain than fine gold. She is more precious
than rubies, and all the things you may desire cannot
compare with her. Length of days is in her right hand,
in her left hand riches and honor. Her ways are
ways of pleasantness, and all her paths are peace.
She is a tree of life to those who take hold of her,
and happy are all who retain her." [38]

(Proverbs 3:13-18)

In the Scriptures, the word *Torah* is synonymous with the word *Wisdom* and also with the expression the *Tree of Life.* Therefore, the Torah is not only God's Teaching and Instruction—Torah represents life itself! The Torah scroll is a visual demonstration of what God has already written on your heart and placed within your mind according to the New Covenant. In other words, the LORD takes these words written on the Torah scroll and makes them come alive to you by the power of the Holy Spirit. The *Tanakh* (Old Testament) uses various words to refer to God's instructions for His people. The most commonly used words are: [39]

Law

Decrees; Statutes

Judgments; Ordinances

Commands; Testimonies

The majority of people and ministers today still see the Torah as law rather than teaching. They're innocent, and the reason they are innocent is because we have failed to teach and disciple them in the Torah. When you look at this list of words: law, commands, decrees, judgments, ordinances, statutes, testimonies, you are going to sense a certain hardness in the translation. But if I translate these words back into their original Hebrew, they become the words, *"Torah," "Chukim," "Mishpatim,"* and *"Mitzvot."*

1. **Law (Torah):**
   If I say the word "law" in English, you may think of the Highway Patrolman pulling you over and writing you a ticket. You hear law, and you naturally think legalism. But, in the Hebrew mindset, Torah is not law as is the Western or Greek understanding of the word. Torah is Teaching, Instruction, Guidance, and Direction leading to life. Torah is practical Godly Instruction for His holy people.

2. **Decrees; Statutes (Chukim):**
   The word *"Chukim"* means image, a lasting impression, or to take upon the image of God. The 613 Principles of the Torah are not intended as harsh, rigid decrees or statutes of Law. They are life-giving Principles which reflect the image—the nature and character—of God. The *Chukim* should create

a *lasting impression* for us and our descendants; an impression that reflects the glory of the Divine nature within us.

3. Judgments; Ordinances (Mishpatim):

The word *"Mishpatim"* actually refers to God's deliverer and deliverance. So how was this word translated as judgment? Whenever you take a word from Hebrew—an action and love language, and then translate it into Greek—a rigid and exacting language, you are going to transmit that hardness in the translation. In the case of *"Mishpatim,"* if I use the word judgment instead of the word deliverance, there's a big difference to your ears! If I come to judge you, it gives a connotation that you are guilty of something. Many, many people live with ambiguous feelings of guilt and shame, but they are actually living in fear. Fear is not absence of the Presence of God; fear is the absence of the presence of *direction.* And what is Torah? Torah is guidance, teaching, and direction. In other words, the Torah written on your heart and mind already has an instruction embedded in you, and when the Holy Spirit embodies and empowers that instruction, it leads to deliverance *(Mishpatim)* and never judgment.

4. Commands; Testimonies (Mitzvot):

A more accurate English translation of the Hebrew word *"Mitzvot"* is deeds, good works, or works of righteousness. This category of Instructions in the Torah is intimately associated with compassion, charity, and alms-giving. It draws on the empathetic reaches of our hearts as fellow human beings, to care for and share with one another.

Law, Decrees, Judgments, Testimonies—these are legal terms, and they illustrate the difference between covenant law, and man's law. In man's law you rely on precedent and statute; you require case law. The words Teaching, Image, Deliverance, and Deeds—these terms come out of covenant law. You're in covenant with God.

You don't have to earn salvation through works. You are not trying to appease a pagan god. In Yeshua, you're no longer under the judgment of the law of sin and death. You are not in pursuit of God; God is in pursuit of you!

Most of the time in the Scriptures, when legal words such as law, statutes, decrees, or testimonies appear in translation, you can restore the intended meaning by substituting the original Hebrew words and meanings back into the Biblical text. The following examples compare several English translations side-by-side with the original Hebrew understanding:

1. Law (Torah): Teaching, Instruction, Guidance

"I delight to do Your will,
O my God,
and Your **law (Torah)**
is within my heart."

"I delight to do Your will,
O my God,
and Your **Teaching (Torah)**
is within my heart." [40]
(Psalms 40:8, emphasis added)

"Blessed is the man whom
You instruct, O Lord,
and teach out of Your
law (Torah)"

"Blessed is the man
whom You instruct,
O Lord, and teach
out of Your
guidance (Torah)" [41]
(Psalms 94:12, emphasis added)

"Give me understanding, and I shall keep Your **law (Torah);** indeed, I shall observe it with my whole heart."

"Give me understanding, and I shall keep Your **Instruction (Torah);** indeed, I shall observe it with my whole heart." [42]

(Psalms 119:34, emphasis added)

2. Decrees; Statutes (Chukim): Image; Lasting Impression; Image of God

"In the day when your walls are to be built, in that day the **decree (chukim)** shall go far and wide."

"In the day when your walls are to be built, in that day the **image of God (chukim)** shall go far and wide." [43]

(Micah 7:11, emphasis added)

"The covenant which He made with Abraham, and His oath to Isaac, and confirmed it to Jacob for a **statute (chukim),** to Israel as an everlasting covenant"

"The covenant which He made with Abraham, and His oath to Isaac, and confirmed it to Jacob for a **lasting impression (chukim),** to Israel as an everlasting covenant" [44]

(Psalms 105:9-10, emphasis added)

3. Judgments; Ordinances (Mishpatim): God's Deliverer; Deliverance

"For when Your **judgments (mishpatim)** are in the earth, the inhabitants of the world will learn righteousness."

"For when Your **deliverers (mishpatim)** are in the earth, the inhabitants of the world will learn righteousness." [45]
(Isaiah 26:9, emphasis added)

For all nations shall come and worship before You, for Your **judgments (mishpatim)** have been manifested."

"For all nations shall come and worship before You, for Your **deliverers (mishpatim)** have been manifested." [46]
(Revelation 15:4, emphasis added)

4. Commands; Testimonies (Mitzvot): Deeds; Works of Righteousness

"You shall diligently keep the commandments of the Lord your God, His **testimonies (mitzvot),** and His statutes which He has commanded you."

"You shall diligently keep the commandments of the Lord your God, His **deeds (mitzvot),** and His statutes which He has commanded you." [47]
(Deuteronomy 6:17, emphasis added)

"All the paths of the Lord
are mercy and truth,
to such as keep His
covenant and His
testimonies (mitzvot)."

"All the paths of the Lord
are mercy and truth,
to such as keep His
covenant and His **works
of righteousness (mitzvot).**"[48]
(Psalms 25:10, emphasis added)

TRANSLATION, TRANSLATION, TRANSLATION

> *The results of interpreting Biblical concepts and Hebrew expressions from a Greek mindset have been disastrous for both Christianity and Judaism. Much of this has happened because the Bible is a Middle-Eastern book that we have read from a Western cultural perspective.*[49]

It's a matter of restoring a Hebrew mindset of the Spirit and life found within the Torah, and removing a negative Greek mindset of *law* that still permeates the Church today. This does NOT mean that I'm against the Church, I teach in churches all the time. The message I'm bringing is a teaching that won't frustrate you, that is not common, and that separates you. This message will cause you to truly prosper and to have gain and increase in your life.

"Therefore lay aside all filthiness and
overflow of wickedness, and receive with meekness the

implanted word, which is able to save your souls.
But be doers of the word, and not hearers only,
deceiving yourselves. For if anyone is a hearer
of the word and not a doer, he is like a man observing his
natural face in a mirror; for he observes himself, goes away,
and immediately forgets what kind of man he was.
But he who looks into the perfect law of liberty
and continues in it, and is not a forgetful hearer
but a doer of the work, this one will be blessed
in what he does."[50]

(James 1:21-25, emphasis added)

Within the Torah are God's Principles that cause you to prosper spiritually, physically, financially, and emotionally. The main reason why so many believers today have lost their fire for God is because they are frustrated. And why are they frustrated? Because they're not walking in God's purpose for their lives. And what is the purpose of God for your life? The Torah.

God is a God of order, and not of chaos. The Torah is a Book of order, and order is the accurate arrangement of all things. God is returning you to the Torah in order to remove those things which are inaccurately arranged in your life. The Torah is light *(or)* in the midst of your darkness. By the Torah, God removes your chaos and brings your life back into order. God has a definitive purpose for your life, and that purpose is the message that people in the Church seem to be starving for.

> *Because of the misunderstandings of the meaning of Torah and its role in the life of the believers today, Paul is often accused of forsaking the Torah, teaching against the Torah, and starting a new religion called Christianity. While tradition says otherwise, Paul was not a Christian in the Western sense, nor did he ever become one! Paul was a Torah-observant Jew.*[51]

"For Christ is the end of the law
for righteousness
to everyone who believes." [52]

(Romans 10:4, emphasis added)

The word "end" in Greek is "telos," and is more properly translated as "goal." Christ is the telos—the ***goal*** *of the law. Paul is not saying that the Torah has "ended," Paul is simply saying that the Torah points people to Jesus, the ultimate goal of the Torah!* [53]

Paul also speaks of different kinds of laws, but this is hard to distinguish because the same Greek word, ***nomos,*** *is used for each reference and translated into English as* ***law*** *without any distinction.*[54]

What was the faith of Paul? It was the Torah! Remember, Paul is writing to those raised in the Torah, those who already understand Torah as teaching and not as legalism. So when you read your Bible, you may have a hard time knowing the difference between *the law of sin and death* and *the law of Christ Jesus.* You have to discern which law are the Scriptures talking about? The first century believers were asking the same questions. That's why, in Romans 3, they came to Paul and questioned, *"Has the Torah been done away with?"* And Paul answered saying, *"Heaven forbid!* God has terminated the law of sin and death, not His holy Law—Torah.

Since Paul's writings do not make a clear distinction between the holy law of God and the law of sin and death, it is easy to get confused and think Paul was writing negatively about the Torah. When Paul seems to be writing negatively about the Torah, he is really writing against the misuse of the Torah as the legalistic system of rules and regulations one must keep in order to be saved. Phrases such as "under the law," "works of the law," or "curse of the law" refer to this misuse or perversion of the law... Paul also speaks against a certain group of Jewish believers called "Judaizers," who taught that the Gentiles had to keep the Torah as a ***requirement*** *for salvation.*[55]

"For the law of the Spirit of Life in Christ Jesus
has made me free from the law of sin and death." [56]

(Romans 8:2)

CHAPTER 5

TORAH: THE FIRST CENTURY CHURCH

The Voice of the Principles, Volume 2, Part 1
To view a video segment of this resource, scan the QR code using your smartphone.

"And when they heard it, they glorified the Lord.
And they said to him, "You see, brother,
how many myriad of Jews there are who have believed,
and they are all zealous for the Law" [1]

(Acts 21:20)

Do the events in Acts Chapter 21 occur before or after Acts 2:38 and the Day of Pentecost (*Shavuot* in Hebrew)? So in other words, in Acts 21 they already had the infilling of the Holy Spirit, they were speaking in tongues, they were on fire for God, they loved the Lord, and yes...they were ***zealous** for the Torah!* Can you imagine that? The Holy Spirit led the first century Church to the Torah.

Again, you are not in pursuit of God; God is in pursuit of you. In fact, countless born again, Spirit-filled Christians around the world are becoming immersed in and returning to the Hebrew roots of the Christian faith. These believers, often to their own amazement, find themselves drawn to their Hebrew roots today, at times even unaware that God prophesied this great restoration of Torah, the Hebrew letters and language of the Bible, and the Jewish culture and lifestyle of Jesus—the full counsel of the Holy Spirit.

What I'm saying is the Holy Ghost *brought* you to what nourishes you *in* the Spirit of God. And when you do the things that nourish the

Spirit of God, you rekindle your fire for God. The Torah is God's orchestration tool that enables you to control your mind and thoughts, or better yet, for the LORD to control who you are, and how you are living as His child.

"Remember the Sabbath Day, to keep it holy." [2]

(Exodus 20:8)

The Sabbath Day? The Sabbath has been around since the seventh day of Creation. If God (Jesus) is truly the same yesterday, today, and forever (Hebrews 13:8), then exactly when and how did the Sabbath Day become a negotiable matter? When you read the Ten Commandments which say, *"You shall not murder,"* then as believers, is it proper to negotiate and say, "We're now under *grace* in the New Testament, and no longer under the law, so we can freely murder!" Is that negotiable? Heaven forbid! The Commandment against murder is not negotiable! So what about the rest of the Commandments, are they negotiable?

As you return to the Hebrew roots of the Christian faith, you will begin to *"Remember the Sabbath Day…"* and find yourself sanctifying, or setting this specific period of time apart. From sundown Friday night to sundown Saturday night you will begin to celebrate the Sabbath. Now you can still worship on Sunday, that's not an issue. You can also worship on Monday, Tuesday, Wednesday, Thursday, and Friday. But you must understand that the foremost appointed time – the God-given, Holy Ghost power-driven, Order of Melchizedek anointing, comes on the Sabbath, in God's preordained time! When you synchronize your life according to God's appointed times (*Moadim*), the Feasts and the Sabbath now draw you. Remember, *"The Sabbath was made for man, man was not made for the Sabbath"* (Mark 2:27).

God ordained specific times throughout the year that you are instructed to enter into His timing. When you do, you are not subject to time, time is subject to you! Written in the Torah is the promise that God will literally add time to your life. How does He add time to your life? While everybody else is growing older on Saturday—washing their cars, having garage sales, etc.—you're absorbing life in the Presence of God where He causes gain and increase in your life. So on the Sabbath, you begin stepping into God's timeless eternity, and that eternity is adding life to yours.

The first century believers accepted Jesus as their Savior and Messiah. They had *also* accepted Jesus' lifestyle of Torah within the context of the Hebrew culture and customs. These were the people in the upper room in Acts 2:38. These were the ones who received the infilling of the Holy Spirit. Those who were speaking in tongues were already *in the Spirit* when the Holy Ghost fell. They believed in Yeshua, risen from the dead, and they were *zealous* for the Torah. If these early disciples were participating in the customs, the culture, and the context of Torah, what should you and I be doing?

THE TROUBLE WITH "GENTILES"

As I mentioned, I don't like using the word *Gentile* because Biblically speaking, the word "Gentile" means "pagan, confused, and without God" (Ephesians 2). When referring to non-Jewish believers, I prefer to use the word "Nations." When we talk about believers around the world returning to the Hebrew roots of the Christian faith—the Torah—we're confirming the Biblical prophecies about the nations returning to their Hebrew roots.

In Genesis 22:17 God confirms by covenant that He will multiply the seed of Abraham as the stars of the heavens and the sand upon the seashore, and God empowers that seed to possess the gates of their enemies. Not surprisingly, Abraham's very name means *"father of a multitude of nations."*

In the New Testament period, many among this *multitude of nations* believed in Jesus as their Lord and Savior. The question soon arose about their responsibility to the Torah, just as it does today. In other words, once we come to believe in the Messiah, what parts of the Torah should we observe?[2]

"Then all the multitude kept silent and listened
to Barnabas and Paul declaring how many miracles
and wonders God had worked through them among
the Gentiles. And after they had become silent,
James answered, saying, "Men and brethren, listen to me:
Simon has declared how God at the first visited
the Gentiles to take out of them a people for His name.
And with this the words of the prophets agree,
just as it is written: 'After this I will return
And will rebuild the tabernacle of David,
which has fallen down; I will rebuild its ruins,
and I will set it up; so that the rest of mankind may
seek the Lord, even all the Gentiles who are called
by My name, says the Lord who does all these things.'
"Known to God from eternity are all His works.
Therefore I judge that we should not trouble those from
among the Gentiles who are turning to God,
but that we write to them to abstain from things polluted
by idols, from sexual immorality, from things strangled,
and from blood. For Moses has had throughout many
generations those who preach him in every city, being read
in the synagogues every Sabbath." [3]

(Acts 15:12-21)

The first century Church was faced with a very similar problem as we encounter today. As the Holy Spirit is leading believers from the nations into an understanding of the Hebrew roots of the Christian faith, how do we begin to teach the Torah to those who were not raised as Jews, and have very little, if any, familiarity with the Torah and its 613 Principles? The Council in Acts decided to begin with four primary instructions. They began by teaching new believers the foundational beliefs and practices called, ***"the four corners of the Torah."***

The Acts Council further reasoned that since *"Moses has had throughout many generations those who preach him in every city, being read in the synagogues every Sabbath,"* these converts from the nations would continue to be taught the Torah as they attended weekly services in the synagogue! The unforeseen circumstance of the Council's decision is that believers, then and now, failed to remain in the synagogues and developed an identity as "Christians" which separated them from their Hebrew heritage, masked the Jewish face of the Messiah, and estranged them from the relevance and application of the Torah Principles for their daily lives.

THE FOUR CORNERS OF THE TORAH

1. Abstain from things polluted by idols.

As a first century believer, and even today, I would have to ask myself, "If I'm instructed to abstain from idols, what is an idol?" I have to search the Scriptures (the Torah) to discover what God calls idolatry.

2. Abstain from sexual immorality.

The typical professional counselor today says as long as it doesn't offend you or your partner, most anything is sexually permissible. What they don't realize is that when you participate in sexual activities that God calls immoral, you enter the Realm of Death. To truly *abstain from sexual immorality,* you have to refer back to the Torah in the Book of Leviticus Chapters 13 and 15 to discover what sexual immorality is in God's eyes.

3. Abstain from things strangled.

"Abstain from things that are strangled?" This is referring to the dietary laws, and what is Biblically considered proper *(kosher)* food. Being scattered among the nations, many of us ate almost anything: pickled pig's feet, chitlins, lobster, shrimp, etc. Yet how many of us were taught the dietary instructions given by the One Who created us? How differently would we think and feel if we ate only the things that God calls food in the Torah?

4. Abstain from blood.

"Abstain from blood. We're supposed to abstain from blood?" How many with German ancestry have eaten blood sausage, or head cheese (ground pig's brains and pig's blood)? From its instructions about the lifeblood of animals (Deuteronomy 12:23), the blood of purity (Leviticus 12:4), and all the way to the caution of never making common the shed blood of our LORD (Hebrews 10:29), the Bible is filled with teachings about the handling or mishandling of blood. Yet this distinction between life and death is largely untaught and mostly unknown to believers today.

Everyone that comes into the Torah by the Holy Spirit is like a brand new child—it's as if you've been born again, *again!* And when a child begins learning how to walk, someone steps with the child encouraging and exhorting, "Come on, you can do it!" As the child takes the first few tentative steps, they may say, "That's great, you're doing it!" Soon the child reaches a little further, and takes another few steps. The child may grab hold of a table or a similar object so they can keep going, and continue to walk, with growing *steadiness and steadfastness,* step-by-step along the way.

So how do I encourage people as they return to their Hebrew roots? What is the discipleship process I use to teach the nations how to walk? Do I just bring everybody in one room and say, "Listen, tomorrow morning at nine o'clock we'll be wrapping *tefillin* and *davening*. I want to make sure you know how to read the blessing on your *Tallit* before you put it on. By the way, your sex life will change effective tomorrow! When your wife is having her monthly cycle, you will not have relations with her; you'll sleep in separate beds, and I expect your diet to be *kosher-certified* by the end of the week!" Is that approach likely to work with most people? Is that what you would want? Or do you want to be able to step in slowly, methodically, like a child learning to walk?

The first century believers were no different. The Council in Acts knew that these believers needed the first important steps—*the four corners of the Torah*—and then as they worshipped God in the synagogues on the Sabbath, they would learn the rest of the Torah and understand how it pointed to Yeshua. Again, the purpose was not **Salvation**—they were already believers! The purpose was **Redemption**—the **redeemed** lifestyle of Torah that would enable them to relate to their already Torah-observant Jewish brothers and sisters. After almost 2,000 years the same questions are being discussed as believers are returning to the Hebrew roots of the Christian faith, and once again asking, *"What is the Torah: Law or Grace?"* [4]

CHAPTER 6
TORAH: THE UNPARALLELED DREAM

How to Witness the Torah, Volume 1, Part 1
To view a video segment of this resource, scan the QR code using your smartphone.

"For the vision is yet for an appointed time,
but in the end it shall speak and not lie.
Though it tarry, wait for it.
Cause it will surely come, it will not tarry." [1]
(Habakkuk 2:3)

God has an unparalleled dream for you called the Torah. The 613 Principles of the redeemed lifestyle are called habits. Again, you don't decide your future, you decide your habits, and your habits decide your future. The Principles of the Torah are the purpose of your design on the earth, and that purpose is not common to the unregenerate man. Torah is the unparalleled dream revealing the purposes of God to you. This unparalleled dream will require unparalleled patience. In other words, a Torah dream will require Torah patience. God brought you into His Kingdom and He no longer sees you as a commoner, because He has made you uncommon.

I want you to know, and I want to say to you from the deepest part of my heart, "Welcome home!" You may not understand all of this right now. It's all brand new to you. But the God of Abraham, Isaac, and Jacob has brought you to your covenant. He has restored you to your inheritance. He's leading you into a higher walk. He is causing you to walk in Biblical faith. God found you in the midst of your exile and He is restoring you to the unparalleled dream of the Torah.

The unparalleled dream is what makes me who I am. I don't want to be common, and I don't want to make God common among people. I want to be able to follow the dream and the passion that God has for me, and inspire you in the passion that God has for you! You must continually visualize this unparalleled dream in your heart and your mind. Habakkuk 2:2 says, *"Write the vision and make it plain upon tables, that he that reads it may run."* You might think, "well then, I need to write the vision down." However, Habakkuk 2 is talking about you and what God has *already* done in you.

"For the earnest expectation of the
creation eagerly waits for the revealing
of the sons of God.
For the creation was subjected to futility,
not willingly, but because of
Him who subjected it in hope;
because the creation itself also will be
delivered from the bondage of
corruption into the glorious liberty
of the children of God." [2]

(Romans 8:19-21)

Believers worldwide, and even creation itself, have been waiting anxiously for the glory of God to appear. This is ultimately the glorious appearing of Messiah at the end of the Age, but remember, Yeshua's most prominent teaching was the Kingdom of Heaven. This activity of God is revealing His glory in the midst of His people—His dwelling place! The Scriptures relate that the abiding Presence of God has appeared only seven times on the earth, and we are in the seventh time!

SEVEN APPEARANCES OF GOD'S ABIDING PRESENCE

Number 1: At the time of Adam.

Number 2: At the time of Noah.

Number 3: At the time of Moses and the mobile, moving Tabernacle.

Number 4: At the time of Solomon's Temple.

Number 5: At the time of Herod's Temple.

Number 6: At the time of Jesus Christ.

Number 7: The last time the Abiding Presence of God has appeared on earth is within You!

"The mystery
which has been hidden
from ages and from generations,
but now has been revealed
to His saints.
To them God willed
to make known what are the
riches of the glory of this mystery
among the Gentiles:
which is Christ in you,
the hope of glory." [3]

(Colossians 1:26-27)

God, Jesus Christ *in you,* is the hope of glory. Remember, when your confession matches your conduct, it's called the *kavod,* the glory of God. Up until this point, Christianity has had the confession (Jesus) down to a science. The Jewish people have focused on the Torah (conduct) regarding how to live your life. Now, within the prophetic end-times move of God (Deuteronomy 30), the House of Judah (Jewish people) is being reunited with the House of Israel (believing Nations). These two Houses are again becoming one in the hand of the Messiah Yeshua (Ezekiel 37). Biblically this movement of God is called the *"Restoration of the House of David."*

God is continuing to advance this restoration whether you and I embrace the Torah or not! God's full covenant commitment resides within the *Renewed* Covenant. God is not manipulated by tears. He is not moved by emotion. God has called us to **"Shema!"** (listen *and* obey). He is a God of covenant, and He does not anoint that which is common.

What *is* common to someone who walks outside of the Torah? Tears! Emotions! Frustration! Anger! Rage! Currently, in the United States, we are building more prisons than we ever have in our history. Why are we doing that? Because people have not been taught how to walk in the lifestyle of the Torah. Coincidentally, the message of Torah is taking off in prisons across the country, right now. And why? Because the prisoners are crying out within themselves saying, "Give me order! Society has not taught me anything. My father or mother couldn't teach me. If I am the temple of the living God, if I contain the glory of God—then God, where are You?"

TORAH IS THE UNPARALLELED DREAM

The Torah will not allow you to make God common. The Torah is birthed in uncommon pain—not the torment of a pagan god, but the discipline of a loving Father. Pain will cause you to search for an answer. Pain and crisis are simply an introduction to a new season in your life, and crisis precedes promotion.

Torah—the unparalleled dream—will require an unparalleled faith.

Faith, again, is confidence or persistence in the Principles. In the Greek mindset, faith is how strongly you believe, how accurately you can confess, etc. But in the Hebrew mindset, faith is the one who is persistent; who knocks on the door and keeps on knocking. God has called you to be an uncommon person, because you serve an incomparable God. He has prepared for you an unparalleled prosperity, an unparalleled healing, and an unparalleled faith.

Torah—the unparalleled dream—must be born within you.

God is unparalleled. He is Elohim, the intensification of all power. He is Adonai, the force of God upon the earth. He has forced His way into your life. He is healing you, He is raising you up, He is bringing you to the forefront, and now He is leading you back to His Teaching and Instruction.

Torah—the unparalleled dream—requires an unparalleled focus.

The reason people fail is due to broken focus. Apart from the Spirit-led lifestyle of the Torah, we often operate in a spirit of confusion. That's why so many are constantly trying to confess things into existence, vainly trying to strengthen their faith and focus. What you don't realize is you are not the one making it happen. God alone is the One making it happen within you. He formed you from a pattern that is unparalleled. When you finally step into your purpose (Torah), you will achieve an unparalleled focus, and your strength and energy will come directly from God.

Torah—the unparalleled dream—requires an unparalleled passion.

The Hebrew root word for passion means energy. When you have a passion for something, you also have energy for it! Passion is energy! Passion is enthusiasm and strength. Passion is a vital clue to the path that the Holy Spirit has chosen for your life. Every unparalleled achievement requires an unparalleled passion that only comes from God.

Torah—the unparalleled dream—requires unparalleled favor with others.

You need unparalleled favor to be able to communicate this message of the Torah to people. Joseph received favor from Pharaoh. Esther received favor from the king. Ruth received favor from Boaz. When the hand of God is upon you, favor will come. One day of favor is worth a lifetime of labor. Sow favor, expect it, protect it, and respect it. When someone shows you favor, sow favor!

Torah—the unparalleled dream—requires unparalleled preparation.

Jesus prepared 30 years for only 3½ years of ministry. Some vocations require many years of college before you are truly prepared to walk in your career. God is preparing you for His millennial reign leading into eternity. He is equipping you as laborers sent out into the great end-times harvest—the greatest evangelistic epoch mobilizing the Gospel to the ends of the earth. You are being taught in a school. Your Teacher (Rabbi) is Yeshua, Jesus Christ, and you are His student. You are learning to walk like the Rabbi walks. You will think like the Rabbi thinks. You will talk like the Rabbi talks. You will learn His ways because you are His disciple.

Torah—the unparalleled dream—qualifies those who deserve access to you.

The Torah imparts Godly discernment to you regarding people. It reveals those who are assigned to walk with you and those who are not. Yeshua passed by the crowds of curious onlookers. He passed through the religious-minded Pharisees and spiritual leaders, yet He shared an entire meal in the home of Zaccheus, the tax-collector.

Torah or Law in the English translation of the Bible means instruction, guidance, teaching, and direction, led of the Holy Spirit for walking with God. Torah does not mean a legalistic set of rules one must follow in order to be saved. The Western view of Torah is legalism, but this is not the Biblical view, nor was it the view that Jesus and Paul held. [4]

NEW TESTAMENT STATEMENTS ABOUT THE TORAH

1. *The hearers of the Torah are not justified before the Lord, but the doers of the Torah will be justified.* (Romans 2:23)
2. Paul taught the Ephesians that the promises of God come out of the law and they were to obey them so things would be well with them and they may live long on the earth. (Ephesians 6:2-3; Exodus 20:12; Deuteronomy 5:16)
3. The writer of the Book of Hebrews confirms that this is the same covenant of God's law (Torah) that He promised to renew by promising to write it on our hearts and our minds. (Hebrews 10:16)
4. James reminds us that if we commit sin we are actually transgressing the Torah. (James 2:11, James 2:8-26)
5. By keeping the Lord's commandments we know that we know Him. (1 John 2:3-4)
6. We have our prayers answered because we keep the Lord's commandments and do those things pleasing in His sight. (1 John 3:22) How do we know what things are pleasing in His sight? They are found in the Torah.
7. As we keep the commandments, God will dwell in us and we will have assurance through His Spirit. (1 John 3:24)
8. By keeping God's commandments, we know that our love for God and His children is real. (1 John 5:2-3)

9. The definition of Biblical love is to walk after God's commandments. (2 John 6)
10. Only those who keep the Lord's commandments will have the right to the Tree of Life. (Revelation 22:14)
11. Referring to the Old Testament Hebrew Scriptures, the only Torah available, James makes this statement, "Whosoever looks into the perfect law of liberty and continues therein, being not a forgetful hearer but a doer of the Word of the Torah shall be blessed in his deeds. (James 1:25)
12. The man who says he loves the Lord but does not keep His commandments is a liar and the truth cannot be within him. (1 John 2:4)[5]

Apostolic Faith Mission at Azusa Street

CHAPTER 7
REVIVAL IN THE TORAH

Pursuing Purpose, Part 1
To view a video segment of this resource, scan the QR code using your smartphone.

"For this is good and acceptable in the
sight of God our Savior, who desires all men
to be saved and come to the knowledge of the truth.
For there is one God and one Mediator between
God and men, the Man Christ Jesus." [1]

(1Timothy 2:3-5)

The truth of the Torah is the hottest message in the country. God is blessing the movement of the Torah and it's going to be taught worldwide. Not just in the United States or North America, but all over the world. Even as I write this, very few people have heard or understand this message…yet!

I was recently speaking at a conference marking the anniversary of the Azuza Street revival (1906-1915 in Los Angeles, CA). People from around the world were awestruck by the message of the Torah, and they recognized that this was the "something" they had been missing. They knew about worship, they were well-practiced in praise, and they already had the confession of Jesus. However, they were missing this critical conduct component of the Christian walk. This walk in the Torah Principles was the message they were starving for.

People came believing that God would speak directly to them; that they would receive a word from God. Much of the conference included the typical teachings heard over and over again. Yet these people were seasoned believers, they didn't come to get saved, this was expected to be a revival. The conference attendees were about to find out what I already knew—the message of the Torah *is* the revival! By the second and third night, the people were saying to me, *"This is the message; this is the revival that we've been looking for!"*

It was absolutely amazing to watch! Over 10,000 people attended the conference. Many were there because something was missing in their lives or in their relationship with the Lord. Something kept nagging at them that there simply had to be more. I began by asking how many were frustrated because they sensed they had been walking outside the purposes of God. Then, when I asked how many wanted to experience the walk of the LORD—5,000 to 8,000 people rushed the stage! I believe this is the beginning, the cutting-edge of one of the greatest revivals in the history of mankind. We are positioned by God with a message to be delivered to the universe and we're not going to miss the opportunity.

During this same conference, I met with a bishop who oversees 10,000 pastors in Africa—10,000 pastors! In the United States, if a church has 10,000 members, it's a mega-church. Here, God gave me the privilege of sitting down and sharing the truth of Torah with this African bishop. Now this one man can impart to 10,000 pastors, with those pastors, in turn, reaching hundreds of thousands of people.

Again, during this conference, I had two internationally-known ministers dialogue with me and say, *"We know that this is the next step, that this is the next way...but are you prepared for it?"* They were talking about being prepared with teachings, books, DVDs, and most importantly *people* who can answer the myriad of questions. Qualified people are needed to teach and minister to the hundreds upon hundreds, thousands upon thousands who are right now returning from the nations of their exile and dispersion.

Why is there such a sense of urgency about the message of Torah? Why is this so important for today? Because the Torah is the walk of

Jesus Christ. Torah is a key to greater empowerment by the Holy Spirit. I believe in and teach the **Salvation** message of Calvary, the atoning blood of Jesus, and the infilling of the Holy Spirit. It is ONLY Jesus' blood that has broken the power of sin and death in our lives, but as believers, we have largely neglected and long ago forgotten the walk of **Redemption**—the redeemed lifestyle of following the Torah *by* the Spirit of Jesus Christ—the Spirit of God in us!

Many believers today simply do not understand the importance of this message. They have never been taught the Redemption component of the Good News! They got saved, but they don't truly know the Man Yeshua, *His* walk and *His* ways. They don't understand that, in His humanity, every part of Jesus' walk aligned with the laws of the universe. Every step was synchronized with the sun, the moon, and the stars. This synchronization is explicitly detailed in the Torah. Jesus lived, died, and rose again in precise accordance with God's preordained timing.

The triumphal entry of Jesus into Jerusalem (John 12) took place on the 10th day of the month, which was exactly the same day that the Passover lambs were being brought into the Holy City. Jesus' crucifixion and death occurred precisely on the evening of Passover, even as the earthly lambs also became offerings. Exactly three days and three nights later, Yeshua's resurrection fulfilled the Feast of First Fruits, forever shattering the grip of death in the birth of eternal life. Only one of the Biblical Spring Feasts (Leviticus 23) then remained. Precisely 50 days later, tarrying in Jerusalem as the Lord had instructed, the Apostles received a great outpouring of the Spirit in fulfillment of the ancient Feast of *Shavuot* (Pentecost)!

Today, when you synchronize your walk with the Feast Days of God, including your worship on the Sabbath, you also are aligning with the sun, the moon, and the stars—the heavenly timing of God. You step into the most positive flow of God's power. The rabbis believe there is a double-portion anointing when you celebrate the Sabbath, and that God then deliberately purposes for you and your lineage to prosper. Assembling on the Sabbath means you are walking in the precision that God has called you to—the exact instruction, at the exact time—causing your entire being to synchronize with everything God has preordained for you!

God created our world by taking a chaotic universe and establishing His order. That same order is now being restored in the midst of His people. The first Creation established order, while the second creation (You) establishes people. The first Creation brought a physical order, this second creation restores a moral order to the universe. This same creative and restorative force of God is expressed by His Word. His Word embodies the foundational Principles of the universe; Principles given to His redeemed people to teach us holy from unholy, clean from unclean, and about the Feast Days of God (Ezekiel 22).

"He who has My Commandments
and keeps them, it is he who loves Me.
And he who loves Me will be loved
by My Father, and I will love him and
manifest Myself to him." [2]

(John 14:21)

"Now by this we know
that we know Him,
if we keep His commandments.
He who says, 'I know Him,'
and does not keep
His commandments, is a liar,
and the truth is not in him.'" [3]

(1 John 2:3-4)

The Holy Spirit manifested on Mount Sinai at the giving Torah. The same Holy Spirit empowered Moses, Joshua, Samson, Gideon, and the great kings of Israel. The Holy Spirit spoke through the prophets Isaiah, Ezekiel, and Joel. God's Spirit spoke to Israel in the wilderness and fell upon the Jewish believers in Acts Chapter 2. This same Holy Spirit now dwells within you! The gift of the Holy Spirit today is the gift of God's Presence and power in us. The Creator of the universe reveals Himself in no other area, and on no other mountain. He manifests His glory in you. This is why the New Testament witnesses confirm that Christ in *you* is the hope of God's glory.

"I have written for him the great things of My law,
but they were considered a foreign thing." [4]

(Hosea 8:12)

The failed teaching by the Jews and the flawed teaching by the Church has largely removed Christianity's relationship with the Torah—God's Teaching and Instruction—and replaced it with confessions of faith, religion, and ritual. We have memorized man's creeds and forgotten God's deeds. We have been deceived into thinking that knowing is the same as doing.[5]

"By this we know that we are in Him. He who says that he
abides in Him ought himself
also to walk just as He walked." [6]

(1 John 2:5-6, emphasis added)

Again we reaffirm, we do NOT obey the Torah to be saved. We obey God's commandments because we are saved and desire to follow and please Him. In the bondage of Egypt, the Israelites were saved ***by grace***

through faith in the blood of the Lamb. Christians today are saved in the same manner. The difference found in the New Covenant is not that the Torah has somehow been replaced or done away with. The difference in the New Covenant is that Jesus has written the Torah on our hearts and minds (Jeremiah 31; Hebrews 8). He has overcome the failure of the covenant made in the wilderness, namely the disobedience of our flesh (Hebrews 8), and Jesus now empowers our obedience by His Holy Spirit in us. He accompanies this obedience with the fullness of the promises reserved for His covenant people in the Torah. The Torah is the Instruction Manual—given to a *redeemed* people to teach us how to walk a *redeemed* lifestyle.

> *During the inter-testamental period there was a gradual change in thinking regarding the role of the Torah. Some rabbis began to teach that keeping the Torah was* ***necessary*** *for redemption rather than the* ***result*** *of redemption. It was during this time that for some, Torah became a legalistic system of rules and regulations people were required to keep in order to earn God's favor, rather than as an expression of grace and faith in their hearts.*[7]

> *By misunderstanding the relationship between grace, faith, and the law, the church has taught that grace means that Christians are free from any* ***Torah*** *in their lives and can live as they please. This unfortunate teaching has contributed significantly to the shallowness of Western Christianity.*[8]

Many believers are surprised to learn that approximately 85% of the New Testament is simply a repeat of the Torah, and in fact, the Book of Leviticus was the second most quoted Book by Jesus in the Gospels. Just how did we ever separate the Old from the New Testament? How did we come to reason, and even teach, that more than two-thirds of the Bible has little or no relevance to believers today? The teaching that genuine redemptive faith leads to works of the Torah is found throughout the New Testament writings.[9]

"What does it profit, my brethren,
if someone says he has faith but
does not have works? Can faith save him?
If a brother or sister is naked and
destitute of daily food,
and one of you says to them,
"Depart in peace, be warmed and filled,"
but you do not give them the things
which are needed for the body,
what does it profit? Thus also **faith by itself,
if it does not have works, is dead.**" [10]

(James 2:14-17, emphasis added)

Faith requires action just as faith requires instruction! In the United States alone, statistics show that upwards of 25,000 people a month are leaving the churches.[11] Why do we see such a lack of fire in the body of Christ? What is the root cause of the countless thousands of "un-churched" people today, disillusioned by religion, disappointed in their spiritual leaders? Could it be that we aren't really operating in our purpose? If the Torah does indeed have significance for the believer today, just what exactly is the purpose of the Torah?

TORAH = PURPOSE

1. PURPOSE DETERMINES DESIGN.

God gave us His design from the foundations of the earth, and when you walk in the ways that He designed for you, He will prosper you, He will advance you, and He will cause your lineage to be advanced. The Torah is the walk of the faithful—faith in Jesus, walking according to the Torah!

2. PURPOSE DETERMINES YOUR POTENTIAL.

The purpose of God was written by "the finger of God" and given to Moses at Mount Sinai. This purpose determines both your short-term and your long-term potential. If you desire to live *life more abundantly* (John 10:10) on the earth and achieve your God-given potential, you will begin to desire and follow His plan, designed to give you the maximum potential benefit—the Torah.

3. PURPOSE DETERMINES NATURAL ABILITIES.

Walking in God's Teaching and Instruction, prepares you to receive the maximum benefit that you can have on the earth, through the supernatural blessings of God and through your own natural abilities. For instance, when you eat right *(kosher),* you feel better and you live longer. What might the results be if you not only eat right, but also treat your spouse right, your children right, and you handle your family right—the way of natural ability. In other words, God gives you the *nature* of the Lord, to walk according to the Torah in a *natural* way.

4. PURPOSE DETERMINES CAPACITY AND ABILITY.

Purpose determines the capacity and the ability you have in your life. When you walk in your natural abilities by the inspiration of the *Ruach HaKodesh* (the Holy Spirit), you contain all of the capacity to do the exact thing that you should do, at the exact moment, at the exact place, at the exact time. You begin maximizing, through Godly precision, the capacity and the abilities that you have on the earth.

5. PURPOSE DETERMINES NATURAL TALENTS.

The Torah imparts your unique and natural talent called an instruction. The instruction is given to you with the expectation that you will use your talent to bring the universe to a higher level. Interestingly, your instruction was not designed for you alone. The instruction that God put within you was designed for you to give it to others.

6. PURPOSE DETERMINES NATURAL DESIRES.

God has put within you the natural desire for His Principles. He has given you the desire to celebrate the Sabbath. He put within you the natural desire for a man to marry a woman, and a woman to marry a man. He gave you a natural desire to eat properly. He didn't design the human body to eat pig, lobster, shrimp, or crab. He created within you the desire to participate in those things which are life and not death.

7. PURPOSE DETERMINES FULFILLMENT AND SATISFACTION.

When you keep the Torah, you have a sense of fulfillment and personal satisfaction. For example, on the Sabbath when a husband prays Proverbs 31 over his wife, or a wife prays Psalms 1 over her husband, or when you pray over your children and they receive a blessing, your children's children will continue to do this same thing for a thousand generations and thus they inherit from you a great personal satisfaction.

8. PURPOSE IS THE SOURCE OF PASSION.

The Body of Christ today is largely anemic and at times, sadly ineffective. The reason we have lost our fire and passion is because we have not served our purpose. Where has the passion gone that we had when we were first born again, when we first met the Lord? We've attached ourselves to things that do not have life in them, and we've detached ourselves from the true Source of passion.

9. PURPOSE GIVES EXISTENCE MEANING.

The Torah gives your very existence meaning. It defines and directs nature, natural events, and the Divine nature within you. It reveals God's purpose in you, and your purpose in Creation.

10. PURPOSE IS THE MEASURE OF SUCCESS AND FAILURE.

Torah teaches you the measure of success or failure. You walk in the assurance that you're going to succeed, not based on your abilities, but supernaturally. When you walk in the Realm of Life, God causes supernatural blessings and creativity to come your way.

CHAPTER 8

NATURAL AND WILD BRANCHES – ONE TREE

Controversy of Tzion, Part 1
To view a video segment of this resource, scan the QR code using your smartphone.

The Apostle Paul understood that the House of Israel's return to the Torah and the restoration of the whole House of Jacob were essential precursors for Messiah's return. He shares a deep truth about this mystery in Romans Chapter 11:

"I say then, has God cast away His people?
Certainly not! For I also am an Israelite,
of the seed of Abraham, of the tribe of Benjamin.
God has not cast away His people whom
He foreknew…Even so then,
at this present time there is a
remnant according to the election of grace.
And if by grace, then it is no longer of works;
otherwise grace is no longer grace.
But if it is of works, it is no longer grace;
otherwise work is no longer work.
What then? Israel has not obtained what it seeks;
but the elect have obtained it,
and the rest were blinded…

11 …I say then, have they stumbled that they should fall?
Certainly not! But through their fall, to provoke them
to jealousy, salvation has come to the Gentiles.

Now if their fall is riches for the world,
and their failure riches for the Gentiles,
how much more their fullness!
For I speak to you Gentiles;
inasmuch as I am an apostle to the Gentiles,
I magnify my ministry, if by any means
I may provoke to jealousy those who are my flesh
and save some of them. For if their being cast away
is the reconciling of the world,
what will their acceptance be
but life from the dead?

23 …And they also, if they do not continue in unbelief,
will be grafted in, for God is able to graft them in again.
For if you were cut out of the olive tree
which is wild by nature, and were grafted
contrary to nature into a cultivated olive tree,
how much more will these,
who are natural branches, be grafted
into their own olive tree? For I do not desire,
brethren, that you should be ignorant of this mystery,
lest you should be wise in your own opinion,
that blindness in part has happened to Israel
until the fullness of the Gentiles has come in.
And so all Israel will be saved, as it is written:
"The Deliverer will come out of Zion,
and He will turn away ungodliness from Jacob;
for this is My covenant with them,
when I take away their sins."
Concerning the gospel they are enemies
for your sake, but concerning the election

they are beloved for the sake of the fathers.
For the gifts and the calling of God are irrevocable.
For as you were once disobedient to God,
yet have now obtained mercy
through their disobedience, even so these also
have now been disobedient, that through the mercy shown
you they also may obtain mercy." [1]

(Romans 11:1-31 abridged)

Several years ago while in Israel, I witnessed for myself the process for growing and grafting olive trees. I share the specifics of this process with you, because within it is a key to understanding Paul's theological discourse in Romans 11. Paul speaks specifically about the Olive Tree representing the whole House of Israel, with its natural and wild branches, and the glory of the Root which sustains the life of the tree.

First, let's look at the prophetic representation of each of the elements in the story:

Olive Tree	=	Israel; Whole House of Jacob
Root of the Tree	=	Jesus; Yeshua
Vinedresser	=	Holy Spirit
Natural Branches	=	Jews; House of Judah
Wild Branches	=	Nations (Gentiles); House of Israel
Sap	=	Revelation of the Torah
Tzion/Zion	=	Grafting Process

To fully perceive the layers of significance contained within Romans 11, we must include one additional Biblical concept:

"Beloved, do not forget this one thing,
that with the Lord one day is as a thousand years,
and a thousand years as one day." [2]

(2 Peter 3:8)

It has been 3,500 (three and a half thousand) years since the giving of the Torah at Mount Sinai. And now, seemingly overnight, the House of Israel is coming out from among the nations of their exile and returning to the God of Abraham, Isaac, and Jacob—and the Torah. Now back to the grafting process!

STEP 1
FROM 0-3½ YEARS:

Olive trees, on average, have twelve branches—a very intriguing correlation to the Twelve Tribes of Israel. From the time an olive seed germinates in the soil, the sapling is allowed to grow for three and a half years at which point a grafting must take place. The natural tree with its natural branches will live for three and a half years, and if a grafting does not take place at the end of that time, the olive tree may die.

STEP 2
AT 3½ YEARS:

At the end of three and a half years (three and a half thousand years since Sinai), the Vinedresser (the Holy Spirit) comes to the Olive Tree (the House of Jacob) and He cuts off a natural branch (House of Judah). Just as in Romans 11, the Vinedresser casts the natural olive branch to the ground, yet remarkably the branch does not die, it only hardens.

STEP 3
AT 3½ YEARS:

The Vinedresser then leaves the garden where the natural tree is growing, and He goes out into the field (the Nations). He searches for a wild olive branch (House of Israel)—the most vigorous of all the branches. He finds a wild branch and brings it from *afar (the ends of the earth)* back to the natural tree. The Vinedresser grafts the wild branch into the exact spot where the natural branch was cut off. The grafting is then wrapped tightly to hold it securely in place. Interestingly enough, in Jewish tradition, the cloths used for this wrap are also referred to as *swaddling clothes,* and the grafting itself, in Hebrew, is called *"Tzion"* or *Zion* in English!

STEP 4
FROM $3^1/_2$ YEARS TO 7 YEARS:

After grafting the wild branch into place, the Vinedresser periodically inspects the tree to see if the wild branch is adapting to the natural tree. He tends the tree for another three and a half years, watching for signs that the wild branch has accepted the "sap of the tree" (revelation of the Torah).

STEP 5
FROM $3^1/_2$ YEARS TO 7 YEARS:

After a total of seven years (representing 7,000 years), if the wild branch has properly become one with the tree, the bark of the wild branch will look like the natural bark. At this point, the Vinedresser picks up the natural branch that was cut off and has hardened on the ground for three and a half years. He grafts the natural branch back into the same tree where the wild and natural branches are together being supported by the Root (Jesus/ Yeshua). After this re-grafting of the natural branch, the whole Olive Tree will begin to grow in height, becoming much more vigorous, even doubly fruitful.

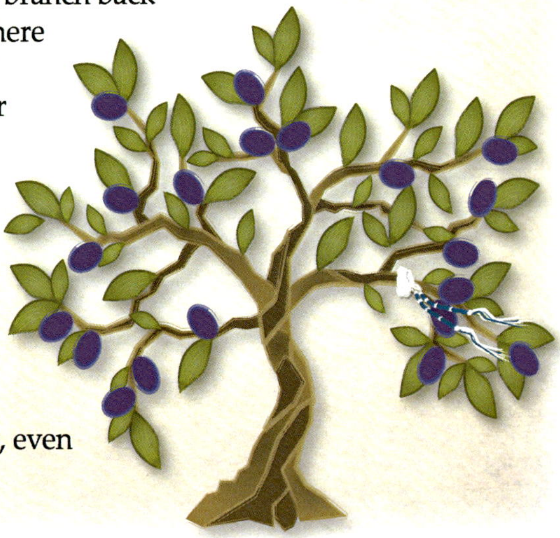

This represents even more than just a deeper insight into Paul's grafting imagery in Romans 11. The complete picture is of Jesus Christ (Yeshua HaMashiach). He was crucified on a tree where a soldier pierced Him with a sword. Out of Yeshua's side flowed water and blood – water representing the "Spirit," and blood commemorating the "Covenant." Into His pierced side the wild branches (Nations; House of Israel) have been grafted. By this grafting you were given access to that which you could never have achieved on your own – life from the dead. When you accept the sap of the Tree (the Torah), the LORD grafts again the natural branches (Jewish people) that were cut off, and the two become one Olive Tree (Israel) supported by the Root (Yeshua).

The Talmud (Commentary on the Torah) teaches that it is literally a miracle for even one from the Gentiles (Nations) to return to the Torah; a miracle equivalent to God placing the stars in the heavens. In fact, the Jews believe that the generations who will actually look upon a Torah scroll are a miracle of the Messiah. So those of you reading this book, who are returning from the nations and being restored to your Hebrew roots – you are a miracle! You are undoubtedly the first of your generations, wild as you may be, to return to God's Teaching and Instruction.

It is *critically* important that you understand that the "Olive Tree" represents the reunified Commonwealth of Israel called, the **Whole House of Jacob.** Romans 11 confirms that as a believer you have been grafted *into* Israel. You are part of Israel, not the other way around. I am not teaching "British Israelism" or "Replacement Theology." We have not in any fashion, form, or way replaced Israel or the Jewish people. This teaching is about the Torah, the whole House of Israel, and the restoration of the Tabernacle of David. This is not about a religion or a religious system. This is about a Kingdom—the Kingdom of Heaven! This is not about trying to become Jewish. You may or may not already be Jewish. The term "Jewish" evolved as a descriptive reference to only three of the Twelve Tribes—the Southern Kingdom of Judah. The bloodline of eternal significance is not earthly, therefore the bloodline we should focus on is that of the Messiah. According to the Bible, by

His blood you *are* a Hebrew, whether of the natural branches or having been grafted in. Like Abraham, you "crossed over" into the fullness of God's blessings. You may be part of the stick of Judah, and his companions, or you may be part of Israel, and his companions (Ezekiel 37), yet in Messiah we are all one Olive Tree called Israel.

"There is neither Jew nor Greek,
there is neither slave nor free,
there is neither male nor female;
for you are all one in Christ Jesus.
And if you are Christ's,
then you are Abraham's seed,
and heirs according to the promise." [3]

(Galatians 3:28-29)

You must remember, as Romans 11 clearly states, that as quickly as you were grafted in, you can be grafted out! Many churches have taught that the Jews must get saved or they're going to Hell. But I remind you that the natural branches were cut off *so that* salvation would come to the Nations (Gentiles). The wild branches are being grafted into the natural Tree, and God is most certainly able to graft the natural branches back in again. Your destiny as the wild olive branch is the same as the natural branch. We are all destined to be part of the same Tree. Those who remain in the wilderness (the Nations), or do not accept the sap of the Tree, will die.

"For if you were cut out of the olive tree
which is wild by nature (the House of Israel),
and were grafted contrary to nature

into a cultivated olive tree,
how much more will these,
who are natural branches (the Jewish people),
be grafted into their own olive tree?
For I do not desire, brethren,
that you should be ignorant of this mystery,
lest you should be wise in your own opinion,
that blindness in part has happened to Israel
(the whole House of Israel) until the
fullness of the Gentiles has come in." [4]
(Romans 11:24-25, emphasis added)

The *"fullness of the Gentiles or Nations"* refers to the House of Israel scattered *afar*—to the *ends of the earth.* Blindness in part has come to the Whole House of Israel, the Jewish people and the Nations, until these Nations return to the Torah. Most of the Church today has missed this crucial point! We're trying to force Jesus on the Jews, yet the Jewish people typically see believers living as pagans, without the Torah, and thus they remain blinded to the Salvation dwelling within you!

However, when the Jewish people see that the returning Nations have begun to follow God's Torah, they realize that you have accepted the sap of the tree. When the scales fall from *your* eyes, and your blindness to the *Torah* is removed, then the Jewish people are aroused to jealousy. Then they will *want* to know Who your God is because they know that only the true Messiah could have brought you back to the Torah. Only then will *their* blindness to Yeshua as the Messiah be healed.

"And so all Israel will be saved, as it is written:
'The Deliverer will come out of Zion (the grafting)'" [5]
(Romans 11:26, emphasis added)

Every believer's life is centered on this incredible story. Whether you are part of the natural or the wild branches, you are participating in the global movement of the House of Judah and the House of Israel becoming one in the hand of the LORD.

"For as you were once disobedient to God,
yet have now obtained mercy
through their disobedience,
even so these also have now been disobedient,
that through the mercy shown you
they also may obtain mercy.
For God has committed them all to disobedience,
that He might have mercy on all.
Oh, the depth of the riches
both of the wisdom and knowledge of God!
How unsearchable are His judgments
and His ways past finding out!
"For who has known the mind of the Lord?
Or who has become His counselor?"
"Or who has first given to Him
And it shall be repaid to him?"
For of Him and through Him and
to Him are all things,
to whom be glory forever. Amen." [6]

(Romans 11:30-36)

THE 7,000-YEAR REDEMPTIVE PLAN OF GOD

Just as Scripture plainly prophesied Israel's exile to the ends of the earth, the Bible also relates God's plan to restore the whole House of Jacob. The redemptive plan of God details this story—"His-story"—the past, present, and future of Israel. This is not a linear timeline as in the Greek mindset. This is the circular Hebrew mindset. We left the Garden of Eden and began an exile of sin and slavery. But God is bringing us full circle, back to Eden, back *to life* (*L'chayim* in Hebrew) and fully restored with Him.

"I make known the
end from the beginning,
from ancient times,
what is still to come.
I say: My purpose will stand, and
I will do all that I please." [7]

(Isaiah 46:10 NIV)

To truly understand the fullness of God's redemptive plan for mankind, we must examine the stark differences between the Greek and Hebrew mindset. Most believers have been taught the Bible from a predominantly Greek perspective and have never heard the Hebraic understanding of His Word. Generally speaking, we have been living in a Greek world attempting to relate to a Hebrew God.

The best way to illustrate these differences between the Greek and Hebrew mindset is to introduce you to two distinctly different models of God's redemption: the Greek model—describing God's judgment on the earth, and the Hebrew model—detailing God's deliverance.

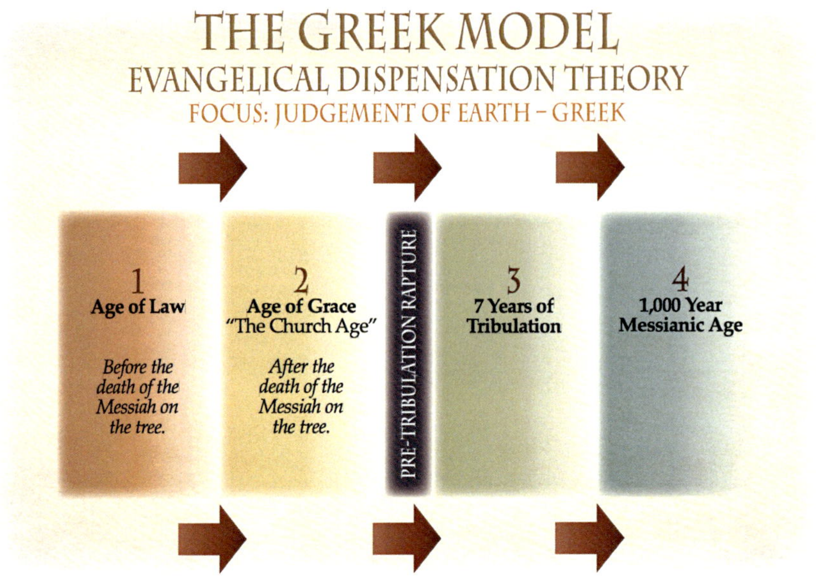

The familiar Evangelical Dispensation theory comes from a Greek model or mindset. This theory is linear, with four primary "ages" or "dispensations" occurring in succession from the beginning to the end. The focus of Dispensationalism is *judgment* on the earth.

EVANGELICAL DISPENSATION THEORY:

1. **Age of Law**
2. **Age of Grace**
   { Rapture }
3. **7-Year Tribulation**
4. **1,000-Year Messianic Age**

1. AGE OF LAW

We begin with the Age of Law, which existed before the death of the Messiah on the tree. This age encompasses:

- Creation
- Adam & Eve and their original sin

- Noah and the flood
- The journeys of the Biblical Patriarchs (Abraham, Isaac, and Jacob) and the Twelve Tribes of Israel
- Moses and the Exodus from Egypt
- The wilderness journey and the Torah at Mount Sinai
- The sacrificial system and the Biblical Feast Days
- The Judges and Kings of Israel
- The major and minor Prophets
- The Writings (Psalms, Proverbs, etc.)
- The birth and life of Jesus the Messiah, with His twelve Apostles, found in the gospels.

2. AGE OF GRACE

The next dispensation in this theory is called the Age of Grace or the "Church" Age. This age begins with the death, burial, and resurrection of the Messiah and includes:

- The development of the Church and its government
- The infilling of the Holy Spirit
- The Epistles and New Testament writings
- The letters to the 7 Churches (Revelation 1-3)

{ RAPTURE }

The rapture or "catching away" of the saints is most commonly taught as a *pre-tribulation* event. This comparatively recent addition to evangelical theology never even existed prior to the early 1800's. One of the first people believed to have taught the idea of a rapture was a young Scottish woman named Margaret Macdonald. Although she was not a theologian or Bible expositor, Macdonald was considered a prophetess in the Irvingite sect (the Catholic Apostolic Church). John Nelson Darby (1800-1882), who has been called the "father of modern Dispensationalism," took Macdonald's new teaching on the rapture and incorporated it into his Dispensational understanding of Scripture and prophecy. Darby would spend the rest of his life speaking, writing, and traveling to spread this new rapture theory.

The person most responsible for the rather widespread acceptance of Pretribulationalism and Dispensationalism among Evangelicals is Cyrus Ingerson Scofield (1843-1921). C.I. Scofield published his Scofield Reference Bible in 1909. This Bible, which espoused the doctrines of Darby in its notes, became very popular in Fundamentalist circles. In the minds of many, Scofield's notes were practically equated with the Word of God itself. [8]

3. 7-YEAR TRIBULATION

Occurring just prior to the seven-year tribulation, the rapture provides a way of escape from the wrath and judgment coming on the earth. For those "left behind" after the rapture, the tribulation immediately begins. The events of the tribulation are described in the Book of Revelation, events which include:

- 3½ years of peace and security in the Land of Israel, at the end of which the Anti-Christ is revealed.
- 3½ years of wrath and judgment poured out upon earth.
- The sealing of the 144,000
- The appearance of Yeshua as King of kings
- The opening of the seven Seals of Revelation
- The sounding of the seven Trumpets of Revelation
- The outpouring of the seven Bowls of wrath
- The defeat of the Anti-Christ and False Prophet
- The binding of Satan (Dragon) for 1,000 years

4. 1,000-YEAR MESSIANIC AGE

We now enter the Messianic Age, when the Messiah begins His 1,000-year reign on the earth. This final dispensation or age is characterized by true peace as the LORD establishes His throne on the earth. Those believers who reign with Messiah on the earth wait in anticipation for their ultimate destination, heaven.

Now let's compare this Evangelical Dispensation theory to the 7,000-Year Redemptive Plan of God!

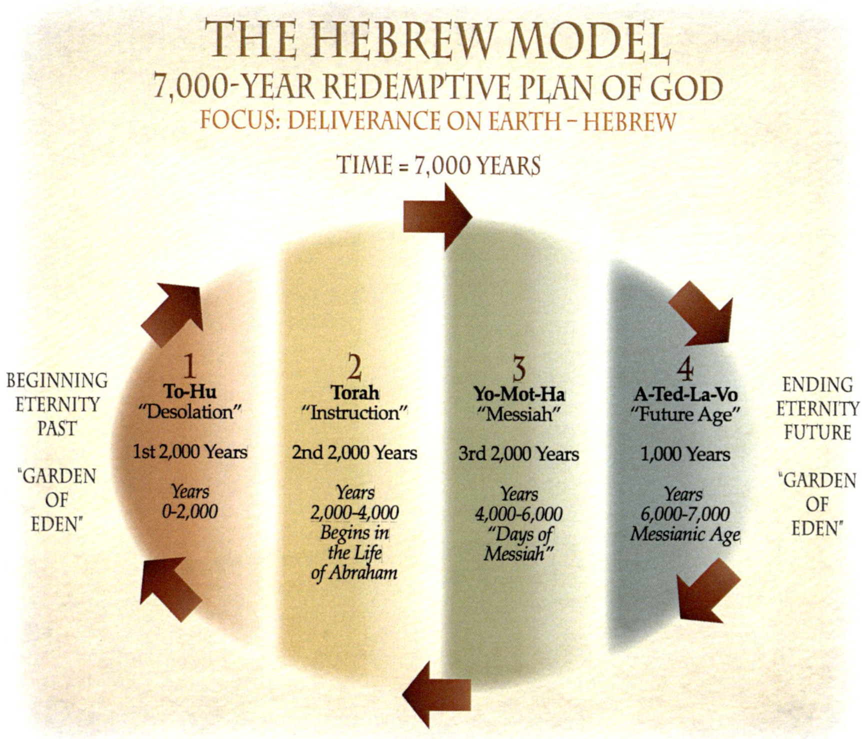

This Hebrew model depicts the redemptive plan of God with its focus on deliverance, and not on judgment. It is cyclical rather than strictly linear in nature and begins in the Garden of Eden called "Eternity Past." The Hebrew model completes a cycle from Eternity Past to Eternity Future (Garden of Eden) spanning four primary periods of time.

7,000-YEAR REDEMPTIVE PLAN OF GOD:

1. **Tohu (Desolation)**
2. **Torah (Instruction)**
3. **Yomot Ha (Days of Messiah)**
4. **Ated Lavo (Future Age)**

1. TOHU (DESOLATION)

The paradise of Eden was short-lived and the sin and fall of Adam became the indictment of all mankind. Thus began the first period of 2,000 years called Desolation or *Tohu* in Hebrew. During this era of time from 0-2,000 years, mankind lived apart from God, devoid of the knowledge of God's Word, without Messiah, and without the inspiration of the Holy Spirit. Man was in a state of darkness and sin was the rule of the day. Similar to the Greek model, this first 2,000-year period encompasses the life and generations from Adam to Noah as well as the judgment on earth from the waters of the Flood.

2. TORAH (INSTRUCTION)

Next begins the second 2,000 year period on earth. This era of time from the years 2,000-4,000 is known as *Torah* in Hebrew, or Teaching. The journey of Abraham begins this era of time as Abraham enters into covenant with God. Abraham becomes the father of a multitude of nations and the inheritor of the Land of Promise.

God's redemptive plan continues through Isaac and Jacob, the Twelve Tribes of Israel, the descent of Jacob's household into Egypt, and the emergence of Moses in God's deliverance of Israel through the Exodus. God nourishes and sustains His people through the wilderness journey, the giving of the Torah, the sacrificial system and the Biblical Feast Days (Moadim). God's Spirit inspires the Judges and Kings ruling over Israel, the major and minor Prophets (Nevi'im), and the era concludes with the Wisdom Writings (Ketuvim).

3. YOMOT HA (MESSIAH)

The third span of 2,000 years is known as *Yomot HaMashiach* in Hebrew, or the Days of Messiah. The years are 4,000-6,000 beginning with the Incarnation of Yeshua as the Messiah. God's Torah, written on tablets of stone, has now been placed within the heart and mind of the man—tablets of flesh (2 Corinthians 3). The Word of God becomes wrapped in flesh, and Jesus becomes the ultimate manifestation of God and Man as One (*Echad* in Hebrew).

4. ATED LAVO (FUTURE AGE)

The fourth span of time is 1,000 years in duration and begins at the year 6,000. It is known as the Future Age or Messianic Age—*Ated Lavo* in Hebrew. This significant period of time combines the era of Torah and the Messiah. Those who enter into this era have God's Torah written on their hearts and minds (Jeremiah 31; Hebrews 8), and are filled with the Spirit of God, enabling them to walk according to the Torah on the earth (Ezekiel 36). God is made known and His glory is being manifested through His people Israel. Man becomes God's dwelling place and His instrument for expanding His Kingdom and establishing His government in the earth. Man's dominion, previously lost in exile, is restored as it had originally existed in Eternity Past—the Garden of Eden.

There are striking distinctions between the Greek and Hebrew models of Salvation and Redemption. The Greek model is largely based on a religious system, while the Hebrew model is entirely founded upon a Kingdom. Syncretism, assimilation, and translation shifts from Hebrew to Greek to English have caused us to move from God's redemptive plan of deliverance, to man's dispensational theory of judgment. The Hebrew model originated, as did Creation, within the thoughts and Word of a Hebrew-speaking God. The Greek model originated and evolved, as did man, through an assimilated Greek mindset.

"For I have bent Judah, My bow,
fitted the bow with Ephraim,
And raised up your sons, O Zion,
against your sons, O Greece,"[9]

(Zechariah 9:13)

God's movement on the earth—the Kingdom of Heaven—is establishing the New Covenant through His people and by His Spirit. To more fully perceive God's eternal plan, we must understand the Bible

...s foundational Hebrew perspective. The 7,000-Year Redemptive ... of God is revealed throughout the pages of the Bible from Genesis to Revelation. God's Salvation (Yeshua) has been revealed, and His Redemption (Torah) complete. Through types and shadows, prophecy and history, exile and restoration; from the beginning (Genesis—Eternity Past) to the New Jerusalem (Revelation—Eternity Future), the King of kings and Lord of lords has made His glory known!

Remember...God's Redemptive Plan includes removing the blindness of Israel (Romans 11)—all of Israel! According to His Plan, the House of Judah (Jewish people) will recognize and receive Yeshua as Messiah (Salvation) when the House of Israel (Nations) recognizes and returns to the Torah by the Holy Spirit (Redemption).

"Now it shall come to pass,
when all these things come upon you,
the blessing and the curse which I have set before you, and
you call them to mind among all the nations
where the LORD your God drives you,
and you return to the LORD your God and obey His voice,
according to all that I command you today,
you and your children, with all your heart and
with all your soul, that the LORD your God will
bring you back from captivity, and have compassion on you,
and gather you again from all the nations
where the LORD your God has scattered you.
If any of you are driven out to the farthest parts
under heaven, from there the LORD your God
will gather you, and from there He will bring you." [10]

(Deuteronomy 30:1-4)

CHAPTER 9
LAZARUS COME FORTH!

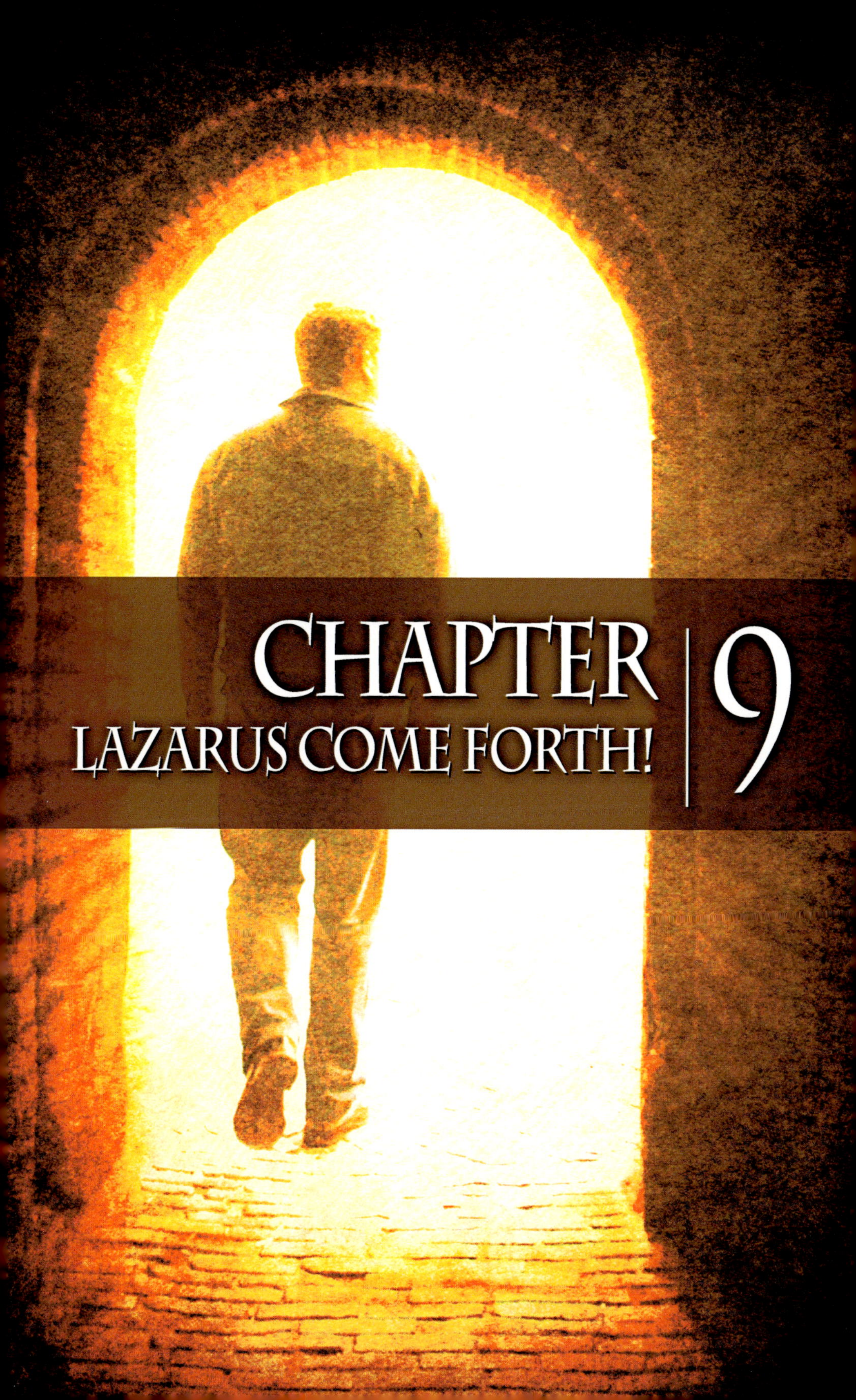

Lazarus Raised, Part 1
To view a video segment of this resource, scan the QR code using your smartphone.

The Bible overflows with type-and-shadow illustrations about the restoration of the whole House of Jacob—the House of Judah and the House of Israel being reunited. Let's look at an excellent example of this from the Gospel story of Lazarus being raised from the dead. Your biggest struggle as you revisit this illustration is going to be your familiarity with the story. Take a moment and ask the Holy Spirit to guide you beyond the literal *(peshat)* meaning, because we're going into the deeper or hidden *(sod)* meaning. First, you need to understand that Lazarus refers to you, as part of Israel, being brought back from the nations.

"Now a certain man was sick, Lazarus of Bethany,
the town of Mary and her sister Martha.
It was that Mary who anointed the Lord
with fragrant oil and wiped His feet with her hair,
whose brother Lazarus was **sick.**" [1]

(John 11:1-2, emphasis added)

The word "sick" (Strong's #770) used in John 11 cannot simply be referring to Lazarus' physical condition, as that would be a dramatic understatement for a man who is about to die! "Sick" in this context also refers to being "outside of the Torah." As previously mentioned, to live according to the Torah Principles is also called living in the Realm of Life. Conversely, we find that the grave physical condition of Lazarus is reflecting a lifestyle lived outside of the Torah, also called the

Realm of Death. This is equally conveyed within the name of Lazarus' hometown of Bethany—a combination of two Hebrew words:

Beit (Strong's #1004): house, dwelling, household
Aniy (Strong's #6041): poor, afflicted, lowly, misery

So Bethany = *beit* (House) + *aniy* (poor, afflicted, lowly, misery) confirms the story context with the location name of Bethany (House of the poor)—those who are poor, afflicted, and lowly; walking outside of the Torah in the realm of darkness and even death. With this understanding, we can begin to uncover how the person Lazarus is also a picture of the people Israel in exile.

"Awake, awake! Stand up, O Jerusalem,
you who have drunk at the hand
of the LORD the cup of His fury;
you have drunk the dregs of the cup of trembling,
and drained it out. There is no one to guide
her among all the sons she has brought forth;
nor is there any who takes her by the hand
among all the sons she has brought up...
Therefore please hear this, you afflicted,
and drunk but not with wine.
Thus says your Lord, the LORD and your God,
who pleads the cause of His people:
"See, I have taken out of your hand
the cup of trembling,
the dregs of the cup of My fury;
you shall no longer drink it." [2]

(Isaiah 51:17-22)

It doesn't matter which culture or ethnic group you identify with: Black, White, Latino, Asian, etc. The branches of your recent ancestry and the hardships suffered by those cultures are not at the root of your affliction. You inherited affliction because your forefathers in Israel went into pagan idolatry worship, and God, by His plan, scattered them to the nations. That is why the affliction and sickness of Lazarus has come upon you. You may be part of the generations that will see your ancestors afflicted. But you are also part of the generations that will, by God's Redemptive Plan, teach your children and your children's children the Torah, so that they will not experience what it is like to be poor, afflicted, and in misery. You are called to finally break the generational transgression and iniquity of your forefathers. It stops with you! Not because of you, but because God has sought you out as a lost sheep and restored you to His fold.

"Surely I will take the children of Israel
from among the nations, wherever they have gone,
and will gather them from every side and
bring them into their own land;
and I will make them one nation in the land,
on the mountains of Israel; and one king shall be
king over them all; they shall no longer be two nations, nor
shall they ever be divided into two kingdoms again. They
shall not defile themselves anymore
with their idols, nor with their detestable things,
nor with any of their transgressions;
but I will deliver them from all their
dwelling places in which they have sinned,
and will cleanse them. Then they shall be My people,
and I will be their God." [3]

(Ezekiel 37:21-23)

Remember, you are not ceasing from the detestable in order to earn your righteousness. The righteousness of salvation is only through the Messiah Yeshua, Jesus Christ. You were fully redeemed at Calvary. But as a redeemed people God intended for you to live a redeemed lifestyle. Now let's be honest, most ministers today do not know or teach about Redemption (Torah) or what it truly means to walk a redemptive lifestyle. What does it mean to be blessed—to *not* walk in poverty and oppression? To *not* walk as if afflicted, poor, and in misery? You can plead the blood of Jesus until you're blue in the face! But until we *also* begin to teach people how to live and walk, and until we truly teach and instruct them in the Principles of the Torah, the abundant life that Jesus promised just simply won't be realized.

"The weak you have not strengthened,
nor have you healed those who were sick,
nor bound up the broken, nor brought back
what was driven away, nor sought what was lost;
but with force and cruelty you have ruled them.
So they were scattered because there was no shepherd;
and they became food for all the beasts of the field
when they were scattered. My sheep wandered
through all the mountains, and on every high hill;
yes, My flock was scattered over the
whole face of the earth, and no one was
seeking or searching for them."
'Therefore, you shepherds, hear the word of the LORD:
"As I live," says the Lord GOD,
"surely because My flock became a prey,
and My flock became food for every beast of the field,
because there was no shepherd,

nor did My shepherds search for My flock,
but the shepherds fed themselves and
did not feed My flock"—therefore, O shepherds,
hear the word of the LORD! Thus says the Lord GOD:
"Behold, I am against the shepherds,
and I will require My flock at their hand;
I will cause them to cease feeding the sheep,
and the shepherds shall feed themselves no more;"

'For thus says the Lord GOD:
"Indeed I Myself will search for My sheep and
seek them out. As a shepherd seeks out his flock
on the day he is among his scattered sheep,
so will I seek out My sheep and
deliver them from all the places
where they were scattered on a cloudy and dark day.
And I will bring them out from the peoples and
gather them from the countries,
and will bring them to their own land;
I will feed them on the mountains of Israel,
in the valleys and in all the inhabited places
of the country. I will feed them in good pasture,
and their fold shall be on the high mountains of Israel.
There they shall lie down in a good fold and
feed in rich pasture on the mountains of Israel.
I will feed My flock, and I will make them lie down,"
says the Lord GOD. "I will seek what was lost and
bring back what was driven away, bind up the broken
and strengthen what was sick; but I will destroy the fat
and the strong, and feed them in judgment." [4]

(Ezekiel 34:4-16)

Generally speaking, most spiritual leaders do not understand the Hebrew roots of the Christian faith. They have learned and therefore "innocently" taught a different Sabbath day and different Feasts. Instead of Passover, First Fruits and Tabernacles, we have celebrated Christmas, Easter, and other pagan holidays that were syncretized into Christianity. This is what you were taught. Your ways became different from the ways of God, which Biblically means you walked into a Realm of Death. Again, my intent is not to cast blame, but simply to shed *light (or)* on to the darkness of the past.

That may sound like a hard or even judgmental word! But remember, your teachers are innocent and you are innocent. This message in NO way suggests that you should be judgmental of your spiritual leaders or your forefathers. They led you, they fed you, and they did what they knew to do. But now God is bringing you into an age of major prophetic fulfillment. You have been born into the generations that are returning to the Torah. The Lord prophesied that He would deliver ***you*** just as He delivered your ancestors before you. With an outstretched arm and by the mighty hand of God, with great signs and wonders, you and a *"multitude of nations"* with you are experiencing the global movement of the Greater Exodus (Jeremiah 16).

"Now a certain man was sick,
Lazarus of Bethany,
the town of Mary and her sister Martha.
It was that Mary who anointed the Lord
with fragrant oil and wiped
His feet with her hair,
whose brother Lazarus was sick.
Therefore the sisters sent to Him, saying,
'Lord, behold, he whom You love is sick.'" [5]

(John 11:1-3)

We've already looked at the significance of the "sickness" of Lazarus, and by extension, the exiled people of Israel. Now we're going to cross-reference John Chapter 11 with Deuteronomy Chapter 7 to better establish just who on the earth the Lord loves, and who it is in fact, that is sick.

"The LORD did not set His love
on you nor choose you because
you were more in number than any other people,
for you were the least of all peoples;
but because the LORD loves you,
and because He would keep the oath
which He swore to your fathers," [6]

(Deuteronomy 7:7-8)

Therefore the sisters sent to Him, saying,
"Lord, behold, he whom You love is sick." [7]

(John 11:3)

The Bible is again utilizing the prophetic imagery associated with God's Redemptive Plan. The one Jesus loves is sick. Not Lazarus alone, but all those whose sickness necessitated Jesus' healing atonement on Calvary. These are the ones Yeshua died for—all those He loves. He came for "the lost sheep of the House of Israel" (Matthew 15:24) who were separated from the Torah and scattered among the nations. He died to re-gather and ingather those who were dispersed and exiled—sick, poor, and afflicted.

"The word of the LORD came again to me, saying:
"Son of man, there were two women,

the daughters of one mother.
They committed harlotry in Egypt,
they committed harlotry in their youth…
Their names: Oholah the elder and
Oholibah her sister; they were Mine,
and they bore sons and daughters." [8]

(Ezekiel 23:1-4)

These two daughters in Ezekiel 23, *Oholah* and *Oholibah,* are a precise representation of the two kingdoms of Israel divided on the Land. As you look at Ezekiel's prophecy you see an illustration of the House of Israel and the House of Judah—two sisters born of one mother (Israel)—who can be further likened allegorically to Christianity and Judaism.

"As for their names, Samaria is Oholah,
and Jerusalem is Oholibah.
'Oholah played the harlot even though she was Mine;
And she lusted for her lovers,
the neighboring Assyrians,
who were clothed in purple, captains and rulers,
all of them desirable young men,
horsemen riding on horses.
Thus she committed her harlotry with them,
all of them choice men of Assyria;
and with all for whom she lusted, with all their idols,
she defiled herself. She has never given up
her harlotry brought from Egypt…
Therefore I have delivered her
into the hand of her lovers,

into the hand of the Assyrians,
for whom she lusted.
They uncovered her nakedness,
took away her sons and daughters,
and slew her with the sword;
she became a byword among women,
for they had executed judgment on her.
Now although her sister Oholibah saw this,
she became more corrupt in her lust than she,
and in her harlotry more corrupt than her sister's harlotry…
Then the Babylonians came to her,
into the bed of love, and they defiled her
with their immorality; so she was defiled by them,
and alienated herself from them.
She revealed her harlotry and
uncovered her nakedness. Then I alienated
Myself from her, as I had alienated Myself
from her sister. 'Yet she multiplied her harlotry
in calling to remembrance the days of her youth,
when she had played the harlot in the land of Egypt.'"[9]

(Ezekiel 23:4-19)

The continual enticement to assimilate into the cultures and pagan practices of her neighboring civilizations eventually took Israel into idolatry and obscurity. Estranged and wandering from the protective Principles of the Torah, stiff-necked, hard-hearted, and spiritually adulterous, God sorrowfully surrendered both kingdoms of Israel to their foreign suitors. The Northern Kingdom of Ephraim was soon conquered by Assyria (c. 722-721 B.C.E.) and exiled or "lost" among the nations. The Southern Kingdom of Judah was later defeated by the Babylonians (c. 586 B.C.E.), the holy Temple destroyed, and the Land of Promise once again overrun by foreigners.

This theme of the two sisters in Ezekiel (*Oholah* and *Oholibah*) carries through to the Gospels and the setting for the story of Lazarus and his two sisters, Mary and Martha. As suggested, the story of Lazarus is also a prophetic illustration of the whole House of Jacob being literally raised up during the last days. As we continue in the story of Lazarus, you will see how Oholah and Oholibah, as well as Mary and Martha in the house of Lazarus, represent Ephraim and Judah. The names Mary and Martha both originate from the same Hebrew root word, *"mara,"* meaning rebellious and bitterness:

Mara (Strong's #4755): rebellious; bitter; bitterness
Oholah = Martha—Northern Kingdom (House of Ephraim)
Oholibah = Mary—Southern Kingdom (House of Judah)

"So when Jesus came, He found that
he had already been in the tomb four days…
Then Martha said to Jesus, "Lord,
if You had been here,
my brother would not have died.
But even now I know that whatever You ask of God,
God will give You." Jesus said to her,
"Your brother will rise again."
Martha said to Him, "I know that he
will rise again in the resurrection
at the last day."Jesus said to her,
"I am the resurrection and the life.
He who believes in Me, though he may die,
he shall live. And whoever lives and
believes in Me shall never die.
Do you believe this?" [10]

(John 11:17-25)

The Bible clearly establishes that the resurrection of Lazarus was an actual event. Yet, interestingly enough, the account of this miracle includes two corresponding statements about the amount of time Lazarus has been in the tomb. Have you ever wondered about the significance of this timeframe and why it is repeated twice in such a relatively short Biblical narrative?

Tradition at the time of Yeshua (and even to this day) relates four specific miracles that only the true Messiah will be able to perform: [11]

1. Cleansing of lepers
2. Healing of a person born blind
3. Casting out of certain demons
4. Raising one who has been dead for more than three days and three nights.

In an unmistakable foreshadowing of His own resurrection after three days and three nights, Yeshua is about to call Lazarus forth from the grave on the fourth day. The multitudes and the Apostles had seen Yeshua perform countless miracles and remarkable healings. But now, in Bethany, Yeshua will demonstrate that sickness and even the grip of death are not strong enough to withstand the miracle-working power of the Kingdom of Heaven.

Jesus said to her, "Did I not say to you
that if you would believe you would see
the glory of God?" Then they took away the stone
from the place where the dead man was lying…
Now when He had said these things,
He cried with a loud voice, **"Lazarus, come forth!"**
And he who had died came out bound
hand and foot with graveclothes,

and his face was wrapped with a cloth. Jesus said to them, "Loose him, and let him go." Then many of the Jews who had come to Mary, and had seen the things Jesus did, believed in Him." [12]

(John 11:40-45, emphasis added)

It has been nearly 4,000 years since the giving of the Torah at Mount Sinai. If *"a day is as a thousand years"* (Psalms 90; 2 Peter 3), then we are quickly approaching the fourth day of Israel's sickness, sleep, and death. You, like Lazarus, were sick, poor, and miserable—you were living outside the Torah. Yet this sickness *and* your healing were foretold by God even before your ancestors were lured away from the Torah by idolatry and harlotry, plagued by sickness and disease, conquered and dispersed to the nations.

"When Jesus heard that He said,
'This sickness is not unto death,
but for the glory of God, that the Son of God
may be glorified through it.'" [13]

(John 11:4)

When you return to the Torah, you are responding to God's Redemptive Plan, bringing glory to the LORD. God's movement on the earth today—the Kingdom of Heaven—is awakening people from their "sleep" likened unto Lazarus being miraculously raised from the dead! They're not physically dead, it's a spiritual realm of death for those who have been taught that the Torah is law or no longer relevant for believers. In other words, they have been starving for the nourishment of the Torah—God's Teaching and Instruction. His Word is again bringing order to chaos, light *(or)* in the midst of darkness, and life from the dead!

"Behold, the days are coming,"
says the Lord God,
"That I will send a famine on the land,
not a famine of bread, nor a thirst for water,
but of hearing the words of the Lord.
They shall wander from sea to sea,
and from north to east;
they shall run to and fro,
seeking the word of the Lord,
but shall not find it." [14]

(Amos 8:11-12)

Many today are crying out for God's glory, hungering for that undefined "something" that seems to be missing from the churches. They're looking for sustenance, not superficiality. Not just any sustenance, but the spiritual truth that brings deliverance, healing, and restoration.

"Therefore we were buried with Him
through baptism into death, that just as
Christ was raised from the dead by the
glory of the Father, even so
we also should walk in newness of life.
For if we have been united together
in the likeness of His death,
certainly we also shall be in the
likeness of His resurrection, knowing this,
that our old man was crucified with Him,

that the body of sin might be done away with,
that we should no longer be slaves of sin." [15]

(Romans 6:4-6)

The prophets of the *Tanakh* and the Divinely inspired writers of the New Testament describe the return of the House of Israel from the nations as equivalent to a resurrection from the dead. Jesus also, three days and three nights after His crucifixion, emerged from the grave, *the firstfruits of those who have fallen asleep* (Romans 9).

One of the clearest Biblical statements about the prophetic purpose of Jesus' death and resurrection, comes from Caiaphas, a High Priest of Israel at the time of Yeshua's earthly ministry.

"Then many of the Jews who had come to Mary,
and had seen the things Jesus did, believed in Him.
But some of them went away to the Pharisees
and told them the things Jesus did.
Then the chief priests and the Pharisees
gathered a council and said, "What shall we do?
For this Man works many signs.
If we let Him alone like this,
everyone will believe in Him,
and the Romans will come and take away
both our place and nation."
And one of them, Caiaphas,
being high priest that year, said to them,
"You know nothing at all, nor do you consider
that it is expedient for us that
one man should die for the people,

and not that the whole nation should perish."
Now this he did not say on his own authority;
but **being high priest that year he prophesied**
that Jesus would die for the nation,
and not for that nation only,
but also that He would gather together
in one the children of God
who were scattered abroad." [16]
(John 11:45-52, emphasis added)

Caiaphas and the religious leaders of his day were concerned, deeply concerned, about the conspicuous impact of Yeshua's teachings and miracles. Fear and the oppression of the Roman Empire blinded the eyes of the spiritual leaders to the greater truth of Who Jesus is (Salvation) and how Jesus lived (Torah). The restoration and re-gathering of the whole House of Jacob would begin with the death, burial, and resurrection of Yeshua. Yet, the ultimate fulfillment of the High Priest's words would not be realized until the prophetic times and movement that are predicted to occur in preparation for the *return* of Yeshua at the end of the age.

"Remember the Law of Moses, My servant,
which I commanded him in Horeb for all Israel,
with the statutes and judgments.
Behold, I will send you Elijah the prophet
before the coming of the great and dreadful day
of the LORD. And he will turn
the hearts of the fathers to the children,
and the hearts of the children to their fathers,
lest I come and strike the earth with a curse." [17]
(Malachi 4:4-6)

The prophecy in Malachi 4 reminds us that the Torah (Law) of Moses will be revived and remembered by God's people *before* the return of the LORD. During this same period of revival, Malachi says the hearts of the children will return to their fathers. Which fathers? Not the early Church fathers and the erroneous teaching that led us away from the Torah. God prophesies that we will return to our Hebrew fathers—Abraham, Isaac, and Jacob—who kept the Torah and received God's covenant blessings, including the continuation of the earthly lineage which brought forth Yeshua the Messiah.

"LAZARUS, COME FORTH!"

"THIS SICKNESS IS NOT UNTO DEATH, BUT FOR THE GLORY OF GOD, THAT THE SON OF GOD MAY BE GLORIFIED THROUGH IT."

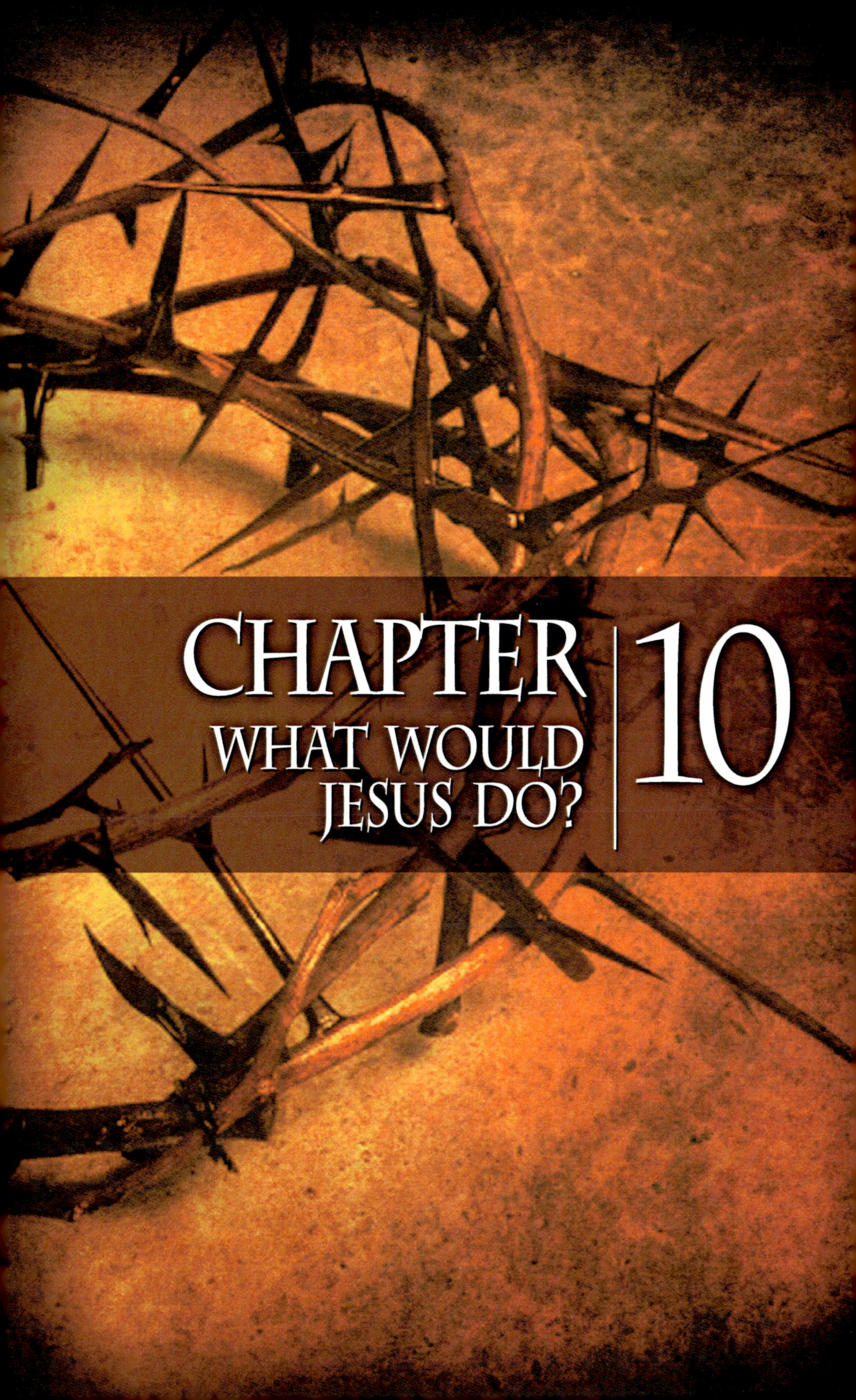

CHAPTER 10
WHAT WOULD JESUS DO?

Controversy of Tzion, Part 2
To view a video segment of this resource, scan the QR code using your smartphone.

"Do not think that I came to destroy the Law or the Prophets. I did not come to destroy but to fulfill. For assuredly, I say to you, till heaven and earth pass away, one jot or one tittle will by no means pass from the law till all is fulfilled. Whoever therefore breaks one of the least of these commandments, and teaches men so, shall be called least in the kingdom of heaven; but whoever does and teaches them, he shall be called great in the kingdom of heaven." [1]

(Matthew 5:17-19)

Yeshua cautions His followers against even thinking that He came to do away with the Torah saying, *"I did not come to destroy (the Law or the Prophets), but to fulfill."* To fulfill in Hebrew means to bring a greater understanding. So what lack of understanding or misunderstanding could Jesus be warning His listeners about? Could it be the very thing that we have taught erroneously for generations—that Jesus came to do away with the Torah?

Yeshua continues His caution saying, *"...till heaven and earth pass away, one jot or one tittle will by no means pass from the law till all is fulfilled."* Again, due to translation, the words jot and tittle have little or no frame of reference for the casual English reader. However, when you return these words to their Hebrew origins, "jot" becomes *"yod"* in Hebrew, and "tittle" becomes *"tagin."* The *yod* is the smallest of the 22 letters in the Hebrew language, and the *tagin* (also called a "crown") is a tiny adornment found near the top of most of the other letters. Yeshua is making an incredibly powerful point to His *Hebrew* listeners. It's a point that outside of its proper context is difficult to discern across the many years and obscurity of translation. Yeshua is saying that believers should not reason that He came to destroy the Torah, and in fact, not even the smallest letter *(yod)* of the Torah, nor the tiniest stroke of a single letter *(tagin)* will pass from the Law until it is all fulfilled!

How have we missed this caution given by the LORD Himself in the Gospels? How can we still entertain the notion that the Torah has been done away with? How could ministers and spiritual leaders not take note of Jesus' final warning in this Matthew Chapter 5 passage:

"Whoever therefore breaks one of the
least of these commandments,
and teaches men so,
shall be called least in the kingdom of heaven;
but whoever does and teaches them,
he shall be called
great in the kingdom of heaven."

Where did we get the concept that God wrote the Torah on Mount Sinai and gave it to Moses, and then when Jesus arrived on the earth He said, "What is this Torah for? Let's do away with this." In reality, Yeshua took hold of the Torah, lived and taught its Principles, and spoke of an even greater fulfillment of the Torah by the empowering of the Holy Spirit. When you say that you have faith in God, you are declaring that you have the faith of Jesus. And what was the faith of Jesus? The Torah!

NEW CONTRACT OR NEW COVENANT?

- A Contract is an agreement between two or more parties which creates an obligation to do or not to do some particular action.
- A Contract is uniquely western or "Greco-Roman" in thought and practice.
- A Contract is written on paper.
- A Contract can be broken.
- A Covenant is a promise between two or more parties—especially for the performance of some action.
- A Covenant is uniquely eastern or "Hebrew" in thought and practice.
- A Covenant is cut in blood.
- A Covenant is eternal.

"Therefore remember that you,
once Gentiles in the flesh…
at that time you were without Christ,
being aliens from the commonwealth of Israel
and strangers from the covenants of promise,
having no hope and without God in the world.
But now in Christ Jesus you who once were far off
have been brought near by the blood of Christ." [2]

(Ephesians 2:11-13)

Again, the term Gentile is not the most accurate description of believers today. Biblically speaking, by the blood of Messiah all believers have been grafted into and become part of Israel. In other words, in Yeshua you *are* an Israelite, and *no longer a stranger to the covenants of promise.* Therefore, the covenants that God made with Israel apply to you as a believer in the Messiah.

The distinction between a contract (Greek mindset) and a covenant (Hebrew mindset) is profound. After all, you have not entered into a breakable "contract" with God or a temporary agreement regarding your Salvation and Redemption. You are in a *covenant relationship* with YHWH and YHWH has made His covenants with you. The Commonwealth of Israel and God's covenant promises that Paul speaks of in Ephesians Chapter 2, are found throughout the Scriptures from Genesis through Revelation. There are seven distinct covenants progressively revealing and fulfilling the 7,000-Year Redemptive Plan of God.

UNIVERSAL COVENANTS MADE WITH ALL MANKIND

- Edenic Covenant – The Covenant in Creation
- Adamic Covenant – The Covenant with Adam
- Noahdic/Noahic Covenant – The Covenant with Noah

COVENANTS MADE WITH ISRAEL

- Abrahamic Covenant – The Covenant with Abraham
- Mosaic Covenant – The Covenant with Moses
- Davidic Covenant – The Covenant with King David
- The Renewed or "New" Covenant – The Covenant in Yeshua (Jesus)

Revealed within these seven covenants are the familiar Biblical themes of progression from darkness to light and from death into life. One method of following the covenants of God through the Scriptures is by cross-referencing the key words found in the covenant passages of the Bible. Let's begin by identifying and defining some of these terms and their Hebrew root words. These covenant terms convey the redemptive plan of God for mankind and they are found in the Hebrew words translated as: **darkness, water, sea, sleep, rib, bone, ark, reeds, tabernacle,** and **nation.**

Darkness (*chôshēch* in Hebrew) – Hebrew root words: dark; darkness; misery; destruction; death; ignorance; sorrow; wickedness; night; obscurity; deep sleep; death.

Water (*mayim* in Hebrew) – Hebrew root words: water; waters; water springs; washing; watercourse; flood; watering; wasting.

Sea (*yām* in Hebrew) – Hebrew root words: sea; seas; west; westward; west side; seafaring; men; people.

Sleep (*tardēmâ* in Hebrew) – Hebrew root words: lethargy; trance; deep sleep; darkness; dread; death.

Rib (*sēlā* in Hebrew) – Hebrew root words: side; chamber; boards; corners; rib; another; beams; halting; leaves; planks.

Bone (*ētsom* in Hebrew) – Hebrew root words: bone; body; substance; selfsame; life; strength.

Ark (*tēbâ* in Hebrew) – Hebrew root words: box; ark.

Reeds (*sûf* in Hebrew) – Hebrew root words: red; flags; weeds; reed; papyrus.

Tabernacle (*sûkka* in Hebrew) – Hebrew root words: hut; lair; booth; cottage; covert; pavilion; tabernacle; tent.

Nations (*gôyeem* in Hebrew) – Hebrew root words: nation; foreign nation; heathen; Gentiles; people.

To move from one covenant to the next is commonly known in the Hebrew mindset as "progressive revelation." The ratification of a new covenant does not in any way eliminate or do away with any prior covenant. Quite the contrary! The "progressive" cutting of an additional covenant intentionally builds upon the revelation and promises of each of the previous covenants.

"LET THERE BE LIGHTS IN THE
FIRMAMENT OF THE HEAVENS
TO DIVIDE THE DAY FROM THE NIGHT;
AND LET THEM BE FOR SIGNS AND
SEASONS, AND FOR DAYS AND YEARS"

1. THE EDENIC COVENANT – THE COVENANT IN CREATION

"The earth was without form, and void; and **darkness (sleep)** was on the face of the deep. And the Spirit of God was hovering over the face of the waters." [3]

(Genesis 1:2, emphasis added)

Creation provides mankind with one of the greatest revelations of God. God's first covenant in Creation, known as the Edenic Covenant, brought light to the darkness, order to the chaos, and life from the dead. The word "darkness" in Hebrew (*chôshēch*) is synonymous (by other root words) with the Hebrew word for sleep. In the beginning, there was no life on earth. It was dead or asleep—and then God spoke!

"Then God said, 'Let the waters
under the heavens be gathered together into one place,
and let the dry land appear'; and it was so.
And God called the dry land Earth, and the gathering
together of the waters He called **Seas (People)**." [4]

(Genesis 1:9-10, emphasis added)

The gathering of the waters He called "Seas," which is another term for people. In this covenant God introduced His plan of redemption, to bring His people together as one in covenant with Him. The Edenic Covenant had no conditions and was enacted by God alone. God did not need Man to invoke this covenant, but introduced mankind in the gathering of the seas and gave Man a place to dwell with Him—earth.

"IT IS NOT GOOD THAT MAN
SHOULD BE ALONE; I WILL MAKE HIM
A HELPER COMPARABLE TO HIM."

2. THE ADAMIC COVENANT– THE COVENANT WITH ADAM

"And the Lord God
caused a **deep sleep** to fall on Adam,
and he slept; and He took one
of his ribs, and closed up the flesh in its place.
Then the **rib** which the Lord God had taken
from man He made into a woman,
and He brought her to the man." [5]

(Genesis 2:21-22, emphasis added)

Adam was created in the image of God, given dominion in the earth, and placed in the paradise of Eden where God ratified His covenant with him. God removed a rib from Adam's side as he "slept." He took this rib *afar* and fashioned Eve, then God returned her back to Adam. This story is a type and shadow of God's redemptive plan to likewise fashion the Bride of Messiah while she is still scattered *afar*—to the *ends of the earth.*

"And Adam said:
'This is now **bone**
(substance and strength) of my bones
and flesh of my flesh;
She shall be called Woman,
because she was taken out of Man.'" [6]

(Genesis 2:23, emphasis added)

The rib taken from Adam was his very own substance and strength. The Hebrew word for "bone" is *"etsom"* also meaning branch, side, substance, or strength. The additional meanings of the word provide a key to interpreting other Scripture passages related by these same words. Israel, in her entirety (twelve tribes) is known as the substance and strength of God. Again, the redemptive plan is revealed with God and Man dwelling together as one in fellowship. The Adamic Covenant is the second unconditional covenant given to all mankind.

3. THE NOAHDIC/NOAHIC COVENANT–THE COVENANT WITH NOAH

"Noah opened the window of the **ark**
which he had made. Then he sent out a raven,
which kept going to and fro until the waters
had dried up from the earth. He also sent out
from himself a dove, to see if the waters had
receded from the face of the ground.
But the dove found no resting place
for the sole of her foot,
and she returned into the ark to him,
for the waters were on the face of the whole earth.
So he put out his hand and took her,
and drew her into the ark to himself.
And he waited yet another seven days,
and again he sent the dove out from the ark.
Then the **dove (Holy Spirit)** came to him
in the **evening (Noah in a deep sleep),** and behold,
a freshly plucked **olive leaf (branch)**

"THIS IS THE SIGN OF THE COVENANT WHICH I HAVE ESTABLISHED BETWEEN ME AND ALL FLESH THAT IS ON THE EARTH."

was in her mouth; and Noah knew
that the **waters (judgment)**
had receded from the earth." [7]

(Genesis 8: 6-11, emphasis added)

The story of Noah is a clear depiction of judgment and deliverance simultaneously being enacted on earth. Noah built the Ark according to God's precise instructions. Then, by this Ark and in the midst of judgment, God provided deliverance for His people. The Noahdic Covenant is the third unconditional covenant made with all mankind. The sign in the earth of the Noahdic covenant is the rainbow (Genesis 9).

As the floodwaters began to subside, Noah tested the water levels on the earth by first sending out a raven and then a dove from the Ark. The window in the side of the ark reveals an opening to be used for God's purpose. It compares to the "side" of Adam from which God took a rib and fashioned Eve. It is also a clear foreshadowing of Yeshua's side that was pierced at His crucifixion.

The dove returning to the Ark with the olive leaf or "branch" is a further illustration of Adam's side, and the Bride of Messiah being brought from "afar" (the Nations). Noah becomes a type and shadow of Yeshua. He reaches out his hand and draws the dove in through the "side" of the protective Ark. In like manner, you will be drawn to God during the time of judgment and your deliverance is certain.

4. THE ABRAHAMIC COVENANT–THE COVENANT WITH ABRAHAM

"'Bring Me a three-year-old heifer,
a three-year-old female goat,
a three-year-old ram,
a turtledove, and a young pigeon.'
Then he brought all these to Him
and cut them in two,
down the middle, and placed
each piece opposite the other;
but he did not cut the birds in two.
And when the vultures came
down on the carcasses,
Abram drove them away.
Now when the sun was going down,
a **deep sleep** fell upon Abram; and behold,
horror and **great darkness** fell upon him." [8]

(Genesis 15:12, emphasis added)

At the cutting of the Abrahamic Covenant, Abraham falls into a "deep sleep" and experiences an unusual "dread" and "darkness." God tells Abraham that his descendants will not retain their initial possession of the Promised Land shown to Abraham. God explains that Israel will serve a foreign people (Egypt) for more than 400 years, and then afterwards they will be restored to the Land with great signs and wonders. Although this is a clear prophecy of the Egyptian slavery and Exodus, the story continues the now familiar themes of exile and return, and a bride or branch being brought from *afar* and returning to God's covenants.

"LOOK NOW TOWARD HEAVEN,
AND COUNT THE STARS IF
YOU ARE ABLE TO NUMBER THEM...
SO SHALL YOUR DESCENDANTS BE."

"And it came to pass,
when the sun went down and it was **dark,**
that behold, there appeared a **smoking oven**
and a **burning torch** that passed
between those pieces.
On the same day the Lord made
a covenant with Abram, saying:
To your descendants I have given this land,
from the river of Egypt to the great river,
the River Euphrates'" [9]

(Genesis 15:17-18, emphasis added)

In cutting the Abrahamic Covenant, God manifests in the form of a smoking oven and a burning torch and walks between the divided pieces of the offering. The imagery reflects God's redemptive plan to move in the midst of fragmented Israel, once sown in the Land, yet scattered to the nations. The Abrahamic Covenant is an unconditional covenant of faith given to Israel, Abraham's seed. The sign in the earth of the Abrahamic Covenant is circumcision cut in the flesh of man.

5. THE MOSAIC COVENANT– THE COVENANT WITH MOSES

"Then the daughter of Pharaoh
came down to bathe at the river.
And her maidens walked along the riverside;

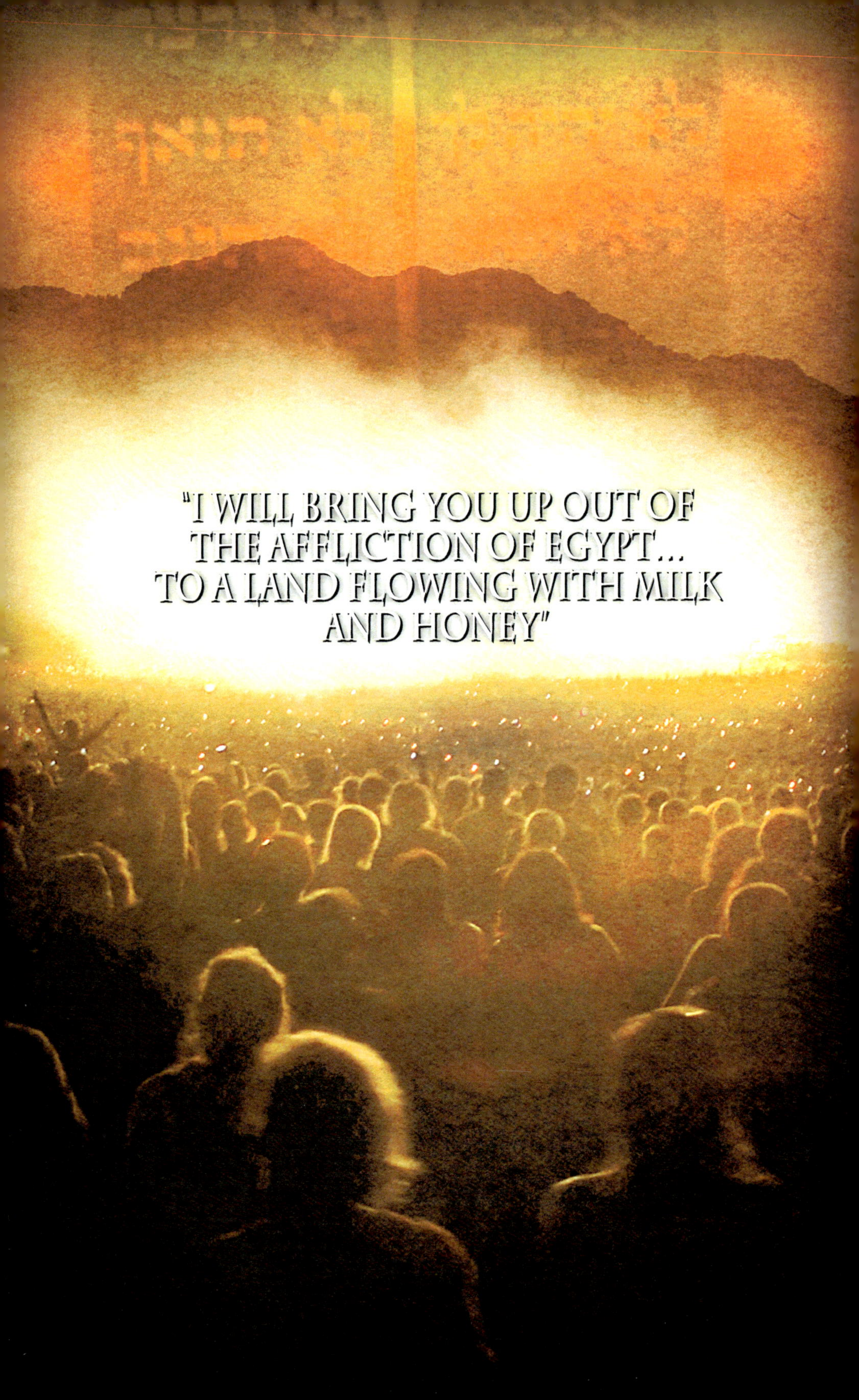
"I WILL BRING YOU UP OUT OF
THE AFFLICTION OF EGYPT...
TO A LAND FLOWING WITH MILK
AND HONEY"

and when she saw the ark **among the reeds,**
she sent her maid to get it.
And when she had opened it,
she saw the child, and behold, the baby wept.
So she had compassion on him, and said,
"This is one of the Hebrews' children."
Then his sister said to Pharaoh's daughter,
"Shall I go and call a nurse for you
from the Hebrew women,
that she may nurse the child for you?"
And Pharaoh's daughter said to her, "Go."
So the maiden went
and called the child's mother." [10]

(Exodus 2:6-7, emphasis added)

The miraculous saga of Moses' birth and deliverance from certain death is filled with redemptive comparisons and covenant language. Within the palace of Pharaoh (the very ruler who uttered the death sentence for the Hebrew boys) Moses will be nursed by his own mother, and nurtured as a prince of Egypt. To preserve his life, Moses' mother had placed him within an "ark" or basket, and set him adrift on the Nile. The ark was fashioned together with asphalt and pitch, the same material used in the construction of Noah's ark. The reeds, in Hebrew, refer to the nations. God had hidden His deliverer among the nations in preparation for His future deliverance. As Moses "sleeps" the ark rests above the waters and life again emerges from darkness and death.

As God's redeemer, Moses will lead the Children of Israel out of their bondage, also emptying Egypt of its treasures, gold, and silver. After the Exodus, God established the Mosaic Covenant with His people through the impartation of the Torah at Mount Sinai as the ***redeemed*** inheritors of the Land of Promise. God's redemptive plan through Moses is a foreshadowing of Yeshua as the great Redeemer.

"I WILL RAISE UP THE TABERNACLE
OF DAVID... AND REBUILD IT
AS IN DAYS OF OLD"

The Mosaic Covenant is a conditional covenant given to Israel. The Torah establishes God's government and constitution. The covenant language stipulates blessings for obedience and curses for disobedience to God's instructions. The earth sign of the Mosaic covenant is the Sabbath.

6. THE DAVIDIC COVENANT–THE COVENANT WITH KING DAVID

"For surely I will command,
and will sift the house of Israel among all nations,
as grain is sifted in a sieve;
yet not the smallest grain shall fall to the ground...
On that day I will raise up the tabernacle of David,
which has fallen down, and repair its damages;
I will raise up its ruins,
and rebuild it as in days of old." [11]

(Amos 9:9-11)

The Davidic Covenant assures that God will rebuild His dwelling place on the earth. A physical Tabernacle will again stand on the Temple Mount in Jerusalem, and its ruins will be built up as in days of old. Amos even prophesies the timing for this restoration of the Tabernacle of David. The rebuilding will take place during the days of the ingathering and re-gathering of the House of Israel, once scattered among the nations. God will restore His people to their Land, raise up His Temple, and cause the House of Judah and the House of Israel to become one in His hand (Ezekiel 37)—the movement called, *"The Restoration of the Tabernacle of David."*

We are seeing this prophetic move of God on the earth today! God's redemptive plan is causing the *multitude of nations* to return to the Torah, led by His Holy Spirit. You are God's dwelling place on the earth, restored as His temple (1 Corinthians 3)—Messiah *in* you, the hope of glory (Colossians 1), and the "one new man" of Ephesians Chapter 2.

7. THE RENEWED OR "NEW" COVENANT–THE COVENANT IN YESHUA (JESUS)

"But one of the soldiers pierced His side with a spear,
and immediately blood and water came out.
And he who has seen has testified,
and his testimony is true;
and he knows that he is telling the truth,
so that you may believe.
For these things were done that the
Scripture should be fulfilled,
"Not one of His bones shall be broken."
And again another Scripture says,
"They shall look on Him whom they pierced." [12]

(John 19:34-37)

The piercing of Yeshua's "side" caused an opening from which both blood and water flowed. Like the opening in Adam's side to remove the "rib" that God fashioned into Eve, and the opening in the side of Noah's ark, the pierced side of Yeshua fulfills the pattern of God's redemptive plan.

Into Yeshua's side we have been grafted, whether of the natural or the wild branches. The deception of the enemy and the defeat of sin are temporary in the eternal "light" of Salvation and Redemption in

"I WILL PUT MY LAWS IN
THEIR MIND AND
WRITE THEM ON THEIR HEARTS"

Messiah. The devastating effects of exile and assimilation are ended. Even the weakness of the Mosaic Covenant is overcome by this Renewed Covenant in Yeshua.

"Because finding fault with them,
He says: "Behold, the days are coming,
says the Lord, when I will make a **new (renewed)**
covenant with the house of Israel and
with the house of Judah—not according
to the covenant that I made
with their fathers in the day
when I took them by the hand
to lead them out of the land of Egypt;
because they did not continue in My covenant,
and I disregarded them, says the Lord.
For this is the covenant that I will make
with the house of Israel after those days, says the Lord:
I will put My laws in their mind and
write them on their hearts; and I will be their God,
and they shall be My people." [13]

(Hebrews 8:8-10, emphasis added)

Far from isolated examples of exegesis, nearly every parable, prophecy, and miracle in the Bible is a further setting of the stage for the restoration and reunification of the whole House of Jacob—the House of Judah with the House of Ephraim/Israel. Yeshua spoke of the great harvest at the end of the age. Jeremiah, a prophet who witnessed and experienced the siege and exile of Israel to Babylon, encouraged his listeners by reminding them of Israel's restoration still to come—the last and greater Exodus!

"Because your fathers have forsaken Me,'
says the Lord; 'they have walked after other gods
and have served them and worshiped them,
and have forsaken Me and not kept My law.
And you have done worse than your fathers,
for behold, each one follows the dictates
of his own evil heart, so that no one listens to Me.
Therefore I will cast you out of this land
into a land that you do not know,
neither you nor your fathers;
and there you shall serve other gods day and night,
where I will not show you favor.'
"Therefore behold, the days are coming,"
says the Lord, "that it shall no more be said,
'The Lord lives who brought up the
children of Israel from the land of Egypt,' but,
'The Lord lives who brought up **the children of Israel
from the land of the north and from all the lands
where He had driven them.'
For I will bring them back into their land
which I gave to their fathers.'"** [14]

(Jeremiah 16:11-15, emphasis added)

This is why we are seeing the worldwide "birth pangs" of the Messiah (Matthew 24). The world at large is being prepared for the appearing of the King of kings upon the earth. Yet the Bride of Messiah must first emerge in preparation for the Great Marriage Supper of the Lamb (Revelation 19). God is moving by His Spirit, to call you from your place of exile, to remove the blindness of Israel (Romans 11), to raise you up from *afar* (the ends of the earth), and restore you to your original heritage and covenant blessings.

God promised that He would teach you the Torah while you were yet in the nations. The very fact that believers around the world are being awakened to their Hebrew roots and learning the Torah is a direct fulfillment of end-times prophecy and a sign to Jews and Christians alike that the Messianic Era is upon us.

"As for you, son of man,
take a stick for yourself and write on it:
'For Judah and for the children of Israel,
his companions.' Then take another stick
and write on it, 'For Joseph, the stick of Ephraim,
and for all the house of Israel, his companions.'
Then join them one to another for yourself
into one stick, and they will become one in your hand.
"And when the children of your people speak to you,
saying, 'Will you not show us
what you mean by these?'—
say to them, 'Thus says the Lord GOD:
"Surely I will take the stick of Joseph,
which is in the hand of Ephraim,
and the tribes of Israel, his companions;
and I will join them with it,
with the stick of Judah, and make them one stick,
and they will be one in My hand."'
And the sticks on which you write
will be in your hand before their eyes.
"Then say to them, 'Thus says the Lord GOD:
"Surely I will take the children of Israel
from among the nations, wherever they have gone,

and will gather them from every side
and bring them into their own land;
and I will make them one nation in the land,
on the mountains of Israel;
and one king shall be king over them all;
they shall no longer be two nations,
nor shall they ever be divided into two kingdoms again.
They shall not defile themselves anymore
with their idols, nor with their detestable things,
nor with any of their transgressions;
but I will deliver them from all their
dwelling places in which they have sinned,
and will cleanse them.
Then they shall be My people,
and I will be their God." [15]

(Ezekiel 37:15-23)

Ezekiel clearly prophesies that the whole House of Jacob—the House of Judah and the House of Israel—shall be gathered from the nations and become one nation in God's hand.

"I am the good shepherd; and I know My sheep,
and am known by My own.
As the Father knows Me, even so I know the Father;
and I lay down My life for the sheep.
And other sheep I have which are not of this fold;
them also I must bring, and they will hear My voice;
and there will be one flock and one shepherd.
Therefore My Father loves Me,

because I lay down My life
that I may take it again.
No one takes it from Me,
but I lay it down of Myself.
I have power to lay it down,
and I have power to take it again.
This command I have received
from My Father." [16]

(John 10:14-18)

As He speaks these words recorded in the Gospel of John, Yeshua is standing with the House of Judah—descendants of the Jews who had returned from the Babylonian exile—telling them that He would lay down His life, not only for them, but also for these "other sheep" that were not in that day identified with the Jews—the "lost sheep of the House of Israel." Yeshua refers to the House of Israel by name, first when He sends out His twelve Apostles:

"But go rather to the lost sheep of
the house of Israel." [17]

(Matthew 10:6)

Later when Yeshua reminds the Apostles about the purpose of His ministry, He says:

"I was not sent except to the
lost sheep of the house of Israel." [18]

(Matthew 15:24)

When the House of Israel returns to the Torah, the House of Judah will recognize the Messiah in them. When Yeshua says that He came to fulfill the Law (Matthew 17), He is saying that in Him is the fulfillment of **God's Teaching and Instruction—the Torah.** In Yeshua, both the Person (Salvation) and the Principles (Redemption) of God exist. He lived His life according to the Torah, and His Incarnation is the complete picture of God dwelling within mankind.

God has called us to be a holy people, set apart unto Him. You have been called out of the nations to the redeemed lifestyle (Torah) that restores your God-given dominion on the earth, the dominion that God destined for you from the beginning.

Surely, we are living in the Messianic Age, the final era of the 7,000-Year Redemptive Plan of God. You are the witnesses of God's eternal Salvation (Yeshua) and you are the bearers of this message of God's Redemption (Torah). Your life will never be the same!

The Nations returning to the Torah is a fulfillment of the Messianic prophecies and evidence of the miracle-working power of the *Ruach HaKodesh*—the Holy Spirit. At that time and in these days, the blindness of Israel will be healed. The House of Judah will clearly see the face of Yeshua, and the House of Israel will have their eyes forever opened to the eternal words of the Torah.

CONCLUSION: AMAZING GRACE

Bringing Honor in the Midst of Jezebel, Part 1
To view a video segment of this resource, scan the QR code using your smartphone.

The English word "grace" derives from the Latin *gratia* meaning "gratitude" or "thanks."

The Greek word which is translated as "grace" is *charis*. From charis we derive such words as "charisma" and "charity" and ideas generally associated with charm or beauty.

The Hebrew word which is often translated into English as grace is *chen* meaning beauty, elegance, and favor. Another Hebrew word related to grace is *chesed*, most often translated as mercy.

It is clear that the word "grace" has diverse origins and usage. It also becomes clear that the original concept presented in the Hebrew Scriptures has not necessarily been properly represented by the word "grace" in the English language. This can lead to a misconception that there is little to no grace found in the Old Testament, when, in fact, the Hebrew word *chesed* (grace and favor) occurs 274 times, and the Hebrew *chen* (grace and mercy) occurs 69 times.

There are also numerous other Hebrew words which express the concepts of mercy, compassion, patience, goodness, favor, and kindness—all of these additional elements are included within the revelation of "grace." Ironically, even though grace is a foundational cornerstone, Western Christianity has developed an extremely narrowed doctrine and understanding of Biblical grace.

"For by grace you have been
saved through faith,
and that not of yourselves;
it is the gift of God." [1]

(Ephesians 2:8)

Simply put, without God's outpouring of grace, no one could be saved! Grace is the conduit for salvation. Grace is the unmerited gift that is freely given so that none can boast that they somehow earned or were deserving of His salvation. Without exception, the Scriptures confirm that no one can be saved apart from the grace of YHWH.

A grave misunderstanding of the Bible quickly arises when this grace is viewed as something new or mutually exclusive from the Torah. Teachings and doctrines have emerged that even posit the Torah and grace as adversarial rivals, with grace having somehow won the struggle and replaced the Torah. Many Christians have been taught that grace came only through Jesus in the New Testament and that the Old Testament has been nullified because there is no grace in the Torah.

"Then the Lord saw that the
wickedness of man was great in the earth,
and that every intent of the
thoughts of his heart was only evil continually.
And the Lord was sorry that He had made man
on the earth, and He was grieved in His heart...
but Noah found **grace** in the eyes of the Lord." [2]

(Genesis 6:5-8, emphasis added)

What preserved Noah and his family was most certainly not the wickedness and corruption of mankind. Likewise, the inhabitants on board Noah's ark were not saved by the physical structure which rose above the waters of judgment. What saved Noah and all those with him was the grace of God, and it was this grace which was manifested within the protective confines of an earthly vessel.

"And the LORD passed before him
and proclaimed, 'The **LORD,** the **LORD God,**
merciful and **gracious, longsuffering,** and abounding
in **goodness** and **truth, keeping mercy** for thousands,
forgiving iniquity and transgression and sin,
by no means clearing the guilty,
visiting the iniquity of the fathers upon the children
and the children's children to the third
and the fourth generation.'" [3]

(Exodus 34:6-7, emphasis added)

The very word grace, with all its related Hebrew words, is the central theme of the revelation of God's Name given to Moses. Again, in Hebrew thought, names are not nouns or titles. God's Name reveals His nature, character, action, and activity. To even suggest that grace is a New Testament concept only is to diminish the very Name and nature of God.

God has progressively revealed Himself throughout the Scriptures, from the first words of Genesis to the last verse of Revelation. The Voice of Creation is *Elohim.* To Abraham He is *El Shaddai.* From Mount Sinai He is *YHWH.* And as Salvation He is called *Yeshua.* The Voice of Creation is the Voice of the Torah, and the Voice of YHWH is the Voice of the Principles.

"Therefore know this day,
and consider it in your heart,
that the **LORD** Himself is **God in heaven above**
and **on the earth beneath;** there is no other." [4]
(Deuteronomy 4:39, emphasis added)

Elohim: God (Genesis 1:1)
YHWH Elohim: The LORD God (Genesis 2:4)
YHWH: LORD (Genesis 4:1)
El Elyon: The Most High God (Genesis 14:18)
Davar YHWH: The Word of the LORD (Genesis 15:1)
El Roi: The God Who Sees (Genesis 16:13)
El Shaddai: The God Who is Sufficient (Genesis 17:1)
El Olam: The Everlasting God (Genesis 21:33)
YHWH Yireh: The LORD will be seen (Genesis 22:13)
Ehyeh Asher Ehyeh: I AM that I AM (Exodus 3:14)
YHWH Ropheka: The LORD your Healer (Exodus 15:26)
YHWH Eloheikem: The LORD your God (Exodus 16:12)
YHWH Nissi: The LORD my Miracle (Exodus 17:15)
YHWH Mikadoshchem: The LORD Who sanctifies (Exodus 31:13)
YHWH Shalom: The LORD is Peace (Judges 6:24)
YHWH Tzavaot: The LORD of Hosts (Isaiah 1:9)
Immanuel: God with us (Isaiah 7:14)
YHWH Tzidkeinu: The LORD our Righteousness (Jeremiah 23:6)
YHWH Yeshua: The LORD my Salvation (Revelation 22:21)

"And in that day you will say...
Behold, God is my salvation, I will trust and not be afraid;
'For **Yah,** the **LORD,** is my strength and song;
He also has become **my salvation**.'" [5]
(Isaiah 12:2, emphasis added)

Isaiah confirms the "Good News" of the Gospel revealed throughout the pages of the Bible: the LORD YHWH has become our Salvation—Yeshua, Jesus Christ. The greatest revelation of God, His Name and His nature, took on physical form and dwelt among us. The two components of this Gospel message are God's Salvation and Redemption—the Person Yeshua and the Principles of Yeshua. The Torah reveals God to us: His nature and His ways, God's mercy and justice, His longsuffering and forgiveness, God's Teaching *and* God's Grace.

"And the Word became flesh, and dwelt among us,
and we saw His glory, glory as of the
only begotten from the Father,
full of grace and truth.
John testified about Him and cried out, saying,
This was He of whom I said,
'He who comes after me has a higher rank than I,
for He existed before me.'
For of His fullness we have all received,
and **grace upon grace.**
For the Law was given through Moses;
grace and truth were realized through Jesus Christ." [6]
(John 1:14-17 NAS, emphasis added)

As John introduces his Gospel narrative, beautifully expressing the Incarnation of the Word, he expounds upon this unique revelation of YHWH in the Person Jesus Christ. As a Hebrew, John certainly understood that Jesus had not come to abolish the Torah in favor of a new concept called grace. In fact, John writes that through Jesus, we have all received grace *upon* grace. Perhaps to absolutely clarify this point, John continues by stating that the Law (the second "grace" of John's *grace upon grace* statement) was given through Moses, and grace and truth (the first "grace" of John's statement) were realized through Jesus Christ. For John, the Torah was a revelation of God *and* His grace, just as Jesus is the ultimate revelation of this same YHWH God and His same grace—grace *upon* grace, the Torah pointing to Yeshua—Amazing Grace!

It is the eternal and steadfast grace of YHWH that draws you to His Salvation (Yeshua), and it is this same grace of YHWH that draws you to His Redemption (Torah)—*that you may have life (YHWH), and have life more abundantly (Torah)* (John 10).

The Voice of YHWH…
The Grace of Salvation (Yeshua)!

The Voice of the Principles…
The Grace of Redemption (Torah)!

"Therefore I make known to you that
no one speaking by the Spirit of God
calls Jesus accursed, and no one can say
that **Jesus is LORD (YHWH)**

except by the Holy Spirit.
There are diversities of gifts, but the same Spirit.
There are differences of ministries, but the same LORD.
And there are diversities of activities,
but it is the same God who works all in all." [7]
(1 Corinthians 12:3-6, emphasis added)

I conclude this book as I began it—with a question. In the end it doesn't matter what anyone else thinks or concludes about the Torah. It makes absolutely no difference to me what congregation or denomination you belong to, or how dearly you hold to the teachings you grew up with. My purpose is not to dishonor any of those who have gone before us, and certainly not to discredit those who labor with us in the work of the Kingdom.

It's not ultimately about what your Pastor, Priest, Minister, or Bishop believes. It's also not about conforming to or pridefully confronting the beliefs of your family, friends, father, mother, sister, or brother. In the final analysis, God's Word is the ultimate authority and the standard of truth we are each accountable to. The understanding of this Word comes only by His Holy Spirit within you, the mobilization of God's action and activity on the earth—the Kingdom of Heaven.

In the end, it comes down to you! What do you believe? What will you do with the truth that God has revealed to you? What is the Spirit speaking by His Voice of the Principles within you? *What is the Torah: Law or Grace?*

GLOSSARY

A

Abraham: Biblical patriarch; literally, "father of a multitude of nations."

Adonai: *(Hebrew)* Name of God, meaning the force of God upon the earth; literally "my Master."

Adonai YHWH: *(Hebrew)* The LORD my Master.

Afar: Biblical metaphor for "the nations" or "the ends of the earth."

Arianism: Beliefs based on the heretical teachings of Arius (c. 300 A.D.) which denied the Divinity of Yeshua.

Anti-Semitism: Prejudice against or hostility towards the Jewish people.

Aquinas: Early Church father, considered to be the Church's greatest theologian and philosopher.

Ark of the Covenant: Gold covered box containing the stone tablets of Moses that rested within the Holy of Holies. Ark Cover was called the "Mercy Seat" of God.

Assyria: Kingdom in Mesopatamia responsible for the defeat and exile of the northern kingdom of Israel c. 781 B.C.E.

Ated Lavo: *(Hebrew)* Future Age.

Atlantic Triangle: Slave-trade route connecting Europe, Africa, North and South America.

Augustine: Early Church father who promoted Marcion's heretical ideas of a two-Deity principle.

Azuza Street Revival: Pentecostal revival in Los Angeles, CA from early 1906 to 1915.

B

Babylon: Kingdom in Mesopatamia responsible for the defeat and exile of the southern kingdom of Israel c. 586 B.C.E.

Bethany: Hometown of Lazarus, Mary, and Martha; literally, "house of the poor."

Boaz: Kinsman redeemer in Biblical story of Ruth.

Breastplate: Part of the High Priest's garments; woven of gold, wool, and linen, covered with 12 stones, each identifying one of the tribes of Israel.

British Israelism: Belief that Western Europeans are direct descendants of the Ten Lost Tribes of Israel.

C

Chatah: *(Hebrew)* Sin; literally, "to miss the mark."

Choshech: *(Hebrew)* Darkness.

Chrysostom: 4th century Bishop of Church at Antioch.

Chukim: *(Hebrew)* Image; Lasting impression; Image of God.

Circumcision: Sign of Abrahamic Covenant; removal of foreskin on the 8th day for Hebrew males.

Commonwealth: Community founded for the common good; Biblically the Commonwealth of Israel.

Constantine: Roman Emperor who convened the Council of Nicea in 325 A.D.

Contract: Uniquely Western or Greco-Roman agreement which creates an obligation.

Covenant: Uniquely Eastern or Hebraic promise, especially for the performance of some action.

D

Darby, John Nelson (1800-1882): Known as the "father of Modern Dispensationalism.

Davar YHWH: *(Hebrew)* The Word of the LORD.

Davening: *(Hebrew)* Bowing motion during Hebrew prayer or liturgy.

Decalogue: The Ten Commandments; literally "Ten Utterances."

Dispensationalism (also Evangelical Dispensation Theory): Greek model of successive dispensations or ages of time, focused on Judgment on the earth .

Drash: *(Hebrew)* Discussion; Allegory; Midrash.

E

Easter: Ancient pagan ritual on Spring Equinox syncretized into Christianity as celebration of Jesus' resurrection.

Eber: *(Hebrew)* to cross over.

Ehyeh Asher Ehyeh: I AM that I AM.

El Elyon: The Most High God.

Elohim: *(Hebrew)* Name for God, meaning the intensification of all power.

El Olam: *(Hebrew)* The Everlasting God.

El Roi: *(Hebrew)* The God Who Sees.

El Shaddai: *(Hebrew)* Name for God; literally, "God Who is Sufficient."

Equinox: Bi-annual alignment between the earth's equator and the linear plane of the Sun.

Esther: Biblical heroine considered to have prevented the destruction of the Jewish people c. 522 B.C.E.

Etsom: *(Hebrew, plural of Eytz)* Bone, Rib, Side, Branch.

Eusebius: Early Church father, considered to be the father of Church history.

Exegesis: Scriptural Interpretation.

F

Faith: Obedience in action.
First Fruits: Biblical Spring Feast fulfilled in Yeshua's Resurrection.
Fulfill: Bring to a greater understanding.

G

Gentile: Common term for non-Jewish people; Biblical definition, "pagan; confused; without God."
Golden Altar: Altar of Incense within the Sanctuary.
Grafting: Joining the branches of a plant or tree into the stock of a host tree.

H

HASHEM: Substitute term for YHWH; the Tetragrammaton.
Heresy: Conflicting change to a system of beliefs.
Holy of Holies: Innermost part of the Sanctuary; resting place of the Ark of the Covenant.
House of Ephraim: Northern kingdom of Israel *(also House of Israel, or "Ten Lost Tribes").*
House of Jacob: House of Judah and House of Ephraim combined.
House of Judah: Southern kingdom of Israel.
House of Israel: Northern kingdom of Israel *(also House of Ephraim, or "Ten Lost Tribes").*

I

Immanuel: *(Hebrew)* God with us.
Ineffable: Unspeakable.
Israel: *(Hebrew)* Name of Jacob, collective name for the 12 tribes; literally, "to overcome with God."

J

Jew: People belonging to the Tribe or House of Judah.
Jot: *(Yod in Hebrew)* Smallest of the 22 Hebrew letters.

K

Kashrut: *(Hebrew)* Kosher; Fit; Proper.
Kavod: *(Hebrew)* Glory.
Ketuvim: 3rd major section of the Tanakh; literally, Writings.
Kidron Valley: Expanse between Mount of Olives and Mount Moriah.
King David: Biblical king who reigned over a united Israel forty years c. 1005-965 B.C.E.
King Rehoboam: Biblical king under whose reign Israel divided into two distinct kingdoms c. 913 B.C.E.
King Solomon: Son of King David who reigned over a united Israel forty years c. 965-923 B.C.E.
Kohen Gadol: *(Hebrew)* High Priest.
Kosher: Fit; Proper.

L

Law of Christ: Eternal fulfillment and interpretation of the Mosaic Covenant.

Law of Sin and Death: Judgment and penalties defined in the Torah and Mosaic Covenant.

L'Chayim: *(Hebrew)* Common Hebrew expression meaning "to life!"

Levites: Priests.

Lineage: Descendants from a common ancestor.

Luther: German priest and theologian who initiated the Reformation or Protestant Reformation.

M

Macdonald, Margaret: Young Scottish woman who initiated the belief in a pre-tribulation rapture of believers.

Marcion: Early Church father best known for his heretical teaching of a two-Deity principle.

Mary: Sister of Lazarus and Martha; literally, "bitter."

Melchizedek: High Priest of God (Genesis 14); literally "King of Righteousness."

Mercy Seat: Lid or Cover of the Ark of the Covenant.

Messianic Era: Period of time culminating in the appearing of the Messiah and His 1,000-year Reign.

Mishpatim: *(Hebrew)* God's deliverer; Deliverance.

Mithra: Pagan deity whose birthday celebration on December 25th was syncretized into Christianity as the Birth of Jesus.

Mitzvot: *(Hebrew)* Deeds; Works of righteousness.

Moadim: *(Hebrew)* Biblical Feast and Festivals; God's appointed times; literally, "Rehearsals."

Modalism: Belief that God has revealed Himself in different "modes" throughout time.

Monotheism: Belief in One God.

Mount Moriah: Temple Mount in Jerusalem; literally, "mountain of God's teaching."

Mount of Olives: Probable site of Jesus' crucifixion; opposite Mount Moriah in Jerusalem.

Mount Sinai: *(also Horeb)* Mountain of God where Moses received the Torah.

N

Nevi'im: *(Hebrew)* 2nd major section of the Tanakh; literally, "Prophets."

Niddah: *(Hebrew)* Biblical instructions for purity; separation, especially as related to sexual relations.

Northern Kingdom: Kingdom of Ephraim; Kingdom of Israel; "Ten Lost Tribes"; Conquered and exiled by Assyria c. 721 B.C.E.

O

Or: *(Hebrew)* Light.

Oholah: *(Hebrew)* Samaria in Biblical prophecy.

Oholibah: *(Hebrew)* Jerusalem in Biblical prophecy.

Old Testament: Western term for Tanakh or Hebrew Scriptures.

Origen: Early Church father, considered to be the foremost Greek scholar and theologian.

Order of Melchizedek: Eternal priestly order of Yeshua the Messiah.

P

Passover: Biblical Spring Feast fulfilled in Yeshua's death as the Passover Lamb.
Pentateuch: Greek term for the Torah; First five Books of Moses.
Peshat: *(Hebrew)* Literal; Simple.
Pharisees: Religious sect of teachers and students at the time of Yeshua.
Polytheism: Belief in multiple gods.
Promised Land: Biblical land of Israel.

R

Rabbi: Teacher.
Rambam: Rabbi Moshe ben Maimon—12th Century Rabbi who derived the list of 613 Commands in the Torah.
Rapture: *(also Pre-tribulation Rapture)* Recent Doctrine added to Dispensational Theology c. 1830; Belief in the "catching away" of believers just prior to the 7-year Tribulation.
Realm of Death: Outside of or disobeying the Torah; not observing the Torah Principles.
Realm of Life: Obedience to and observance of Torah Principles.
Redemption: The Principles of Yeshua; Lifestyle characterized by the 613 Principles of the Torah.
Reformation: *(also Protestant Reformation)* European Christian reform movement initiated by Luther.
Remez: *(Hebrew)* Refer; Hint.
Replacement Theology: Teaching that the Church has replaced Israel in God's promise and prophecy.
Restoration of the House of David: Reuniting of the whole House of Jacob.
Ruach HaKodesh: *(Hebrew)* The Holy Spirit.

S

Sabbath: Day of rest; Sundown Friday to sundown Saturday.
Sadducees: Religious sect of teachers and students at the time of Yeshua.
Salvation: The Person Yeshua, Jesus Christ.
Saturnalia: Pagan ritual of Winter Solstice in December.
Scofield, C.I. (1843-1921): Dispensationalist and rapture proponent; Published Scofield Reference Bible furthering Evangelical Dispensation Theology.
Shavuot (Pentecost): Biblical Spring Feast fulfilled in Exodus 19 and Acts Chapter 2; literally, "weeks."
Shema: *(Hebrew)* Declaration of God's Oneness (Dt. 6:4); literally "Hear."
Sod: *(Hebrew)* Hidden; Secret.
Solstice: Bi-annual astronomical event of Sun's appearing at earth's northern and southern poles.
Southern Kingdom: Kingdom of Judah; House of Judah.
Spanish Inquisition: 1478 A.D. Catholic tribunal intended to protect the Church from heresy but resulting in severe persecution of Jews and Christians.
Syncretism: Combining paganism and the Torah.
Sukkot: *(Hebrew)* Biblical Fall Feast fulfilled in Yeshua's 1,000-year reign on earth; literally, "Tabernacles."
Synagogue: Jewish/Hebrew House of Worship.

T

Talmidim: *(Hebrew)* Disciples; Students of a Rabbi.
Talmud: *(Hebrew)* Oral Commentary on the Torah.
Tanakh: *(Hebrew)* Acronym for three main divisions of the Scriptures: Torah (Teaching), Nevi'im (Prophets), Ketuvim (Writings).
Tefillin: *(Hebrew)* Scripture boxes worn on the arm and forehead during prayer (also Phylacteries).

Telos: *(Greek)* Goal, Purpose; End.

Temple Mount: Site in Jerusalem of the first two and future third Temples; Mount Moriah.

Ten Lost Tribes: Northern Kingdom of Israel; House of Ephraim; House of Israel.

Tertullian: Early Church father (c. 200 A.D.) and notable Christian apologist.

Tetragrammaton: YHWH; four-letter Name of God.

Tittle: Tagin *(Hebrew),* "crown" or adornment on most Hebrew letters.

Tohu: *(Hebrew)* 2,000-year era from Creation to Abraham; literally, "destruction."

Tohu v'bohu: *(Hebrew)* Biblical description of earth prior to Creation; literally, "chaos and emptiness."

Torah: *(Hebrew)* 1st major division of the Tanakh; literally, Teaching; Instruction.

Trias: *(Greek)* used by Theophilus of Antioch (c. 180 A.D.) in reference to God, His Word, and His Wisdom; literally, "a set of three."

Tribulation: 7-year reign of Anti-Christ and the False Prophet detailed in the Book of Revelation.

Trinitarianism: Christian doctrine of the Trinity; three separate, distinct, and eternal Persons of the Godhead.

Trinitas: *(Latin)* referring to the Father, Son, and Holy Spirit; translated "Trinity" in English.

Trinity: Christian doctrine that God eternally exists in three distinct persons: The Father, Son, and Holy Spirit.

Two-Deity Principle: Heretical teaching of a harsh God in the Tanakh and a merciful God, Jesus in the New Testament.

Tzion/Zion: *(Hebrew)* Jerusalem; Israel, specifically glorified and restored Israel.

Y

Yarah: *(Hebrew)* to shoot an arrow.
Yeshua: Hebrew Name of Jesus.
Yeshua HaMashiach: *(Hebrew)* Jesus the Messiah.
YHWH: *(Hebrew)* Name for God; often translated as Yahweh, Lord, or LORD.
YHWH Eloheikem: *(Hebrew)* The LORD your God.
YHWH Elohim: *(Hebrew)* The LORD God.
YHWH Mikadoshchem: *(Hebrew)* The LORD Who sanctifies.
YHWH Nissi: *(Hebrew)* The LORD my Miracle.
YHWH Ropheka: *(Hebrew)* The LORD your Healer.
YHWH Shalom: *(Hebrew)* The LORD is Peace.
YHWH Tzavaot: *(Hebrew)* The LORD of Hosts.
YHWH Tzidkeinu: *(Hebrew)* The LORD our Righteousness.

YHWH Yeshua: *(Hebrew)* The LORD my Salvation.
YHWH Yireh: The LORD will be seen.
Yom Kippur: *(Hebrew)* Biblical Fall Feast fulfilled in Yeshua's atonement; literally, "Day of Atonement" or "Day of Covering."
Yomot HaMashiach: *(Hebrew) (also Yomot Ha)* 2,000-year era beginning with the Incarnation of Yeshua.

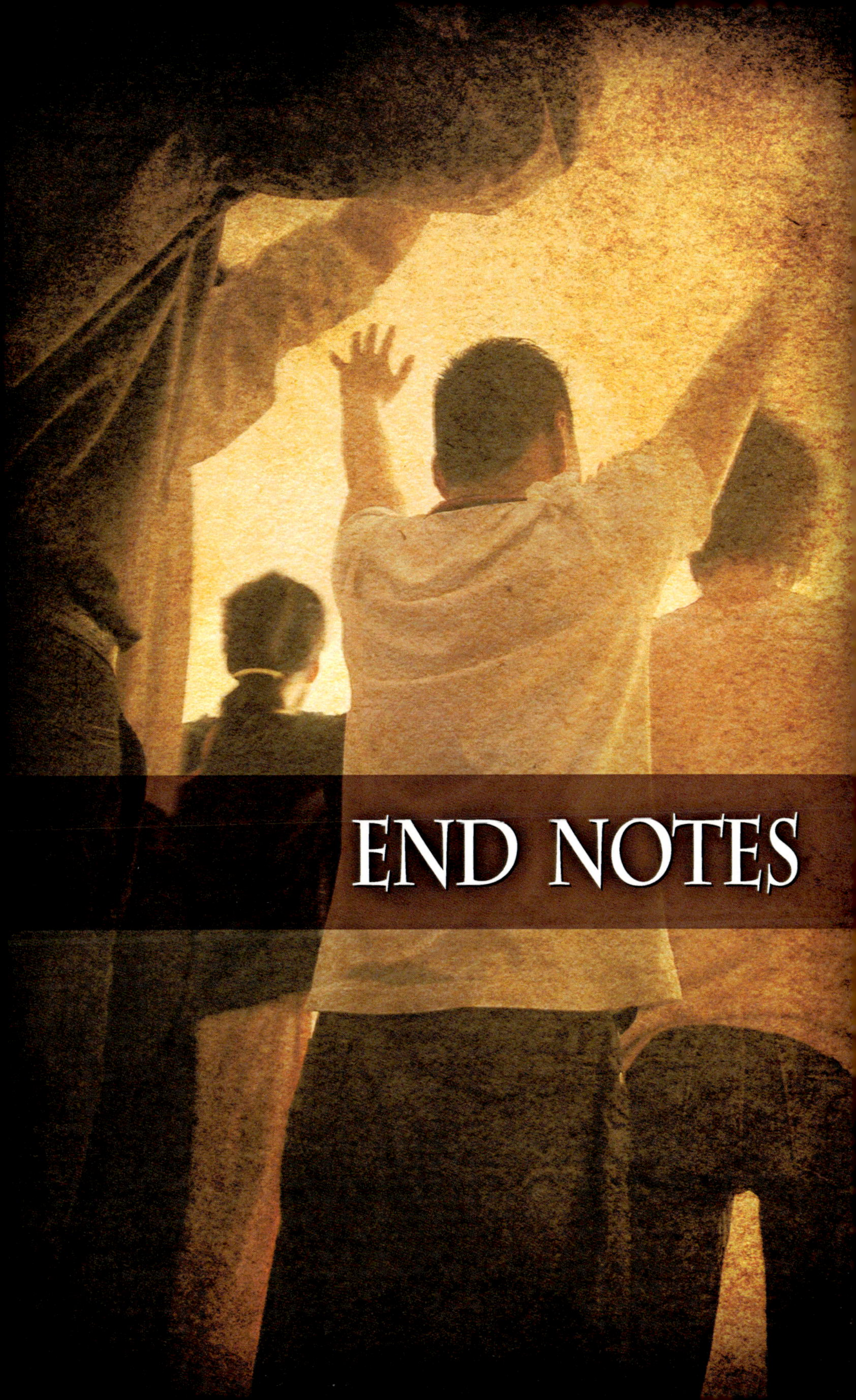

END NOTES

Simchat Torah Beit Midrash® gratefully acknowledges the following individuals and organizations for their excellent work and source material:

Dr. Richard Booker—Institute for Hebraic-Christian Studies and Sounds of the Trumpet, Inc. Publishing.

Dr. Marvin Wilson—Professor, Gordon-Conwell Theological Seminary and William B. Erdsman Publishing.

The late **Dr. Dwight A. Pryor**—Founder of The Center for Judaic-Christian Studies.

Dr. Brad Young—Jerusalem School of Synoptic Research and Hendrickson Publishers.

FOREWORD

1. Simcha Jacobovici, *The Quest for the Lost Tribes* (by A&E Home Video, 2008)

INTRODUCTION

1. *The Bible—New King James Version®* (Nashville, TN: by Thomas Nelson Publishers, 1982), Genesis Ch. 1
2. ibid, John Ch. 1
3. ibid, Genesis Ch.2

CHAPTER ONE
TORAH: THE HISTORICAL UNDERSTANDING

1. *The Bible—New King James Version®*, Genesis Ch. 1
2. ibid, Psalms Ch. 33
3. Rabbi Nosson Scherman, *The Chumash—Artscroll Series/ Stone Edition* (Brooklyn, NY: by Mesorah Publications, Ltd., 1998), p. xxv
4. Richard Booker, *Torah: Law or Grace?*, (Woodlands, TX: by Sounds of the Trumpet, Inc., 2001), p. 17
5. ibid, p. 17
6. Talmud, tractate Makkoth, 23b
7. Scherman, *The Chumash,* p. xxi
8. *The Bible—New King James Version®*, Matthew Ch. 22
9. ibid, Genesis Ch. 2
10. Barney Kasdan, *God's Appointed Times,* (Baltimore, MD: by Messianic Jewish Publishers, 1993), p. 117
11. *The Bible—New King James Version®*, Exodus Ch. 6
12. ibid, Exodus Ch. 34
13. ibid, Psalms Ch. 118
14. ibid, John Ch. 17
15. ibid, Matthew Ch. 4
16. Booker, *Torah: Law or Grace?*, p. 18
17. *The Bible—New King James Version®*, Jeremiah Ch. 31; Hebrews Ch. 8

CHAPTER TWO
TORAH: WORKS OR GRACE?

1. Booker, *Torah: Law or Grace?*, p. 1
2. ibid, p. 1
3. ibid, p. 2
4. *Complete Jewish Bible* (Clarksville, MD: by Jewish New Testament Publications, Inc., 1998), Romans Ch. 3
5. *The Bible—New King James Version®*, Ephesians Ch. 2
6. www.theopedia.com/Trinity

7. The Bible—New King James Version®, Deuteronomy Ch. 6
8. ibid, Exodus Ch. 20
9. ibid, Deuteronomy Ch. 6
10. ibid, John Ch. 10
11. ibid, Exodus Ch. 3
12. ibid, John Ch. 8
13. ibid, Deuteronomy Ch. 32
14. ibid, John Ch. 8
15. ibid, Deuteronomy Ch. 4
16. ibid, John Ch. 3
17. ibid, Isaiah Ch. 45
18. ibid, Titus Ch. 2
19. ibid, Isaiah Ch. 44
20. ibid, Revelation Ch. 1
21. ibid, Isaiah Ch. 9
22. ibid, John Ch. 14
23. ibid, Psalms Ch. 23
24. ibid, John Ch. 10
25. ibid, Isaiah Ch. 40
26. ibid, Matthew Ch. 24
27. ibid, Deuteronomy Ch. 33
28. ibid, Jude Ch. 1

CHAPTER THREE
THE HEBREW ROOTS OF THE CHRISTIAN FAITH

1. *The Bible—New King James Version®*, 1 Cor. Ch. 3
2. Rabbi Stanley Wagner, Rabbi Emeritus, BMH-BJ Congregation, Denver, Colo.
3. Booker, *Torah: Law or Grace?*, p. 3
4. ibid, p. iii
5. ibid, p. 3
6. ibid, p. 4
7. ibid, p. 3
8. *The Bible—New King James Version®*, Acts Ch. 24

9. ibid, Acts Ch. 21
10. ibid, Acts Ch. 28
11. Booker, *Torah: Law or Grace?*, p. 27
12. Talmud, tractate Bamidbar, Rabba 13:15
13. *The Bible—New King James Version®*, Mark Ch. 11

CHAPTER FOUR
THE LANGUAGE OF EXILE

1. *The Bible—New King James Version®*, Genesis Ch. 35
2. ibid, Amos Ch. 9
3. ibid, Isaiah Ch. 43
4. Abraham J. Karp, *From the Ends of the Earth,* (Washington, DC: Library of Congress, 1991), p. 151
5. Christopher L. Miller, *The French Atlantic Triangle,* (Durham & London: by Duke University Press, 2008), p.3
6. *The Bible—New King James Version®*, 2 Corinthians Ch. 5
7. ibid, Romans Ch. 10
8. *The Hebrew Names Version* (Public Domain), Ephesians Ch. 2
9. *The Bible—New King James Version®*, John Ch. 15
10. ibid, Ezekiel Ch. 36
11. Booker, *Torah: Law or Grace?*, p. 19
12. *The Bible—New King James Version®*, Acts Ch. 4
13. ibid, John Ch. 16
14. ibid, Genesis Ch. 1
15. ibid, Nehemiah Ch. 9
16. ibid, Nehemiah Ch. 9
17. ibid, Isaiah Ch. 42
18. ibid, Isaiah Ch. 44
19. ibid, Isaiah Ch. 61; Luke Ch. 4
20. ibid, Ezekiel Ch. 37
21. ibid, Joel Ch. 2
22. ibid, Zechariah Ch. 4
23. ibid, Psalms 51
24. ibid, Psalms 104

25. ibid, Matthew Ch. 12
26. ibid, John Ch. 14
27. ibid, Acts Ch. 1
28. ibid, Acts Ch. 20
29. ibid, Romans Ch. 8
30. ibid, Romans Ch. 8
31. ibid, Ephesians Ch. 1
32. ibid, 1 Corinthians Ch. 2
33. ibid, 1 Corinthians Ch. 3
34. ibid, 2 Corinthians Ch. 3
35. ibid, 2 Timothy Ch. 1
36. ibid, Revelation Ch. 22
37. ibid, Deuteronomy Ch. 32
38. ibid, Proverbs Ch. 3
39. Booker, *Torah: Law or Grace?*, p. 21
40. *The Bible—New King James Version®*, Psalms 40
41. ibid, Psalms 94
42. ibid, Psalms 119
43. ibid, Micah Ch. 7
44. ibid, Psalms 105
45. ibid, Isaiah Ch. 26
46. ibid, Revelation Ch. 15
47. ibid, Deuteronomy Ch. 6
48. ibid, Psalms 25
49. Booker, *Torah: Law or Grace?*, p. 4
50. *The Bible—New King James Version®*, James Ch. 1
51. Booker, *Torah: Law or Grace?*, p. 23
52. *The Bible—New King James Version®*, Romans Ch. 10
53. Booker, *Torah: Law or Grace?*, p. 29
54. ibid, p. 28
55. ibid, p. 28
56. *The Bible—New King James Version®*, Romans Ch. 8

CHAPTER FIVE
TORAH: THE FIRST CENTURY CHURCH

1. *The Bible—New King James Version*®, Acts Ch. 21
2. Booker, *Torah: Law or Grace?*, p. 25
3. *The Bible—New King James Version*®, Acts Ch. 15
4. Booker, *Torah: Law or Grace?*, p. 26

CHAPTER SIX
TORAH: THE UNCOMMON DREAM

1. *The Bible—New King James Version*®, Habukkuk Ch. 2
2. ibid, Romans Ch. 8
3. ibid, Colossians Ch. 1
4. Booker, *Torah: Law or Grace?*, p. 18
5. Ron Moseley, *The Spirit of the Law,* (Sherwood, AK: Mozar Research Foundation, 1993), p. 22-24

CHAPTER SEVEN
REVIVAL IN THE TORAH

1. *The Bible—New King James Version*®, 1 Timothy Ch. 2
2. ibid, John Ch. 14
3. ibid, 1 John Ch. 2
4. ibid, Hosea Ch. 8
5. Booker, *Torah: Law or Grace?*, p. 33
6. *The Bible—New King James Version*®, 1 John Ch. 2
7. Booker, *Torah: Law or Grace?*, p. 31
8. ibid, p. 32
9. ibid, p. 11
10. *The Bible—New King James Version*®, James Ch. 2

CHAPTER EIGHT
NATURAL AND WILD BRANCHES

1. *The Bible—New King James Version®*, Romans Ch. 11
2. ibid, 2 Peter Ch. 3
3. ibid, Galatians Ch. 3
4. ibid, Romans Ch. 11
5. ibid, Romans Ch. 11
6. ibid, Romans Ch. 11
7. *The Bible—New International Version®* (Grand Rapids, MI: by Biblica, Inc.™, Zondervan, 1973), Isaiah Ch. 46
8. Dave MacPherson, *The True Story of the Pre-Trib Rapture* (Plainfield, NJ: Logos International, 1975), p. 93
9. *The Bible—New King James Version®*, Zechariah Ch. 9
10. ibid, Deuteronomy Ch. 30

CHAPTER NINE
LAZARUS COME FORTH!

1. *The Bible—New King James Version®*, John Ch. 11
2. ibid, Isaiah Ch. 51
3. ibid, Ezekiel Ch. 37
4. ibid, Ezekiel Ch. 34
5. ibid, John Ch. 11
6. ibid, Deuteronomy Ch. 7
7. ibid, John Ch. 11
8. ibid, Ezekiel Ch. 23
9. ibid, Ezekiel Ch. 23
10. ibid, John Ch. 11
11. ibid, Mosely, *Yeshua, A Guide to the Real Jesus and the Original Church,* p.22
12. *The Bible—New King James Version®*, John Ch. 11
13. ibid, John Ch. 11
14. ibid, Amos Ch. 8
15. ibid, Romans Ch. 6
16. ibid, John Ch. 11
17. ibid, Malachi Ch. 4

CHAPTER TEN
WHAT WOULD JESUS DO?

1. *The Bible—New King James Version®*, Matthew Ch. 5
2. ibid, Ephesians Ch. 2
3. ibid, Genesis Ch. 1
4. ibid, Genesis Ch. 1
5. ibid, Genesis Ch. 2
6. ibid, Genesis Ch. 2
7. ibid, Genesis Ch. 8
8. ibid, Genesis Ch. 15
9. ibid, Genesis Ch. 15
10. ibid, Exodus Ch. 2
11. ibid, Amos Ch. 9
12. ibid, John Ch. 19
13. ibid, Hebrews Ch. 8
14. ibid, Jeremiah Ch. 16
15. ibid, Ezekiel Ch. 37
16. ibid, John Ch. 10
17. ibid, Matthew Ch. 10
18. ibid, Matthew Ch. 15

CONCLUSION:
AMAZING GRACE

1. *The Bible—New King James Version®*, Ephesians Ch. 2
2. ibid, Genesis Ch. 6
3. ibid, Exodus Ch. 34
4. ibid, Deuteronomy Ch. 4
5. ibid, Isaiah Ch. 12
6. *The New American Standard Bible®*, (La Habra, CA: by The Lockman Foundation, 1995), John Ch. 1
7. *The Bible—New King James Version®*, 1 Corinthians Ch. 12

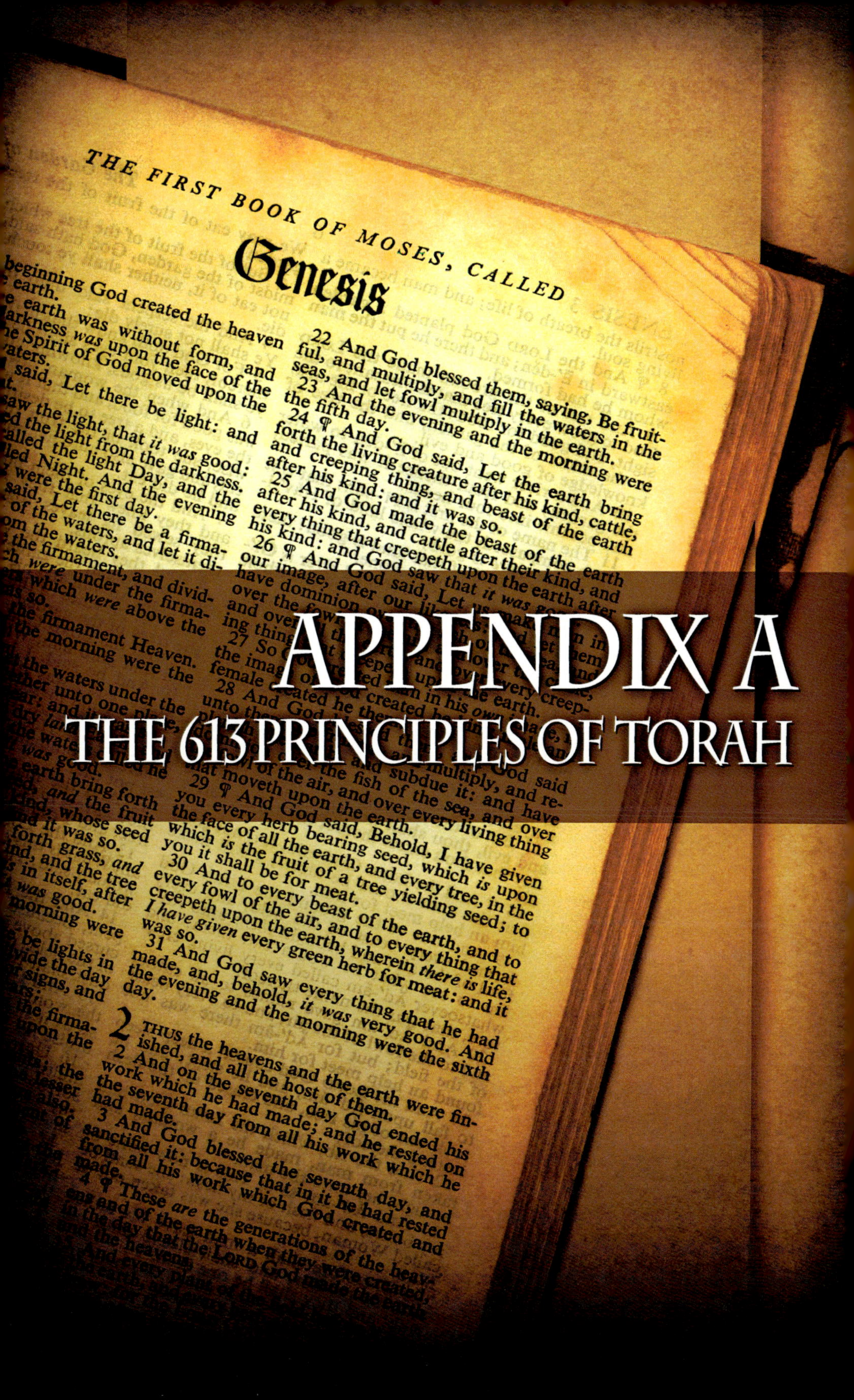

APPENDIX A

THE 613 PRINCIPLES OF TORAH

Simchat Torah Beit Midrash presents the 613 Principles of the Torah as categorized by the "Ten Commandments." Each one of the Ten Commandments heads a list followed by the additional Principles that fall within that catergory. These 613 Torah Principles are listed here in the exact order that God gave them in the Bible—Genesis through Deuteronomy.

THE FIRST COMMANDMENT—(EXODUS 20:2-3)

"I am the LORD, your God, Who has taken you out of the land of Egypt, from the house of slavery."

1. "I Am the Lord your God" (Ex. 20:2)
2. "You shall not recognize the gods of others in My Presence" (Ex. 20:3)
3. "You shall not mention the names of the gods of others" (Ex. 23:13)
4. "Your mouth shall not cause the names of the gods to be heard" (Ex. 23:13)

5. "You shall worship the LORD your God" (Ex. 23:25)
6. "You shall not seal a covenant with the Canaanite nations or their gods" (Ex. 23:32)
7. "You shall not practice sorcery" (Lev. 19:26)
8. "You shall not believe in lucky times" (Lev. 19:26)
9. "You shall make tzitzit with a thread of blue" (Num. 15:38)
10. "You shall not explore after your heart and after your eyes after which you stray" (Num. 15:39)
11. "Hear O Israel: The LORD our God, the LORD is One" (Deut. 6:4)
12. "You shall love the LORD your God with all your heart, with all your soul, and with all your resources" (Deut. 6:5)
13. "You shall teach the Torah thoroughly to your children and you shall speak of the commands while you sit in your home, while you walk on the way" (Deut. 6:7)
14. "You shall recite the Shema every morning and evening" (Deut. 6:7)
15. "You shall bind the Torah on your head" (Tefillin) (Deut. 6:8)
16. "You shall bind the Torah on your hand" (Tefillin) (Deut. 6:8)
17. "You shall write the Torah on your doorposts and your gates" (Mezuzah) (Deut. 6:9)
18. "You shall fear the LORD your God" (Deut. 6:13)
19. "You shall not test the LORD your God" (Deut. 6:16)
20. "You shall not fear the enemies in the Land" (Deut. 7:21)
21. "You shall eat and be satisfied, and bless the LORD your God" (Deut. 8:10)
22. "You shall cleave to the LORD your God" (Deut. 10:20)
23. "You shall not add to the commandments of Torah" (Deut. 13:1)
24. "You shall not subtract from the commandments of Torah" (Deut. 13:1)
25. "You shall not listen to one who prophesies in the name of the gods of others" (Deut. 13: 3-4)
26. "You shall not practice divination" (Deut. 18:10)
27. "You shall not practice astrology" (Deut. 18:10)
28. "You shall not read omens or practice sorcery" (Deut. 18:10)
29. "You shall not practice the art of an animal charmer" (Deut. 18:11)

30. "You shall not practice necromancy by inquiring of Ov" (Deut. 18:11)
31. "You shall not practice necromancy by inquiring of Yidoni" (Deut. 18:11)
32. "You shall not practice necromancy by consulting the dead" (Deut. 18:11)
33. "You shall hearken to the Prophet" (Deut. 18:15)
34. "You shall not fear the false prophet" (Deut. 18:22)
35. "You shall not allow the Canaanite nations to live" (Deut. 20:16)
36. "You shall destroy the Canaanite nations" (Deut. 20:17)
37. "You shall not allow an Ammonite or Moabite to enter the congregation, to the tenth generation" (Deut. 23:74)
38. "You shall remember what Amalek did to Israel when leaving Egypt" (Deut. 25:17)
39. "You shall destroy the seed of Amalek" (Deut. 25:19)
40. "You shall wipe out the memory of Amalek from under heaven" (Deut. 25:19)
41. "You shall observe God's Torah and walk in His ways" (Deut. 28:9)
42. "You shall write a copy of the Torah for yourself" (Deut. 31:19)

THE SECOND COMMANDMENT—(EX. 20:4-5)

"You shall have no other gods before Me.
You shall not make yourself a carved image nor any likeness
of that which is in the heavens above or on the earth below
or in the water beneath the earth. You shall not prostrate
yourself to nor worship them, for I am the LORD,
your God—a jealous God."

43. "You shall not make for yourself carved images" (Ex. 20:4)
44. "You shall not bow down to carved images" (Ex. 20:5)
45. "You shall not worship carved images" (Ex. 20:5)
46. "You shall not make images of gods of silver or gods of gold (Ex. 20:20)
47. "You shall not build an Altar of hewn stones" (Ex. 20:22)
48. "You shall not ascend the Altar on steps" (Ex. 20:23)
49. "You shall not allow the pagan nations to dwell in the Land of Israel" (Ex. 23:33)

50. "You shall build a Sanctuary for God" (Ex. 25:8)
51. "You shall not remove the staves from their rings in the Ark" (Ex. 25:15)
52. "You shall place the Showbread on the Table in the Sanctuary, continually"
(Ex. 25:30)
53. "You shall kindle the Menorah of the Sanctuary, continually" (Ex. 27:21)
54. "You shall make the Priestly garments" (Ex. 28:2)
55. "You shall not loosen the Breastplate from the Ephod" (Ex. 28:28)
56. "You shall not tear the High Priest's robe" (Ex. 28:32)
57. "You shall eat the meat of the Inauguration-Offering" (Ex. 29:33)
58. "A Kohen shall not eat the First Fruits Offering outside the Sanctuary" (Ex. 29:33)
59. "You shall offer incense on the Golden Altar twice daily" (Ex. 30:7-8)
60. "You shall not offer foreign incense on the Golden Altar" (Ex. 30:9)
61. "You shall wash your hands and feet upon entering the Sanctuary" (Ex. 30:19)
62. "You shall make the holy anointing oil" (Ex. 30:31)
63. "You shall not duplicate the holy anointing oil for other purposes" (Ex. 30:32)
64. "You shall not smear the holy anointing oil on human flesh" (Ex. 30:32)
65. "You shall not duplicate the holy incense for other purposes" (Ex. 30:37)
66. "You shall bring the Elevation-Offering according to the Torah" (Lev. 1:2)
67. "You shall bring the Meal-Offering of fine flour with oil and frankincense upon it" (Lev. 2:1)
68. "You shall not offer any leaven or fruit-honey upon the Altar" (Lev. 2:11)
69. "You shall salt every Meal-Offering" (Lev. 2:13)
70. "You shall not discontinue the salt of your God's covenant from upon your Meal-Offering" (Lev. 2:13)

71. "You shall bring the Feast Peace-Offering according to the Torah" (Lev. 3:1)
72. "You shall offer a young bull as a Sin-Offering for the entire assembly" (Lev. 4:13)
73. "You shall offer a she-goat as a Sin-Offering for the unintentional sin of an individual" (Lev. 4:27)
74. "You shall bring Offerings in accordance to your means" (Lev. 5:1-11)
75. "You shall not separate a bird slaughtered for a Sin-Offering" (Lev. 5:8)
76. "You shall not place oil on the Meal-Offering for sin" (Lev. 5:11)
77. "You shall not put frankincense on the Meal-Offering for sin" (Lev. 5:11)
78. "You shall bring an unblemished ram as a Guilt-Offering for an unintentional sin against the LORD's holies" (Lev. 5:15)
79. "You shall bring an unblemished ram as a Guilt-Offering for an unintentional sin that violates the Torah" (Lev. 5:17-18)
80. "A Kohen shall separate the ash of the Elevation-Offering and place it next to the Altar" (Lev. 6:3)
81. "You shall keep a perpetual fire on the Altar" (Lev. 6:6)
82. "You shall not extinguish the fire on the Altar" (Lev. 6:6)
83. "The Kohanim shall eat the remainder of the Meal-Offering" (Lev. 6:9)
84. "You shall not bake the remainder of the Meal-Offering with leaven" (Lev. 6:10)
85. "You shall bring the twice daily Meal-Offering of the Kohen on the day of inauguration" (Lev. 6:13)
86. "You shall not eat the Meal-Offering of a Kohen" (Lev. 6:16)
87. "You shall slaughter the Sin-Offering where the Elevation-Offering is slaughtered" (Lev. 6:18)
88. "You shall not eat the Sin-Offering slaughtered within Sanctuary" (Lev. 6:23)
89. "You shall slaughter the Guilt-Offering where the Elevation-Offering is slaughtered" (Lev. 7:1)
90. "You shall burn any remaining part of the Feast-Offering on the third day" (Lev. 7:17)

91. "You shall not intend to eat any remaining part of the Feast-Offering on the third day" (Lev. 7:18)
92. "You shall not eat an Offering that touches anything unclean" (Lev. 7:19)
93. "You shall burn in fire an Offering that touches anything unclean" (Lev. 7:19)
94. "A Kohen shall not leave his head unshorn" (Lev. 10:6)
95. "A Kohen shall not rend his garments" (Lev. 10:6)
96. "A Kohen shall not leave the Holy Place with the holy anointing oil upon him" (Lev. 10:7)
97. "An intoxicated person shall not enter the Holy Place" (Lev. 10:9)
98. "The High Priest shall not come at all times into the Holy of Holies" (Lev. 16:2)
99. "YoushallnotslaughterOfferingsoutsidetheSanctuary" (Lev.17:3-4)
100. "You shall not present any of your children for Molech" (Lev. 18:21)
101. "You shall not make molten gods for yourself" (Lev. 19:4)
102. "You shall not turn to the idols" (Lev. 19:4)
103. "You shall not eat the Feast-Offering beyond on the third day" (Lev. 19:6-8)
104. "You shall not plant your field with mixed seed" (Lev. 19:19)
105. "You shall not turn to the sorcery of the Ovot or Yid'onim" (Lev. 19:31)
106. "You shall not become unclean through the sorcery of the Ovot or Yid'onim" (Lev. 19:31)
107. "A Kohen shall not become unclean for the dead, except for a close relative" (Lev. 21:1)
108. "A Kohen shall become unclean for a close relative who has died" (Lev. 21:2-3)
109. "A Kohen shall not desecrate the Name of their God" (Lev. 21:6)
110. "A Kohen shall not marry a woman who is a harlot" (Lev. 21:7)
111. "A Kohen shall not marry a woman who has been desecrated" (Lev. 21:7)
112. "A Kohen shall not marry a woman who has been divorced" (Lev. 21:7)
113. "You shall sanctify the Kohanim" (Lev. 21:8)

114. "The High Priest shall not come near any dead person" (Lev. 21:11)
115. "The High Priest shall not become contaminated for his father or mother" (Lev. 21:11)
116. "The High Priest shall marry a woman in her virginity" (Lev. 21:13)
117. "The High Priest shall not marry a widow, a divorcee, a desecrated woman, or a harlot" (Lev. 21:14)
118. "The High Priest shall not desecrate his offspring" (Lev. 21:15)
119. "A Kohen with a blemish shall not offer the Fire-Offerings of the LORD" (Lev. 21:17)
120. "A Kohen with any blemish shall not approach to offer the Fire-Offerings of the LORD" (Lev. 21:18)
121. "A Kohen with any blemish shall not approach the Altar" (Lev. 21:23)
122. "A Kohen who is unclean shall not come near the Offerings" (Lev. 22:2)
123. "A Kohen who is unclean shall not eat from the Offerings" (Lev. 22:4)
124. "A person who is not a Kohen shall not eat the Offerings" (Lev. 22:10)
125. "A person who resides with a Kohen shall not eat the Offerings" (Lev. 22:10)
126. "A person who is the laborer of a Kohen shall not eat the Offerings" (Lev. 22:10)
127. "The daughter of a Kohen married to a person who is not a Kohen shall not eat the Offerings" (Lev. 22:12)
128. "The Kohanim shall not desecrate the Offerings" (Lev. 22:15)
129. "You shall not offer a blemished animal on the Altar" (Lev. 22:20)
130. "You shall offer only unblemished offerings" (Lev. 22:21)
131. "You shall not offer a blemished animal as a Free-Will Offering" (Lev. 22:21)
132. "You shall not offer a blemished animal as a Fire-Offering" (Lev. 22:22)

133. "You shall not offer any part of a blemished animal on the Altar" (Lev. 22:22)
134. "You shall not offer a blemished animal on the Altar, or in the Land" (Lev. 22:24)
135. "You shall not offer an animal from the hand of a stranger" (Lev. 22:25)
136. "You shall offer an animal only from its eighth day on as a Fire-Offering" (Lev. 22:27)
137. "You shall not leave any Feast Offering until morning" (Lev. 22:30)
138. "You shall not sell the fields of the open land of the Levites" (Lev. 25:34)
139. "You shall not emplace a flooring stone upon which to prostrate yourself" (Lev. 26:1)
140. "You shall expel from the camp everyone who has tzara'as, a zav-emission, or is contaminated by a dead body" (Num. 5:2)
141. "A unclean person shall not contaminate their camps" (Num. 5:3)
142. "You shall confess your sins of treachery toward the LORD and make restitution" (Num. 5: 6-7)
143. "You shall not pour oil on the Meal-Offering of jealousies" (Num. 5:15)
144. "You shall not place frankincense on the Meal-Offering of jealousies" (Num. 5:15)
145. "The Kohanim shall bless the Children of Israel with the Aaronic Blessing" (Num. 6:23)
146. "The Kohanim shall carry the Ark on the shoulder" (Num. 7:9)
147. "You shall sound the two silver trumpets as a remembrance before God" (Num. 10:9-10)
148. "The Levites shall not perform the work of the Kohanim" (Num. 18:3)
149. "The Levites and the Kohanim shall safeguard the Sanctuary" (Num. 18:4)
150. "An alien shall not approach the Sanctuary" (Num. 18:4)
151. "The Kohanim shall safeguard the Holy Place and the Altar" (Num. 18:5)

152. "The Levite shall perform the work of the Sanctuary" (Num. 18:23)
153. "The Levites shall give a tithe from the tithes of the Children of Israel" (Num. 18:26)
154. "You shall offer male lambs, two a day, as a continual Elevation-Offering" (Num. 28:3)
155. "You shall give cities for dwelling and open space to the Levites" (Num. 35:2)
156. "You shall not show favor to the seven Canaanite nations" (Deut. 7:2)
157. "You shall not take the silver and gold from the carved images of gods" (Deut. 7:25)
158. "You shall not bring an abomination into your home" (Deut. 7:26)
159. "You shall destroy all the places where the nations you shall possess worshiped their gods" (Deut. 12:2)
160. "You shall not bring offerings outside the Sanctuary" (Deut. 12:13)
161. "You shall bring offerings only in the Sanctuary" (Deut. 12:14)
162. "You shall not eat in your cities, the tithe of your grain" (Deut. 12:17)
163. "You shall not eat in your cities, the tithe of your wine" (Deut. 12:17)
164. "You shall not eat in your cities, the tithe of your oil" (Deut. 12:17)
165. "You shall not eat in your cities, the tithe of your firstborn cattle and flocks" (Deut. 12:17)
166. "You shall not eat in your cities, all your vow offerings" (Deut. 12:17)
167. "You shall not eat in your cities, all your free-will offerings" (Deut. 12:17)
168. "You shall not eat in your cities, what you raise up with your hand" (Deut. 12:17)
169. "You shall not forsake the Levite" (Deut. 12:19)
170. " You shall bring your offerings to the Sanctuary" (Deut. 12:26)
171. "You shall not accede to one who entices you secretly" (Deut. 13:9)

172. "You shall not hearken to one who entices you secretly" (Deut. 13:9)
173. "You shall not take pity on one who entices you secretly" (Deut. 13:9)
174. "You shall not be compassionate to one who entices you secretly" (Deut. 13:9)
175. "You shall not conceal one who entices you secretly" (Deut. 13:9)
176. "You shall not allow one who entices to do such an evil thing again in your midst" (Deut. 13:12)
177. "You shall burn in fire completely the city that worships the gods of others"(Deut. 13:17)
178. "You shall not rebuild a city destroyed as punishment for idolatry" (Deut. 13:17)
179. "You shall not take anything from a city that worships the gods of others" (Deut. 13:18)
180. "You shall not plant an idolatrous tree—any tree—near the Altar of the LORD" (Deut. 16:21)
181. "You shall not erect a pillar which the LORD hates" (Deut. 16:22)
182. "You shall not slaughter an ox or a lamb or kid in which there will be a blemish" (Deut. 17:1)
183. "The entire tribe of Levi shall not have an inheritance with Israel, the LORD is their inheritance" (Deut. 18:1)
184. "The entire tribe of Levi shall not share in the spoils of war" (Deut. 18:1)
185. "You shall give the Kohen the foreleg, the jaw, and the maw from every offering" (Deut. 18:3)
186. "You shall give the Kohen the first of your grain, wine, and oil" (Deut. 18:4)
187. "You shall give the Kohen the first of the shearing of your flock" (Deut. 18:4)
188. "The Levites shall minister in the Name of the LORD" (Deut. 18:6-8)
189. "The Kohen shall speak to the people when you draw near to the war" (Deut. 20:2)
190. "You shall not sow your vineyard with a mixture" (Deut. 22:9)

191. "An unclean person shall not enter the midst of the camp" (Deut. 23:11)
192. "There shall not be a promiscuous woman among the daughters of Israel" (Deut. 23:18)
193. "There shall not be a promiscuous man among the sons of Israel" (Deut. 23:18)
194. "You shall not bring a harlot's hire to the House of the LORD" (Deut. 23:18)
195. "You shall not bring the exchange for a dog to the House of the LORD" (Deut. 23:18)
196. "You shall not drink the wine libations used for idols" (Deut. 32:38)

THE THIRD COMMANDMENT—(EX. 20:7)

"You shall not take the Name of the LORD, your God, in vain, for the LORD will not absolve anyone who takes His Name in vain."

197. "You shall circumcise every male among you" (Gen. 17:10)
198. "You shall not eat the displaced sinew on the hip-socket" (Gen. 32:33)
199. "You shall not take the Name of the Lord in vain" (Ex. 20:7)
200. "You shall not eat an animal that was torn" (Ex. 22:30)
201. "You shall not cook a young goat in its mother's milk" (Ex. 23:19)
202. "You shall not cook a young goat in the milk of its mother" (Ex. 34:26)
203. "You shall not eat the fat of oxen, sheep, or goats" (Lev. 7:23)
204. "You shall not consume any blood" (Lev. 7:26)

205. "You may eat the animal that has completely split hooves and chews the cud" (Lev. 11:2-8)
206. "You shall not eat the flesh or touch the carcass of any unclean animal" (Lev. 11:8)
207. "You may eat everything in the water that has fins and scales" (Lev. 11:9)
208. "You shall not eat anything unclean from the creatures in the water" (Lev. 11:11)
209. "You shall not eat any unclean bird" (Lev. 11:13)
210. "You may only eat a flying teeming creature that walks on four legs: one that has jumping legs above its legs" (Lev. 11:21)
211. "You shall not become contaminated by touching unclean carcasses" (Lev. 11: 24)
212. "You shall not become contaminated by touching the carcasses of creeping creatures" (Lev. 11:29-31)
213. "You shall not become contaminated by consuming food or drink which has come into contact with any unclean thing" (Lev. 11:34)
214. "You shall not eat any teeming creature which teems upon the ground" (Lev. 11:41)
215. "You shall not eat anything that creeps on its belly" (Lev. 11:42)
216. "You shall not eat anything that walks on four legs, or numerous legs" (Lev. 11:42)
217. "You shall not become contaminated through any teeming thing that creeps on the earth" (Lev. 11:43-44)
218. "A woman who gives birth to a male shall be ritually unclean for seven days; for 33 days she shall remain in blood of purification. If she gives birth to a female, she shall be ritually unclean for fourteen days; for 66 days she shall remain in blood of purification" (Lev. 12:2-5)
219. "A ritually unclean person may not enter the Sanctuary" (Lev. 12:4)
220. "A woman shall bring the prescribed offering after childbirth and purification" (Lev. 12:6)
221. "The Kohen shall declare the one with tzara'as contaminated" (Lev. 13:3)

222. "You shall not shave a nesek affliction" (Lev. 13:33)
223. "You shall clearly distinguish one who has a tzara'as affliction" (Lev. 13:45)
224. "You shall declare a malignant tzara'as of the garment as contaminated" (Lev. 13:51)
225. "The metzora shall be brought to the Kohen on the day of his purification" (Lev. 14:2)
226. "The metzora shall shave off all his hair, immerse his clothing and immerse his flesh in water" (Lev. 14:9)
227. "The metzora shall bring the prescribed offering on the eighth day of his purification" (Lev. 14:10)
228. "The Kohen shall declare a malignant tzara'as of a house" (Lev. 14:44)
229. "A man who has a discharge from his flesh shall be contaminated" (Zav)(Lev. 15:2)
230. "Anyone who sits on the seat of a zav shall be contaminated until evening" (Lev. 15:6)
231. "A zav shall bring the prescribed offering on the eighth day of his purification" (Lev. 15: 13-15)
232. "A man who has a discharge of semen shall immerse his flesh in water and remain contaminated until evening" (Lev. 15:16)
233. "A woman with a discharge of blood shall remain in her state of separation for a seven-day period" (Lev. 15:19)
234. "A woman who has a discharge of blood outside her period of separation shall remain contaminated" (Zavah)(Lev. 15:25)
235. "A zavah shall bring the prescribed offering on the eighth day of her purification" (Lev. 15: 28-29)
236. "You shall pour out the blood of the clean animal or bird and cover it with earth" (Lev. 17:13)
237. "You shall not swear falsely, thereby desecrating the Name of your God" (Lev. 19:12)
238. "You shall not mate your animal into another species" (Lev. 19:19)
239. "You shall not round off the edge of your scalp" (Lev. 19:27)
240. "You shall not destroy the edge of your beard" (Lev. 19:27)
241. "You shall not place a tattoo upon yourself" (Lev. 19:28)

242. "You shall not follow the traditions of the Canaanite nations" (Lev. 20:23)
243. "You shall sanctify God's holy Name" (Lev. 22:32)
244. "You shall not desecrate God's holy Name" (Lev. 22:32)
245. "A Woman shall submit to the law of jealousies" (Sotah)" (Num. 5:15-27)
246. "The Nazir shall not drink new or aged wine" (Num. 6:3)
247. "The Nazir shall not drink vinegar of wine or aged wine" (Num. 6:3)
248. "The Nazir shall not drink anything in which grapes have been steeped" (Num. 6:3)
249. "The Nazir shall not eat fresh or dried grapes" (Num. 6:3)
250. "The Nazir shall not eat anything made from wine grapes, even the pips or skin" (Num. 6:4)
251. "The Nazir shall not shave his hair during his vow" (Num. 6:5)
252. "The Nazir shall let his hair grow during his vow" (Num. 6:5)
253. "The Nazir shall not become unclean for the dead" (Num. 6:6)
254. "The Nazir shall not contaminate himself for the death of a close relative" (Num. 6:7)
255. "The Nazir shall shave his hair and burn it on the fire of the Altar upon completing his vow" (Num. 6:18)
256. "You shall prepare the ashes of the red heifer used in ritual purification" (Num. 19:2-9)
257. "Anything within the dwelling of a corpse shall be contaminated for seven days" (Num. 19:14)
258. "You shall purify one who touches a dead body with the water of sprinkling" (Num. 19:13, 21)
259. "You shall not test the LORD you God" (Deut. 6:16)
260. "You shall not intermarry with the seven Canaanite nations" (Deut. 7:3)
261. "You shall not worship or bring offerings as the Canaanite nations did" (Deut. 12:4)
262. "You may eat your redeemed animal offerings" (Deut. 12:15)
263. "You may eat from your cattle and flocks" (Deut. 12:21)
264. "You shall not eat the blood, the life with the meat" (Deut. 12:23)

265. "You shall not cut your flesh for a dead person" (Deut. 14:1)
266. "You shall not make a bald spot between your eyes for a dead person" (Deut. 14:1)
267. "You shall not eat any abomination" (Deut. 14:3)
268. "You shall not eat any unclean animal" (Deut. 14:7)
269. "You may eat every clean bird" (Deut. 14:11)
270. "You shall not eat any flying swarming creature" (Deut. 14:19)
271. "You shall not eat any carcass" (Deut. 14:21)
272. "Male garb shall not be on a woman" (Deut. 22:5)
273. "A man shall not wear a woman's garment" (Deut. 22:5)
274. "You shall not plow with an ox and a donkey together" (Deut. 22:10)
275. "You shall not wear combined fibers; wool and linen together" (Deut. 22:11)
276. "A man with crushed testicles or severed organ shall not enter the congregation" (Deut. 23:2)
277. "A mamzer shall not enter the congregation, to the tenth generation" (Deut. 23:3)
278. "An Ammonite or Moabite shall not enter the congregation, to the tenth generation" (Deut. 23:4)
279. "You shall not reject an Edomite" (Deut. 23:8)
280. "You shall not reject an Egyptian" (Deut. 23:8)
281. "You shall have a place outside the camp for sanitation" (Deut. 23:14-15)
282. "You shall carry a shovel with your weapons to bury excrement" (Deut. 23:15)
283. "You shall not remove any signs of tzara'as affliction" (Deut. 24:8)

THE FOURTH COMMANDMENT – (EX. 20:8-11)

"Remember the Sabbath day, to sanctify it.
Six days you shall work and accomplish all your work;
but the seventh day is Sabbath to the LORD, your God;
you shall not do any work—you, your son, your daughter,
your slave, your maidservant, your animal, and your
convert within your gates—for in six days the LORD made
the heavens and the earth, the sea and all that is in them,
and He rested the seventh day. Therefore the LORD
blessed the Sabbath day and sanctified it."

284. "You shall observe the New Moon and the beginning of the months" (Ex. 12:2)
285. "You shall slaughter the Passover lamb on the afternoon of the 14th of Nisan" (Ex. 12:6)

286. "You shall eat the roasted Passover lamb at night on the 15 of Nisan" (Ex. 12:8)
287. "You shall not eat the Passover partially roasted or cooked in water" (Ex. 12:9)
288. "You shall not leave any of the Passover lamb until morning" (Ex. 12:10)
289. "You shall nullify the leaven from your homes on the day before Passover" (Ex. 12:15)
290. "You shall observe a holy convocation on the first day of Passover" (Ex. 12:16)
291. "You shall not do any work on the first day of Passover" (Ex. 12:16)
292. "You shall observe a holy convocation on the seventh day of Passover" (Ex. 12:16)
293. "You shall not do any work on the seventh day of Passover" (Ex. 12:16)
294. "You shall eat Matzot on the first night of Passover" (Ex. 12:18)
295. "You shall not possess or eat leaven during the seven days of Passover" (Ex. 12:19)
296. "An alienated person shall not eat the Passover offering" (Ex. 12:43)
297. "A sojourner and a hired laborer shall not eat the Passover offering" (Ex. 12:45)
298. "You shall not break a bone in the Passover offering" (Ex. 12:46)
299. "You shall not remove the Passover offering from the house to the outside" (Ex. 12:46)
300. "An uncircumcised male shall not eat the Passover offering" (Ex. 12:48)
301. "You shall not eat chametz on Passover" (Ex. 13:3)
302. "You shall eat Matzot for the seven days of Passover" (Ex. 13:7)
303. "You shall not have chametz in your possession or leaven in your borders during Passover" (Ex. 13:7)
304. "You shall tell the story of the Ex. on Passover" (Ex. 13:8)
305. "You shall not leave your place to work on the Sabbath" (Ex. 16:29)

306. "You shall remember the Sabbath day to sanctify" (Ex. 20:8)
307. "You shall not do any work on the Sabbath" (Ex. 20:10)
308. "You shall set free your Hebrew bondsman in the seventh year" (Ex. 21:2)
309. "You shall marry your Hebrew bondswoman or designate her for your son" (Ex. 21:8)
310. "You shall assist in the redemption of a Hebrew bondswoman" (Ex. 21:8)
311. "You shall not sell a Hebrew bondswoman" (Ex. 21:8)
312. "You shall not withhold food, clothing, or marital relations from a Hebrew bondswoman" (Ex. 21:10)
313. You shall leave your land untended and unharvested in the seventh year" (Ex. 23:11)
314. "You shall accomplish your work in six days and rest on the Sabbath" (Ex. 23:12)
315. "You shall celebrate the three annual pilgrimage Festivals during the year" (Ex. 23:14)
316. "You shall not appear before God empty-handed on the pilgrimage Festivals" (Ex. 23:15)
317. "You shall not allow the fat of the offerings to remain overnight" (Ex. 23:18)
318. "You shall desist from plowing and harvesting on the Sabbath" (Ex. 34:21)
319. "All males shall appear before the LORD three times a year" (Ex. 34:23)
320. "You shall not slaughter the Passover lamb while in the possession of leavened food" (Ex. 34:25)
321. "You shall not kindle fire in any of your dwellings on the Sabbath day" (Ex. 35:3)
322. "You shall perform the incense service and offerings on Yom Kippur" (Avodah) (Lev. 16)
323. "You shall afflict yourselves on Yom Kippur" (Lev. 16:29)
324. "You shall have a Sabbath of complete rest on Yom Kippur" (Lev. 16:29, 31)
325. "You shall revere the Sanctuary" (Lev. 19:30)

326. "You shall bring an Omer of your First Fruits on the morrow of the rest day after Passover" (Lev. 23:10)
327. "You shall count the Omer, seven weeks from First Fruits, until the morrow, 50 days" (Lev. 23:15)
328. "You shall bring two loaves of bread as a wave offering on Shavuot" (Lev. 23:17)
329. "You shall have a holy convocation on Shavuot" (Lev. 23:21)
330. "You shall not do any laborious work on Shavuot" (Lev. 23:21)
331. "You shall have a holy convocation; a remembrance with shofar blasts on Yom Teruah" (Lev. 23:24)
332. "You shall not do any laborious work on Yom Teruah" (Lev. 23:25)
333. "You shall not do any work on Yom Kippur" (Lev. 23:29)
334. "You shall have a holy convocation on the first day of Sukkot" (Lev. 23:35)
335. " You shall not do any work on the first day of Sukkot" (Lev. 23:35)
336. "You shall offer the fire-offering on each of the seven days of Sukkot" (Lev. 23:36)
337. "You shall have a holy convocation on the eighth day of Sukkot" (Shemini Atzeret) (Lev. 23:36)
338. "You shall not do any work on the eighth day of Sukkot" (Lev. 23:36)
339. "You shall take from the four species on the first day of Sukkot" (Lulav)(Lev. 23:40)
340. "You shall dwell in booths for a seven-day period during Sukkot" (Lev. 23:42)
341. "You shall not sow your field during the seventh year" (Shemittah) (Lev. 25:4)
342. "You shall not prune your vineyard during the seventh year" (Lev. 25:4)
343. "You shall not reap the aftergrowth of your harvest in the seventh year" (Lev. 25:5)
344. "You shall not pick the grapes set aside for yourself in the seventh year" (Lev. 25:5)

345. "You shall count seven cycles of Sabbatical years; 49 years" (Lev. 25:8)
346. "You shall sound the Shofar on Yom Kippur for the Jubilee year" (Yovel) (Lev. 25:9)
347. "You shall sanctify the 50th year and proclaim freedom throughout the Land" (Lev. 25:10)
348. "You shall not sow in the Jubilee year" (Lev. 25:11)
349. "You shall not harvest the aftergrowth in the Jubilee year" (Lev. 25:11)
350. "You shall not pick what was set aside for yourself in the Jubilee year" (Lev. 25:11)
351. "You shall not sell the Land in perpetuity" (Lev. 25:23)
352. "You shall provide redemption for the Land in the Jubilee year" (Lev. 25:24)
353. "You shall allow the redemption of a house until the end of one year of its sale" (Lev. 25:24)
354. "You shall not work your Hebrew bondsman with slave labor" (Lev. 25:39)
355. "You shall not sell a Hebrew bondsman in the manner of a slave" (Lev. 25:42)
356. "You shall not subjugate a Hebrew bondsman through hard labor" (Lev. 25:43)
357. "You may acquire foreign bondsman to remain yours as an ancestral heritage" (Lev. 25:46)
358. "You shall not allow a foreigner to mistreat a Hebrew bondsman" (Lev. 25:53)
359. "You shall make the second Passover offering on the 14th day of the second month" (Pesach Sheni) (Num. 9:11)
360. "You shall eat the Passover Sheni lamb with matzot and bitter herbs" (Num. 9:11)
361. "You shall not break a bone of the Passover Sheni lamb offering (Num. 9:12)
362. "You shall not leave over any of the Passover Sheni lamb offering until morning" (Num. 9:12)
363. "You shall offer two male lambs as an Elevation-Offering on each Sabbath" (Mussaf) (Num. 28:9)

364. "You shall offer the prescribed Elevation-Offering on your New Moons" (Num. 28:11)
365. "You shall offer the prescribed Elevation-Offering on Shavuot" (Num. 28:26-27)
366. "You shall offer the prescribed Elevation-Offering on Yom Teruah" (Num. 29:1-2)
367. "You shall sound and hear the shofar on Yom Teruah" (Num. 29:1)
368. "You shall offer the prescribed Elevation-Offering on Yom Kippur" (Num. 29:7-8)
369. "You shall offer the prescribed Elevation-Offerings on each day of Sukkot" (Num. 29:13)
370. "You shall offer the prescribed Elevation-Offering on the eighth day of Sukkot" (Num. 29:36)
371. "You shall not demand payment of debts remitted in the 7th year " (Deut. 15:2)
372. "You shall remit the debts of your brother in the 7th year " (Deut. 15:3)
373. "You may demand payment of debts from a gentile—debts not remitted in the 7th year" (Deut. 15:3)
374. "You shall not refuse to lend to your destitute brother because the year of remission is near" (Deut. 15:9)
375. "You shall not send your Hebrew bondservant away empty-handed" (Deut. 15:13)
376. "You shall adorn your Hebrew bondservant generously from your flocks, from your threshing floor, and from your wine cellar" (Deut. 15:14)
377. "You shall not eat leavened bread with the Passover" (Deut. 16:3)
378. "You shall rejoice on your Festivals" (Deut. 16:14)
379. "You shall observe the requirements for taking a woman captured in war as a wife" (Deut. 21:11)
380. "You shall not sell a woman captured in war" (Deut. 21:14)
381. "You shall not enslave a woman captured in war" (Deut. 21:14)
382. "You shall not turn over a slave who is rescued from his master to you" (Deut. 23:16)

383. "You shall not taunt a slave who is rescued from his master to you" (Deut. 23:17)
384. "You shall observe the laws of marriage and divorce" (Deut. 24:1)
385. "A husband shall be free for his home for the first year" (Deut. 24:5)
386. "You shall read the Torah to all of Israel during Sukkot in each Sabbatical year" (Deut. 31:12)

THE FIFTH COMMANDMENT—(EX. 20:12)

"Honor your father and your mother,
that your days will be lengthened upon the land
that the LORD, your God, gives you."

387. "You shall honor your father and your mother" (Ex. 20:12)
388. "You shall not strike your father or mother" (Ex. 21:15)
389. "You shall not curse your father or mother" (Ex. 21:17)
390. "You shall not curse a leader among your people" (Ex. 22:27)
391. "You shall revere your mother and father" (Lev. 19:3)
392. "The tithe of cattle or the flock shall be holy to the LORD" (Lev. 27:33)
393. "You shall only appoint a king whom the LORD will choose from your brethren" (Deut. 17:15)
394. "You shall not appoint a king who is a foreign man, who is not your brother" (Deut. 17:15)

395. "You shall not return to Egypt to dwell there" (Deut. 17:16)
396. "A king shall not have too many horses for himself" (Deut. 17:16)
397. "A king shall not have too many wives" (Deut. 17:17)
398. "A king shall not greatly increase silver and gold for himself" (Deut. 17:17)
399. "The king shall write for himself two copies of the Torah" (Deut. 17:18)
400. "You shall observe the overtures for peace and war" (Deut. 20:11-12)
401. "A man who issues a slander against a virgin of Israel shall be punished" (Deut. 22:18-19)
402. "A man who issues a slander against a virgin of Israel shall not divorce her all his days" (Deut. 22:19)
403. "The bill of divorce shall be a written document" (Deut. 24:1)
404. "You shall not remarry your divorced wife after she has remarried another man" (Deut. 24:4)
405. "A husband shall not be obligated from home for the first year" (Deut. 24:5)
406. "The brother of a man who dies childless shall marry his brother's wife" (Levirate Marriage) (Deut. 25:5)
407. "The childless widow shall not marry anyone except her late husband's brother" (Deut. 25:5)
408. "You shall release the childless widow if her late husband's brother refuses to marry her" (Deut. 25:9)

THE SIXTH COMMANDMENT—(EX. 20:13)

"You shall not murder"

409. "You shall not murder" (Ex. 20:13)
410. "You shall not kidnap" (Ex. 21:16)
411. "You shall not taunt or oppress a stranger" (Ex. 22:20)
412. "You shall not cause pain to any widow or orphan" (Ex. 22:21)
413. "You shall help unload a donkey crouching under its burden" (Ex. 23:5)
414. "You shall not refrain from helping a man or donkey crouching under its burden" (Ex. 23:5)
415. "You shall not curse the deaf" (Lev. 19:14)
416. "You shall not place a stumbling block before the blind" (Lev. 19:14)
417. "You shall not be a gossip monger" (Lev. 19:16)
418. "You shall not stand aside while your neighbor's blood is shed" (Lev. 19:16)

419. "You shall reprove your neighbor and not bear a sin because of him" (Lev. 19:17)
420. "You shall not hate your brother in your heart" (Lev. 19:17)
421. "You shall not put another to shame" (Lev. 19:17)
422. "You shall love your neighbor as yourself" (Lev. 19:18)
423. "You shall not take revenge" (Lev. 19:18)
424. "You shall not bear a grudge" (Lev. 19:18)
425. "You shall rise in the presence of the old and honor the presence of the wise" (Lev. 19:32)
426. "You shall not aggrieve your neighbor" (Lev. 25:17)
427. "You shall love the proselyte for you were strangers" (Deut. 10:19)
428. "You shall not destroy the fruit trees, even in time of war" (Deut. 20:19)
429. "You shall assist the donkey or ox falling on the road" (Deut. 22:4)
430. "You shall make a fence for your roof so you will not place blood in your house if a fallen one falls from it" (Deut. 22:8)
431. "You shall not leave obstacles on a path" (Deut. 22:8)

THE SEVENTH COMMANDMENT—(EX. 20:13)

"You shall not commit adultery"

432. "You shall be fruitful and multiply, fill the earth and subdue it" (Gen. 1:28)
433. "You shall punish a seducer according to the law (Ex. 22:15-16)
434. "You shall not approach your close relative to uncover nakedness" (Lev. 18:6)
435. "You shall not uncover the nakedness of your father" (Lev. 18:7)
436. "You shall not uncover the nakedness of your mother" (Lev. 18:7)
437. "You shall not uncover the nakedness of your father's wife" (Lev. 18:8)
438. "You shall not uncover the nakedness of your sister" (Lev. 18:9)
439. "You shall not uncover the nakedness of your son's daughter" (Lev. 18:10)
440. "You shall not uncover the nakedness of your daughter's daughter" (Lev. 18:10)

441. "You shall not uncover the nakedness of your daughter" (Lev. 18:10)
442. "You shall not uncover the nakedness of your father's wife's daughter" (Lev. 18:11)
443. "You shall not uncover the nakedness of your father's sister" (Lev. 18:12)
444. "You shall not uncover the nakedness of your mother's sister" (Lev. 18:13)
445. "You shall not uncover the nakedness of the wife of your father's brother" (Lev. 18:14)
446. "You shall not lie carnally with your father's brother" (Lev. 18:14)
447. "You shall not uncover the nakedness of your son's wife" (Lev. 18:15)
448. "You shall not uncover the nakedness of your brother's wife" (Lev. 18:16)
449. "You shall not uncover the nakedness of a woman and her daughter" (Lev. 18:17)
450. "You shall not uncover the nakedness of a woman and her son's daughter" (Lev. 18:17)
451. "You shall not uncover the nakedness of a woman and her daughter's daughter" (Lev. 18:17)
452. "You shall not uncover the nakedness of a woman in addition to her sister, to make them rivals, in her lifetime" (Lev. 18:18)
453. "You shall not uncover the nakedness of a woman in her time of separation" (Niddah) (Lev. 18:19)
454. "You shall not lie carnally with your neighbor's wife" (Lev. 18:20)
455. "A man shall not lie carnally with another man, it is an abomination" (Lev. 18:22)
456. "You shall not lie with any animal" (Lev. 18:23)
457. "A woman shall not stand before an animal for mating, it is a perversion" (Lev. 18:23)
458. "A man shall marry the virgin he has seduced and give her father fifty silver shekels" (Deut. 22:29)
459. "A man shall not divorce the virgin he has seduced and married" (Deut. 22:29)

THE EIGHTH COMMANDMENT—(EX. 20:13)

"You shall not steal"

460. "You shall not oppress the stranger among you" (Ex. 22:20)
461. "You shall lend money to the poor of your people without interest" (Ex. 22:24)
462. "You shall not demand payment from a debtor who is unable to pay" (Ex. 22:24)
463. "You shall not act as a creditor in an agreement involving interest" (Ex. 22:24)
464. "You shall leave the corners of your fields" (Lev. 19:9)
465. "You shall leave the gleanings of your field" (Lev. 19:9)
466. "You shall not pick the undeveloped twigs of your vineyard" (Lev. 19:10)
467. "You shall not gather the fallen fruit of your vineyard" (Lev. 19:10)
468. "You shall leave the fallen fruit for the poor and the proselyte" (Lev. 19:10)

469. "You shall leave the undeveloped twigs of your vineyard for the poor and the proselyte" (Lev. 19:10)
470. "You shall not steal" (Lev. 19:11)
471. "You shall not deny falsely" (Lev. 19:11)
472. "You shall not lie to one another" (Lev. 19:11)
473. "You shall not retain a worker's wage overnight until morning" (Lev. 19:13)
474. "You shall not rob" (Lev. 19:13)
475. "You shall not cheat your neighbor" (Lev. 19:13)
476. "You shall not commit a perversion in measurements" (Lev. 19:35)
477. "You shall not commit a perversion in weights" (Lev. 19:35)
478. "You shall have correct scales, correct weights, and correct measures" (Lev. 19:36)
479. "You shall not slaughter an animal and its offspring on the same day" (Lev. 22:28)
480. "You shall not reap the corners of your field and the gleanings of your harvest" (Lev. 23:22)
481. "You shall not aggrieve one another in your buying and selling" (Lev. 25:14)
482. "You shall not give your brother your money for interest" (Lev. 25:37)
483. "You shall not give your brother your food for increase" (Lev. 25:37)
484. "You shall observe the laws of inheritance" (Num. 27:8)
485. "You shall not harden your heart or close your hand against your destitute brother" (Deut. 15:7)
486. "You shall open your hand and lend whatever is lacking" (Deut. 15:8)
487. "You shall not move the boundary markers of your neighbor" (Deut. 19:14)
488. "You shall return the lost property of your brother" (Deut. 22:1)
489. "You shall not hide yourself from any lost property of your brother" (Deut. 22:3)
490. "You shall not to take the mother bird with her young" (Deut. 22:6)
491. "You shall set free the mother bird when taking the young" (Deut. 22:7)

492. "You shall not cause your brother to take interest" (Deut. 23:20)
493. "You may cause a gentile to take interest" (Deut. 23:21)
494. "You shall not take grapes in a vessel from your neighbor's vineyard" (Deut. 23:25)
495. "You may eat grapes to your fill from your neighbor's vineyard" (Deut. 23:25)
496. "You shall not lift a sickle against the standing grain of your neighbor" (Deut. 23:26)
497. "You shall not take a lower or upper millstone as a pledge" (Deut. 24:6)
498. "You shall not enter your neighbor's home to take collateral for a debt" (Deut. 24:10)
499. "You shall not sleep with a poor man's collateral" (Deut. 24:12)
500. "You shall return the collateral of a poor man when the sun sets" (Deut. 24:13)
501. "You shall pay a worker his wages on the day of his hire" (Deut. 24:15)
502. "You shall not take the garment of a widow as collateral" (Deut. 24:17)
503. "You shall leave the forgotten bundle of your harvest in the field" (Deut. 24:19)
504. "You shall not turn back to take a forgotten bundle from your field" (Deut. 24:19)
505. "You shall not muzzle an ox in its threshing" (Deut. 25:4)
506. "You shall not possess false weights and measures" (Deut. 25:13)

THE NINTH COMMANDMENT—(EX. 20:13)

"You shall not bear false witness against your neighbor."

507. "You shall not bear false witness against your neighbor" (Ex. 20:14)
508. "You shall put to death one who kidnaps a man and sells him" (Ex. 21:16)
509. "You shall exact the penalties for a person inflicting injury" (Ex. 21:18)
510. "You shall avenge the death of a servant who has died by the rod" (Ex. 21:20)
511. "You shall observe the penalties for injuries caused by an animal" (Ex. 21:28)
512. "You shall not eat the flesh of a condemned ox" (Ex. 21:28)
513. "You shall exact the penalties for injuries caused by a pit" (Ex. 21: 33-34)
514. "You shall observe the law for the punishment of thieves" (Ex. 21:37-22:3)

515. "You shall exact the penalties for damage caused by an animal" (Ex. 22:4)
516. "You shall exact the penalties for damage caused by a fire" (Ex. 22:5)
517. "You shall observe the law for the guardian of another's property" (Ex. 22:6-8)
518. "The guilty party shall pay double for every item of liability" (Ex. 22:8)
519. "You shall observe the law for the guardian of another's animals" (Ex. 22:9-12)
520. "You shall observe the law for the borrower of another's possessions" (Ex. 22:13)
521. "You shall not permit a sorceress to live" (Ex. 22:17)
522. "You shall not curse a judge among your people" (Ex. 22:27)
523. "You shall not accept a false report" (Ex. 23:1)
524. "You shall not extend your hand with the wicked to be a venal witness" (Ex. 23:1)
525. "You shall not be a follower of the majority for evil" (Ex. 23:2)
526. "You shall not pervert the law by yielding to the majority" (Ex. 23:2)
527. "You shall not glorify a destitute person in his grievance" (Ex. 23:3)
528. "You shall not pervert the judgment of your destitute person in his grievance" (Ex. 23:6)
529. "You shall not execute the innocent" (Ex. 23:7)
530. "You shall not execute the righteous" (Ex. 23:7)
531. "You shall not accept a bribe" (Ex. 23:8)
532. "A person who is a witness shall testify" (Lev. 5:1)
533. "You shall make restitution and add a fifth for anything deprived from the Sanctuary" (Lev. 5:16)
534. "A robber shall restore the article or principal and add its fifth to it" (Lev. 5:23)
535. "You shall judge your neighbor with righteousness" (Lev. 19:15)
536. "You shall not commit a perversion of justice" (Lev. 19:15)
537. "You shall not favor the poor in a perversion of justice" (Lev. 19:15)

538. "You shall not honor the wealthy in a perversion of justice" (Lev. 19:15)
539. "You shall burn a man in fire who shall take a woman and her mother" (Lev. 20:14)
540. "You shall put to death one who pronounces blasphemously the Name of the LORD" (Lev. 24:16)
541. "You shall not allow a killer to die by vengeance without a trial and judgment" (Num. 35:12)
542. "You shall rescue the killer to a to city of refuge for unintentional homicide" (Num. 35:25)
543. "A single witness shall not testify against a person regarding death" (Num. 35:30)
544. "You shall not accept ransom for the life of a killer who is worthy of death" (Num. 35:31)
545. "You shall not accept ransom for the life of a killer who left his city of refuge prematurely" (Num. 35:32)
546. "You shall not show favoritism in judgment" (Deut. 1:17)
547. "You shall not tremble before any man in judgment" (Deut. 1:17)
548. "You shall take oaths only in God's Name" (Deut. 10:20)
549. "You shall investigate well the report of the abomination of worship of the gods of others" (Deut. 13:15)
550. "You shall appoint Judges and Officers in all your cities to judge the people with righteous judgment" (Deut. 16:18)
551. "You shall do according to the judgment of the Kohanim, the Levites, and the Judge" (Deut. 17:11)
552. "You shall not differ from or disobey the judgment of the Kohanim, the Levites, and the Judge" (Deut. 17:11)
553. "You shall not speak in the name of the gods of others" (Deut. 18:20)
554. "You shall not speak falsely in the Name of God" (Deut. 18:20)
555. "You shall establish the Cities of Refuge" (Deut. 19:3)
556. "You shall not pity the one who murdered" (Deut. 19:13)
557. "A single witness shall not stand up against any man for any iniquity, error, or sin" (Deut. 19:15)

558. "A false witnesses shall receive the punishment he conspired to bring upon his neighbor" (Deut. 19:19)
559. "You shall observe the law for the axed heifer for an unsolved murder" (Deut. 21:4)
560. "You shall not work or sow the valley of the axed heifer" (Deut. 21:4)
561. "You shall hang on the gallows a man whose judgment is death" (Deut. 21:22)
562. "You shall bury an executed body on the same day of execution" (Deut. 21:23)
563. "You shall not leave an executed body hanging overnight" (Deut. 21:23)
564. "You shall stone the man and the woman who lies with a betrothed maiden in the city" (Deut. 22:24)
565. "You shall not stone the betrothed maiden who lies with a man in the field" (Deut. 22:26)
566. "Fathers shall not be put to death because of sons, and sons shall not be put to death because of fathers" (Deut. 24:16)
567. "You shall not pervert the judgment of a proselyte or orphan" (Deut. 24:17)
568. "A Judge shall strike a wicked one with lashes, according to his wickedness, by a count" (Deut. 25:2)
569. "A Judge shall not inflict more than forty lashes" (Deut. 25:2-3)
570. "You shall save the life of the one pursued by the avenger of the blood" (Deut. 25:12)
571. "You shall not pity the life of a pursuer, seeking to wrongly avenge the blood" (Deut. 25:12)

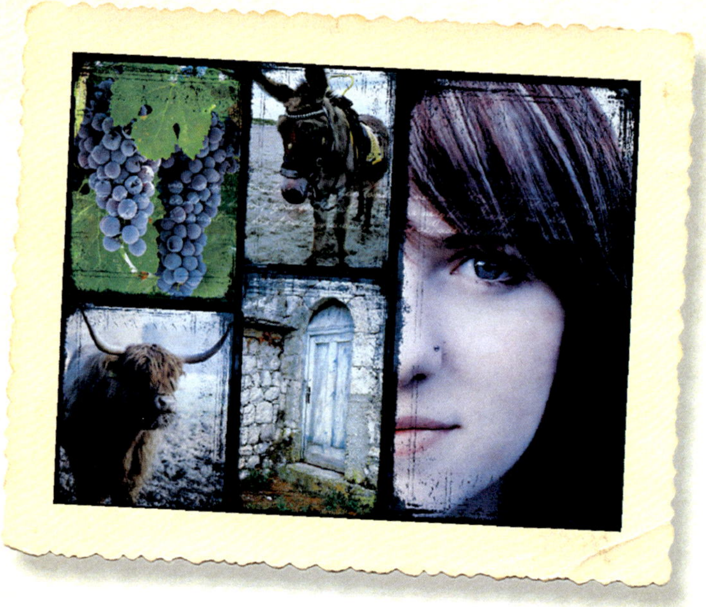

THE TENTH COMMANDMENT—(EX. 20:14)

"You shall not covet your neighbor's house;
you shall not covet your neighbor's wife,
nor his male servant, nor his female servant, nor his ox,
nor his donkey, nor anything that is your neighbor's."

572. "You shall sanctify to the LORD every firstborn of man and beast" (Ex. 13:2)
573. "You shall redeem the firstborn of the unclean animal" (Ex. 13:13)
574. "You shall not covet your neighbor's house. You shall not covet your neighbor's wife, his manservant, his maidservant, his ox, his donkey, nor anything that belongs to your neighbor" (Ex. 20:14)
575. "You shall present the firstborn of your sons to the LORD" (Ex. 22:28)

576. "You shall not delay your Fullness-Offering or your priestly Heave-Offering" (Ex. 22:28)
577. "You shall bring the choicest first fruits of your land to the House of the LORD your God" (Ex. 23:19)
578. "Every male shall give a half-shekel when you take a census" (Ex. 30:12-13)
579. "You shall redeem the firstborn of a donkey" (Ex. 34:20)
580. "You shall not eat the fruit of a tree for its first three years" (Lev. 19:23)
581. "You shall sanctify to the LORD all the fruit of a tree in its fourth year" (Lev. 19:24)
582. "You shall not eat bread of new grain until you bring your First Fruits Offering" (Lev. 23:14)
583. "You shall not eat roasted kernels of a new crop until you bring your First Fruits Offering" (Lev. 23:14)
584. "You shall not eat plump kernels of a new crop until you bring your First Fruits Offering" (Lev. 23:14)
585. "You shall observe the valuations of living beings articulated by vow to the LORD" (Lev. 27: 2-8)
586. "You shall not exchange or substitute an animal articulated by vow to the LORD" (Lev. 27:10)
587. "You shall observe the valuations of unclean animals articulated by vow to the LORD" (Lev. 27:11-12)
588. "You shall observe the valuation of a house articulated by vow to the LORD" (Lev. 27:14)
589. "You shall observe the valuation of a field articulated by vow to the LORD" (Lev. 27:16, 22-23)
590. "You shall segregate the property of a vow as holy to the LORD" (Cherem vow) (Lev. 27:21, 28)
591. "You shall not consecrate by vow to the LORD the firstborn or firstling of animal or flock, it is the LORD's" (Lev. 27:26)
592. "You shall not sell a field segregated by vow as holy to the LORD" (Lev. 27:28)
593. "You shall not redeem a field segregated by vow as holy to the LORD" (Lev. 27:28)

594. "You shall set aside the tithe of the land, of the seed of the land, of the fruit tree, as holy to the LORD" (Lev. 27:30)
595. "You shall tithe from your cattle and flock, the tenth shall be holy to the LORD" (Lev. 27:32)
596. "You shall not substitute the tithe of the cattle or flock" (Lev. 27:33)
597. "You shall set aside a loaf as a portion from the first of your kneading" (Challah) (Num. 15:20)
598. "You shall not redeem the firstborn of clean animals" (Num. 18:17)
599. "You shall fulfill the words of your mouth" (Num. 30:3)
600. "You shall not desecrate your word" (Num. 30:3)
601. "You shall not covet your neighbor's possessions" (Deut. 5:18)
602. "You shall bring your offerings to the Sanctuary" (Deut. 12:5-6)
603. "You shall tithe the entire crop of your planting, the produce of your field, year by year" (Deut. 14:22)
604. "You shall set aside the tithe for the Levite and the proselyte, orphan, and widow, at the end of three years" (Deut. 14:28)
605. "You shall not work with the firstborn of your ox" (Deut. 15:19)
606. "You shall not shear the firstborn of your flock" (Deut. 15:19)
607. "You shall not bring a harlot's hire or the exchange for a dog to the House of the LORD" (Deut. 23:19)
608. "You shall not be late in paying your vow to the LORD" (Deut. 23:22)
609. "You shall observe and carry out what emerges from your lips" (Deut. 23:24)
610. "You shall make the declaration upon bringing First Fruits to the Temple" (Deut. 26:5)
611. "You shall make the declaration over your tithes" (Deut. 26:13)
612. "You shall not consume the tithe while in a state of contamination" (Deut. 26:14)
613. "You shall not consume the tithe while in mourning" (Deut. 26:14)

APPENDIX A – THE PRINCIPLES OF GOD

APPENDIX B

271 COMMANDS FOR ISRAEL IN THE NATIONS

Early in the 1800's, Rabbi Yisrael Meir extracted from the 613 Principles of the Torah, a list of 271 Commands that can still be observed today, despite the fact that the Temple is not standing and much of Israel remains scattered among the nations. These 271 Principles have been categorized for easy reference and application. While the categories differ from the presentation of the entire 613 Principles *(see Appendix A),* these 271 Principles present the Torah that we can obey as a *"Kingdom of Priests and a Holy nation..."* (Exodus 19:6; Revelation 5:10). These are daily instructions for Israel in the nations, for our worship of God, the honor of the Torah, the Sabbath Day, the Feasts and Festivals. There are Commands for dietary laws, purity, and sanctification. The list concludes with Instructions for the community, family, and neighbors, the redeemed of the LORD living a redeemed lifestyle—shining the Light of Messiah to the ends of the earth.

WORSHIP OF GOD

1. "I Am the Lord your God" (Ex. 20:2)
2. "You shall not recognize the gods of others in My Presence" (Ex. 20:3)
3. "You shall not take the Name of the Lord in vain" (Ex. 20:7)
4. "You shall not mention the names of the gods of others" (Ex. 23:13)
5. "Your mouth shall not cause the names of the gods to be heard" (Ex. 23:13)
6. "You shall worship the LORD your God" (Ex. 23:25)

7. "You shall not swear falsely, thereby desecrating the Name of your God" (Lev. 19:12)
8. "You shall not practice sorcery" (Lev. 19:26)
9. "You shall not believe in lucky times" (Lev. 19:26)
10. "You shall sanctify God's holy Name" (Lev. 22:32)
11. "You shall not desecrate God's holy Name" (Lev. 22:32)
12. "You shall make tzitzit with a thread of blue" (Num. 15:38)
13. "You shall not explore after your heart and after your eyes after which you stray" (Num. 15:39)
14. "Hear O Israel:The LORD our God, the LORD is One" (Deut. 6:4)
15. "You shall love the LORD your God with all your heart, with all your soul, and with all your resources" (Deut. 6:5)
16. "You shall recite the Shema every morning and evening" (Deut. 6:7)
17. "You shall fear the LORD your God" (Deut. 6:13)
18. "You shall eat and be satisfied, and bless the LORD your God" (Deut. 8:10)
19. "You shall cleave to the LORD your God" (Deut. 10:20)
20. "You shall take oaths only in God's Name" (Deut. 10:20)
21. "You shall not listen to one who prophesies in the name of the gods of others" (Deut. 13:3-4)
22. "You shall not practice divination" (Deut. 18:10)
23. "You shall not practice astrology" (Deut. 18:10)
24. "You shall not read omens or practice sorcery" (Deut. 18:10)
25. "You shall not practice the art of an animal charmer" (Deut. 18:11)
26. "You shall not practice necromancy by inquiring of Ov" (Deut. 18:11)
27. "You shall not practice necromancy by inquiring of Yidoni" (Deut. 18:11)
28. "You shall not to necromancy by consulting the dead" (Deut. 18:11)
29. "You shall hearken to the Prophet" (Deut. 18:15)
30. "You shall not speak in the name of the gods of others" (Deut. 18:20)
31. "You shall not speak falsely in the Name of God" (Deut. 18:20)
32. "You shall not fear the false prophet" (Deut. 18:22)

TORAH

33. "You shall teach the Torah thoroughly to your children and you shall speak of the commands while you sit in your home, while you walk on the way" (Deut. 6:7)
34. "You shall bind the Torah on your head" (Tefillin)(Deut. 6:8)
35. "You shall bind the Torah on your hand" (Tefillin)(Deut. 6:8)
36. "You shall write the Torah on doorposts and your gates" (Mezuzah)(Deut. 6:9)
37. "You shall not test the LORD you God" (Deut. 6:16)
38. "You shall not add to the commandments of Torah" (Deut. 13:1)
39. "You shall not subtract from the commandments of Torah" (Deut. 13:1)
40. "You shall observe God's Torah and walk in His ways" (Deut. 28:9)
41. "You shall write a copy of the Torah for yourself" (Deut. 31:19)

DIETARY

42. "You shall not eat the displaced sinew on the hip-socket" (Gen. 32:33)
43. "You shall not eat an animal that was torn" (Ex. 22:30)
44. "You shall not cook a young goat in its mother's milk" (Ex. 23:19)
45. "You shall not cook a young goat in the milk of its mother" (Ex. 34:26)
46. "You shall not eat the fat of oxen, sheep, or goats" (Lev. 7:23)
47. "You shall not consume any blood" (Lev. 7:26)
48. "You may eat the animal that has completely split hooves and chews the cud" (Lev. 11:2-8)
49. "You shall not eat the flesh or touch the carcass of any unclean animal" (Lev. 11:8)
50. "You may eat everything in the water that has fins and scales" (Lev. 11:9)
51. "You shall not eat anything unclean from the creatures in the water" (Lev. 11:11)

52. "You shall not eat any unclean bird" (Lev. 11:13)
53. "You may only eat a flying teeming creature that walks on four legs:one that has jumping legs above its legs" (Lev. 11:21)
54. "You shall not become contaminated by touching unclean carcasses" (Lev. 11:24)
55. "You shall not become contaminated by touching the carcasses of creeping creatures" (Lev. 11:29-31)
56. "You shall not become contaminated by consuming food or drink which has come into contacting with any unclean thing" (Lev. 11:34)
57. "You shall not eat any teeming creature which teems upon the ground" (Lev. 11:41)
58. "You shall not eat anything that creeps on its belly" (Lev. 11:42)
59. "You shall not eat anything that walks on four legs, or numerous legs" (Lev. 11:42)
60. "You shall not become contaminated through any teeming thing that creeps on the earth" (Lev. 11:43-44)
61. "You may eat from your cattle and flocks" (Deut. 12:21)
62. "You shall not eat the blood, the life with the meat" (Deut. 12:23)
63. "You shall not eat any abomination" (Deut. 14:3)
64. "You shall not eat any unclean animal" (Deut. 14:7)
65. "You may eat every clean bird" (Deut. 14:11)
66. "You shall not eat any flying swarming creature" (Deut. 14:19)
67. "You shall not eat any carcass" (Deut. 14:21)

SABBATH DAY

68. "You shall not leave your place to work on the Sabbath" (Ex. 16:29)
69. "You shall remember the Sabbath day to sanctify" (Ex. 20:8)
70. "You shall not do any work on the Sabbath" (Ex. 20:10)
71. "You shall accomplish your work on six days and rest on the Sabbath" (Ex. 23:12)

72. "You shall desist from plowing and harvesting on the Sabbath" (Ex. 34:21)
73. "You shall not kindle fire in any of your dwellings on the Sabbath day" (Ex. 35:3)

FEAST DAYS AND FESTIVALS

74. "You shall observe the New Moon and the beginning of the months" (Ex. 12:2)
75. "You shall nullify the leaven from your homes on the day before Passover" (Ex. 12:15)
76. "You shall observe a holy convocation on the first day of Passover" (Ex. 12:16)
77. "You shall not do any work on the first day of Passover" (Ex. 12:16)
78. "You shall observe a holy convocation on the seventh day of Passover" (Ex. 12:16)
79. "You shall not do any work on the seventh day of Passover" (Ex. 12:16)
80. "You shall eat Matzot on the first night of Passover" (Ex. 12:18)
81. "You shall not possess or eat leaven during the seven days of Passover" (Ex. 12:19)
82. "You shall not eat chametz on Passover" (Ex. 13:3)
83. "You shall eat Matzot for the seven days of Passover" (Ex. 13:7)
84. "You shall not have chametz in your possession or leaven in your borders during Passover" (Ex. 13:7)
85. "You shall tell the story of the Ex. on Passover" (Ex. 13:8)
86. "You shall afflict yourselves on Yom Kippur" (Lev. 16:29)
87. "You shall have a Sabbath of complete rest on Yom Kippur" (Lev. 16:29, 31)
88. "You shall count the Omer, seven weeks from First Fruits, until the morrow, 50 days" (Lev. 23:15)
89. "You shall have a holy convocation on Shavuot" (Lev. 23:21)
90. "Not to do no laborious work on Shavuot" (Lev. 23:21)

91. "You shall have a holy convocation; a remembrance with shofars blasts on Yom Teruah" (Lev. 23:24)
92. "You shall not do any laborious work on Yom Teruah" (Lev. 23:25)
93. "You shall not do any work on Yom Kippur" (Lev. 23:29)
94. "You shall have a holy convocation on the first day of Sukkot" (Lev. 23:35)
95. " You shall not do any work on the first day of Sukkot" (Lev. 23:35)
96. "You shall have a holy convocation on the eighth day of Sukkot" (Shemini Atzeret) (Lev. 23:36)
97. "You shall not do any work on the eighth day of Sukkot" (Lev. 23:36)
98. "You shall count seven cycles of Sabbatical years; 49 years" (Lev. 25:8)
99. "You shall sound the Shofar on Yom Kippur for the Jubilee year" (Yovel) (Lev. 25:9)
100. "You shall sanctify the 50th year and proclaim freedom throughout the Land" (Lev. 25:10)
101. "You shall not eat leavened bread with the Passover" (Deut. 16:3)
102. "You shall rejoice on your Festivals" (Deut. 16:14)

IDOLATRY

103. "You shall not make for yourself carved images" (Ex. 20:4)
104. "You shall not bow down to carved images" (Ex. 20:5)
105. "You shall not worship carved images" (Ex. 20:5)
106. "You shall not make images of gods of silver or gods of gold" (Ex. 20:20)
107. "You shall not make molten gods for yourself" (Lev. 19:4)
108. "You shall not turn to the idols" (Lev. 19:4)
109. "You shall not turn to the sorcery of the Ovot or Yid'onim" (Lev. 19:31)
110. "You shall not become unclean through the sorcery of the Ovot or Yid'onim" (Lev. 19:31)

111. "You shall not take the silver and gold from the carved images of gods" (Deut. 7:25)
112. "You shall not bring an abomination into your home" (Deut. 7:26)
113. "You shall not accede to one who entices you secretly" (Deut. 13:9)
114. "You shall not hearken to one who entices you secretly" (Deut. 13:9)
115. "You shall not take pity on one who entices you secretly" (Deut. 13:9)
116. "You shall not be compassionate to one who entices you secretly" (Deut. 13:9)
117. "You shall not conceal one who entices you secretly" (Deut. 13:9)
118. "You shall not allow one who entices to do such an evil thing again in your midst" (Deut. 13:12)
119. "You shall not take anything from a city that worships the gods of others" (Deut. 13:18)

NIDDAH AND PURITY

120. "You shall be fruitful and multiply, fill the earth and subdue it" (Gen. 1:28)
121. "You shall circumcise every male among you" (Gen. 17:10)
122. "A woman who gives birth to a male shall be ritually unclean for seven days; for 33 days she shall remain in blood of purification. If she gives birth to a female, she shall be ritually unclean for fourteen days; for 66 days she shall remain in blood of purification" (Lev. 12:2-5)
123. "A man who has a discharge from his flesh shall be contaminated" (Zav)(Lev. 15:2)
124. "Anyone who sits on the seat of a zav shall be contaminated until evening" (Lev. 15:6)

125. "A man who has a discharge of semen shall immerse his flesh in water and remain contaminated until evening" (Lev. 15:16)
126. "A woman with a discharge of blood shall remain in her state of separation for a seven-day period" (Lev. 15:19)
127. "A woman who has a discharge of blood outside her period of separation shall remain contaminated" (Zavah)(Lev. 15:25)
128. "You shall not approach your close relative to uncover nakedness" (Lev. 18:6)
129. "You shall not uncover the nakedness of your father" (Lev. 18:7)
130. "You shall not uncover the nakedness of your mother" (Lev. 18:7)
131. "You shall not uncover the nakedness of your father's wife" (Lev. 18:8)
132. "You shall not uncover the nakedness of your sister" (Lev. 18:9)
133. "You shall not uncover the nakedness of your son's daughter" (Lev. 18:10)
134. "You shall not uncover the nakedness of your daughter's daughter" (Lev. 18:10)
135. "You shall not uncover the nakedness of your daughter" (Lev. 18:10)
136. "You shall not uncover the nakedness of your father's wife's daughter" (Lev. 18:11)
137. "You shall not uncover the nakedness of your father's sister" (Lev. 18:12)
138. "You shall not uncover the nakedness of your mother's sister" (Lev. 18:13)
139. "You shall not uncover the nakedness of the wife of your father's brother" (Lev. 18:14)
140. "You shall not lie carnally with your father's brother" (Lev. 18:14)
141. "You shall not uncover the nakedness of your son's wife" (Lev. 18:15)
142. "You shall not uncover the nakedness of your brother's wife" (Lev. 18:16)
143. "You shall not uncover the nakedness of a woman and her daughter" (Lev. 18:17)
144. "You shall not uncover the nakedness of a woman and her son's daughter" (Lev. 18:17)

145. "You shall not uncover the nakedness of a woman and her daughter's daughter" (Lev. 18:17)
146. "You shall not uncover the nakedness of a woman in addition to her sister, to make them rivals, in her lifetime"(Lev. 18:18)
147. "You shall not uncover the nakedness of a woman in her time of separation" (Niddah)(Lev. 18:19)
148. "You shall not lie carnally with your neighbor's wife" (Lev. 18:20)
149. "A man shall not lie carnally with another man, it is an abomination" (Lev. 18:22)
150. "You shall not lie with any animal" (Lev. 18:23)
151. "A woman shall not stand before an animal for mating, it is a perversion" (Lev. 18:23)
152. "You shall not mate your animal into another species" (Lev. 19:19)
153. "You shall not round off the edge of your scalp" (Lev. 19:27)
154. "You shall not destroy the edge of your beard" (Lev. 19:27)
155. "You shall not place a tattoo upon yourself" (Lev. 19:28)
156. "Anything within the dwelling of a corpse shall be contaminated for seven days" (Num. 19:14)
157. "You shall not cut your flesh for a dead person" (Deut. 14:1)
158. "You shall not make a bald spot between your eyes for a dead person" (Deut. 14:1)
159. "Male garb shall not be on a woman" (Deut. 22:5)
160. "A man shall not wear a woman's garment" (Deut. 22:5)
161. "You shall not plow with an ox and a donkey together" (Deut. 22:10)
162. "You shall not wear combined fibers; wool and linen together" (Deut. 22:11)
163. "A man who issues a slander against a virgin of Israel shall be punished" (Deut. 22:18-19)
164. "A man who issues a slander against a virgin of Israel shall not divorce her all his days" (Deut. 22:19)
165. "A man shall marry the virgin he has violated and give her father fifty silver shekels" (Deut. 22:29)
166. "A man shall not divorce the virgin he has married" (Deut. 22:29)

167. "You shall carry a shovel with your weapons to bury excrement" (Deut. 23:14)
168. "There shall not be a promiscuous woman among the daughters of Israel" (Deut. 23:18)
169. "There shall not be a promiscuous man among the sons of Israel" (Deut. 23:18)
170. "You shall observe the laws of marriage and divorce" (Deut. 24:1)
171. "The bill of divorce shall be a written document" (Deut. 24:1)
172. "You shall not remarry your divorced wife after she has remarried another man" (Deut. 24:4)

COMMUNITY

173. "You shall honor your father and your mother" (Ex. 20:12)
174. "You shall not murder" (Ex. 20:13)
175. "You shall not bear false witness against your neighbor" (Ex. 20:14)
176. "You shall not covet your neighbor's house. You shall not covet your neighbor's wife, his manservant, his maidservant, his ox, his donkey, nor anything that belongs to your neighbor" (Ex. 20:14)
177. "You shall not strike your father or mother" (Ex. 21:15)
178. "You shall not kidnap" (Ex. 21:16)
179. "You shall not curse your father or mother" (Ex. 21:17)
180. "You shall exact the penalties for a person inflicting injury" (Ex. 21:18)
181. "You shall observe the penalties for injuries caused by an animal" (Ex. 21:28)
182. "You shall not eat the flesh of a condemned ox" (Ex. 21:28)
183. "You shall exact the penalties for injuries caused by a pit" (Ex. 21:33-34)
184. "You shall observe the law for the punishment of thieves" (Ex. 21:37-22:3)
185. "You shall exact the penalties for damage caused by an animal" (Ex. 22:4)

186. "You shall exact the penalties for damage caused by a fire" (Ex. 22:5)
187. "You shall observe the law for the guardian of another's property" (Ex. 22:6-8)
188. "The guilty party shall pay double for every item of liability" (Ex. 22:8)
189. "You shall observe the law for the guardian of another's animals" (Ex. 22:9-12)
190. "You shall observe the law for the borrower of another's possessions" (Exodus 22:13)
191. "You shall not taunt or oppress a stranger" (Ex. 22:20)
192. "You shall not cause pain to any widow or orphan" (Ex. 22:21)
193. "You shall lend money to the poor of your people without interest" (Ex. 22:24)
194. "You shall not demand payment from a debtor who is unable to pay" (Ex. 22:24)
195. "You shall not act as a creditor in an agreement involving interest" (Ex. 22:24)
196. "You shall not curse a leader among your people" (Ex. 22:27)
197. "You shall not accept a false report" (Ex. 23:1)
198. "You shall not extend your hand with the wicked to be a venal witness" (Ex. 23:1)
199. "You shall not be a follower of the majority for evil, or pervert the law by yielding to the majority" (Ex. 23:2)
200. "You shall not pervert the law by yielding to the majority" (Ex. 23:2)
201. "You shall not glorify a destitute person in his grievance" (Ex. 23:3)
202. "You shall help unload a donkey crouching under its burden" (Ex. 23:5)
203. "You shall not refrain from helping a man or donkey crouching under its burden" (Ex. 23:5)
204. "You shall not pervert the judgment of your destitute person in his grievance" (Ex. 23:6)
205. "You shall not execute the innocent or the righteous" (Ex. 23:7)
206. "You shall not accept a bribe" (Ex. 23:8)

207. "A person who is a witness shall testify" (Lev. 5:1)
208. "A robber shall restore the article or principal and add its fifth to it" (Lev. 5:23)
209. "You shall revere your mother and father" (Lev. 19:3)
210. "You shall not steal" (Lev. 19:11)
211. "You shall not deny falsely" (Lev. 19:11)
212. "You shall not lie to one another" (Lev. 19:11)
213. "You shall not retain a worker's wage overnight until morning" (Lev. 19:13)
214. "You shall not rob" (Lev. 19:13)
215. "You shall not cheat your neighbor" (Lev. 19:13)
216. "You shall not curse the deaf" (Lev. 19:14)
217. "You shall not place a stumbling block before the blind" (Lev. 19:14)
218. "You shall judge your neighbor with righteousness" (Lev. 19:15)
219. "You shall not commit a perversion of justice" (Lev. 19:15)
220. "You shall not favor the poor in a perversion of justice" (Lev. 19:15)
221. "You shall not honor the wealthy in a perversion of justice" (Lev. 19:15)
222. "You shall not be a gossipmonger" (Lev. 19:16)
223. "You shall not stand aside while your neighbor's blood is shed" (Lev. 19:16)
224. "You shall reprove your neighbor and not bear a sin because of him" (Lev. 19:17)
225. "You shall not hate your brother in your heart" (Lev. 19:17)
226. "You shall not put another to shame" (Lev. 19:17)
227. "You shall love your neighbor as yourself" (Lev. 19:18)
228. "You shall not take revenge" (Lev. 19:18)
229. "You shall not bear a grudge" (Lev. 19:18)
230. "You shall rise in the presence of the old" (Lev. 19:32)
231. "You shall honor the presence of the wise" (Lev. 19:32)
232. "You shall not commit a perversion in measurements" (Lev. 19:35)
233. "You shall not commit a perversion in weights" (Lev. 19:35)
234. "You shall have correct scales, correct weights, and correct measures" (Lev. 19:36)

235. "You shall not aggrieve one another in your buying and selling" (Lev. 25:14)
236. "You shall not aggrieve your neighbor" (Lev. 25:17)
237. "You shall not give your brother your money for interest" (Lev. 25:37)
238. "You shall not give your brother your food for increase" (Lev. 25:37)
239. "You shall fulfill the words of your mouth" (Num. 30:3)
240. "You shall not desecrate your word" (Num. 30:3)
241. "You shall not show favoritism in judgment" (Deut. 1:17)
242. "You shall not tremble before any man in judgment" (Deut. 1:17)
243. "You shall not covet your neighbor's possessions" (Deut. 5:18)
244. "You shall love the proselyte for you were strangers" (Deut. 10:19)
245. "You shall not harden your heart or close your hand against your destitute brother" (Deut. 15:7)
246. "You shall open your hand and lend whatever is lacking" (Deut. 15:8)
247. "A single witness shall not stand up against any man for any iniquity, error, or sin" (Deut. 19:15)
248. "You shall not destroy the fruit trees, even in time of war" (Deut. 20:19)
249. "You shall return the lost property of your brother" (Deut. 22:1)
250. "You shall not hide yourself from any by lost property of your brother" (Deut. 22:3)
251. "You shall assist the donkey or ox falling on the road" (Deut. 22:4)
252. "You shall not to take the mother bird with her young" (Deut. 22:6)
253. "You shall set free the mother bird when taking the young" (Deut. 22:7)
254. "You shall make a fence for your roof so your will not place blood in your house if a fallen one falls from it" (Deut. 22:8)
255. "You shall not leave obstacles on a path" (Deut. 22:8)
256. "You shall observe and carry out what emerges from your lips" (Deut. 23:24)
257. "You shall not cause your brother to take interest" (Deut. 23:20)
258. "You may cause a gentile to take interest" (Deut. 23:21)

259. "You shall not take a lower or upper millstone as a pledge" (Deut. 24:6)
260. "You shall not enter your neighbor's home to take collateral for a debt" (Deut. 24:10)
261. "You shall not sleep with a poor man's collateral" (Deut. 24:12)
262. "You shall return the collateral of a poor man when the sun sets" (Deut. 24:13)
263. "You shall pay a worker his wages on the day of his hire" (Deut. 24:15)
264. "Fathers shall not be put to death because of sons, and sons shall not be put to death because of fathers" (Deut. 24:16)
265. "You shall not pervert the judgment of a proselyte or orphan" (Deut. 24:17)
266. "You shall not take the garment of a widow as collateral" (Deut. 24:17)
267. "You shall not muzzle an ox in its threshing" (Deut. 25:4)
268. "The brother of a man who dies childless shall marry his brother's wife" (Levirate Marriage)(Deut. 25:5)
269. "The childless widow shall not marry anyone except her late husband's brother" (Deut. 25:5)
270. "You shall release the childless widow if her late husband's brother refuses to marry her" (Deut. 25:9)
271. "You shall not possess false weights and measures" (Deut. 25:13)

RECOMMENDED RESOURCES

To order any of the resources listed on the following pages, please call 1-866-TORAH-TV or visit store.torah.tv by scanning the QR code using your smartphone.

ADDITIONAL WORKS FROM THE AUTHOR

TORAH 101®

An Introduction to the Hebrew Roots of Your Faith

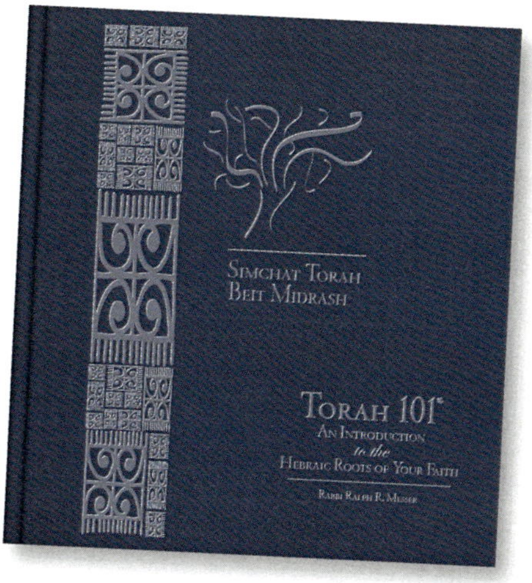

STBM's Award-winning Torah 101® Textbook. Hardcover and full-color design creates a striking companion textbook that appeals to every type of student, especially the audio-visual learner. Including on-screen material and room for note-taking, the Torah 101® Companion Textbook is a finely-crafted component of the complete ICTS curriculum.

Torah 101®–An Introduction to the Hebrew Roots of Your Faith, $125.00/#15000; ICTS Torah 101® student discount, $75.00

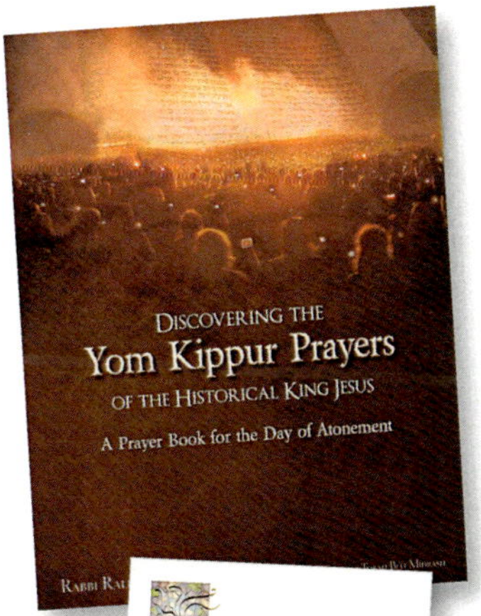

YOM KIPPUR PRAYERS

STBM's own Yom Kippurim Prayer book. Now you can follow along as we go through the Yom Kippurim prayers. Our new prayer book gives the the distinctive Simchat Torah perspective to these fabulous prayers.

Yom Kippur Prayer Book, $10.00/#2518

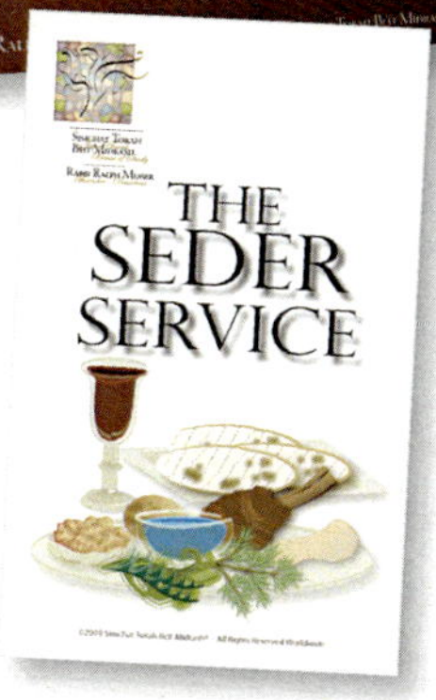

THE SEDER SERVICE

Simchat Torah's version of the Passover Haggadah. Celebrate deliverance from bondage through Yeshua Ha'Mashiach.

Soft-cover, $5.00/#894; Buy 4–get 1 free, $20.00; Buy 8–get 2 free, $40.00

FEATURED TEACHINGS BY RABBI MESSER

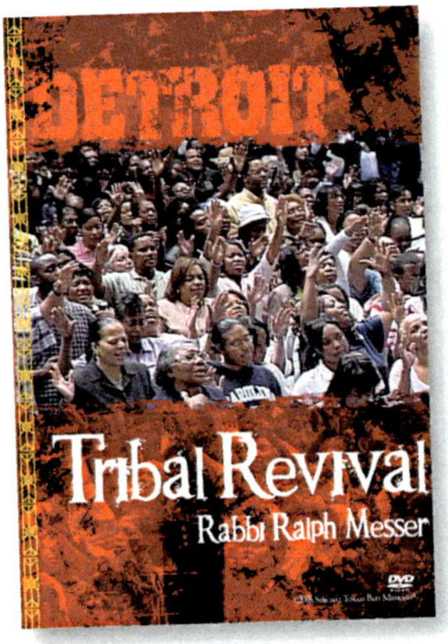

DETROIT TRIBAL REVIVAL

Rabbi Messer's breakthrough teachings from Word of Faith International Christian Center in Detroit, Michigan. Over a series of weeks Rabbi took the city of Detroit by storm, calling down strongholds, and strongly-held misconceptions. It's a Journey of Hebrew Roots and Black Heritage from Africa to present day.

Detroit Tribal Revival DVD, $43.00/#3249

ONE GOD

"Hear O Israel, the Lord our God, the Lord is One!" (Deuteronomy 6:4) How does this foundational concept in Judaism fit with a mainstream Christian teaching of the Trinity? If God is One, then Who did Jesus pray to? You'll be challenged and changed as Rabbi Messer teaches you about Yeshua, Adonai, and Elohim.

One God DVD, $15.00/#127
One God CD, $8.00/#2260
One God Study Course, $36.00/#1567

TORAH: LAW OR GRACE?

How did we come to view Judaism as a religion of law and works while Christianity is viewed as a religion of faith and grace? Follow Rabbi Ralph Messer through the history of the Western church and see how the heresy of one age becomes the orthodoxy of the next.

Torah: Law or Grace? DVD, $43.00/#3248
Torah: Law or Grace? CD, $22.00/#2788

THE VOICE OF THE PRINCIPLES, VOL. 1 & 2

Have the commandments in the Old Testament been replaced by faith in Yeshua? Yeshua speaks through the Principles, the Principles speak through the Holy Spirit, and the Holy Spirit speaks to you! Volume 2 of Rabbi Messer's inspiring series on walking in Faith, the Holy Spirit, and the 613 Principles of Torah.

The Voice of the Principles, Vol. 1 DVD, $29.00/#4276; Vol. 1 CD, $15.00/#4277; The Voice of the Principles, Vol. 2 DVD, $36.00/#4525; Vol. 2 CD, $19.00/#4526

HOW TO WITNESS THE TORAH, VOLUME 1

Many have never heard the word "Torah." Others see Torah as outdated religious observance that Jesus came to do away with. So how can you witness the Torah to others? Your witness of His Word can manifest His Ways—raising the dead to new life!

How to Witness the Torah DVD, $57.00/#3979
How to Witness the Torah CD, $29.00/#3980

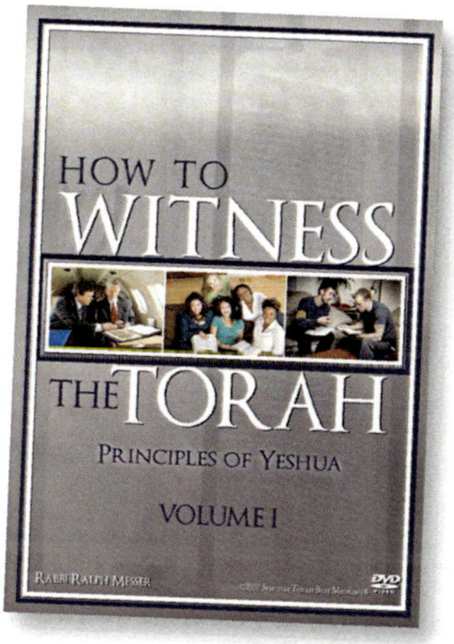

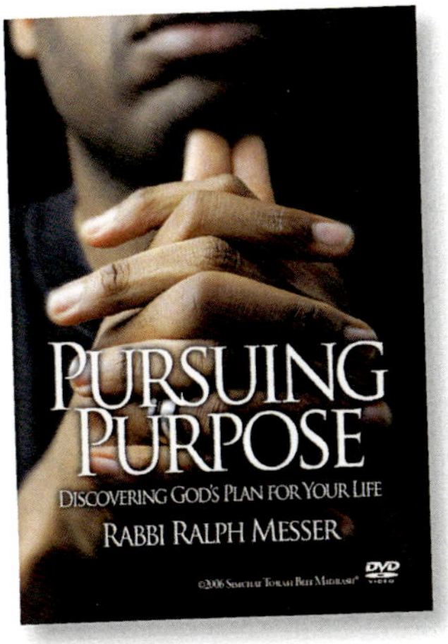

PURSUING PURPOSE

Does God's plan for your life lie hidden within your deepest desire? Pursuing Your Purpose will help you step into Eternity and take hold of your future!

Pursuing Purpose DVD, $29.00/#1105
Pursuing Purpose CD, $15.00/#2462

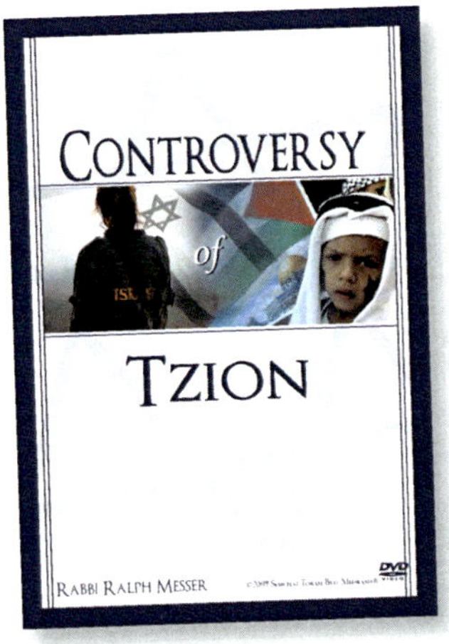

CONTROVERSY OF TZION

While international pressure continues to increase surrounding the Land of Israel, God is preparing His bride and restoring Israel as the Promised Land.

Controversy of Tzion DVD, $29.00/#3937
Controversy of Tzion CD, $15.00/#3938

LAZARUS RAISED

In Lazarus Raised, you'll hear the Lord speaking prophetically—3,500 years into the future—calling You forth, from death into Life! Listen to the Davidic heart of Rabbi Ralph Messer as he brings the beauty and truth of our identity into focus. Hear how he weaves the living Word of God into a beautiful tapestry of who you are and what His ultimate destiny is for you.

Lazarus Raised DVD, $22.00/#1929;
Lazarus Raised CD, $12.00/#2262
Lazarus Raised Study Course, $42.00/#1715

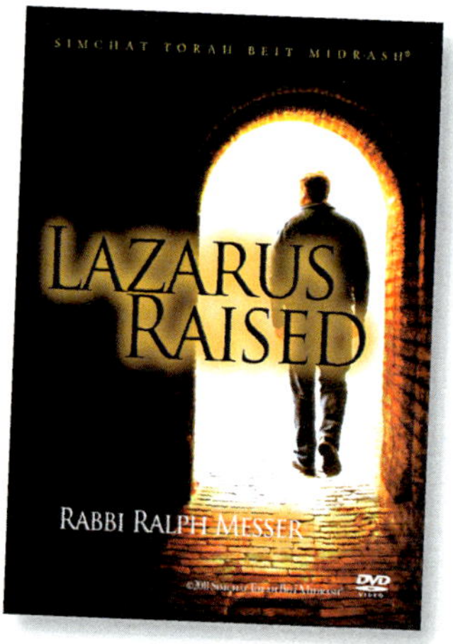

BRINGING HONOR IN THE MIDST OF JEZEBEL

Jezebel manifests to undermine Godly authority. Learn how to bring honor to God first by honoring those around you.

Bringing Honor in the Midst of Jezebel DVD, $29.00/#3891; Bringing Honor in the Midst of Jezebel CD, $15.00/#3892

ALSO FROM SIMCHAT TORAH BEIT MIDRASH

WEEKLY TEACHING SUBSCRIPTIONS

Experience what it's like to sit in a live service at Simchat Torah Beit Midrash! See and feel Rabbi Messer's passion, excitement and energy as he delivers God's Word to the Nations. Perfect for the audio-visual learner—Rabbi Messer's teachings are delivered to your mailbox every month. All of our teachings are made available on DVD, CD or as an online subscription at www.Torah.tv

LET IT RAIN!

Weekly Shabbat Service
DVD Subscription: $50.00/month #1234
Audio CD Subscription: $30.00/month #1234
Let It Rain™ Online Subscription: $19.99/month #1234
Let It Rain!™ Home & Go™: $65.00/month #1234

GIDEON 300 CLUB

Weekly Torah Study
Complete Year–Over 5,000 hours of teaching
Year 1–DVD set: $475.00 #3022; CD set: $230.00 #3033
Year 2–DVD set: $475.00 #3772; CD set: $230.00 #3773
Year 3–DVD set: $475.00 #3837; CD set: $230.00 #3838

ALSO FROM SIMCHAT TORAH BEIT MIDRASH®

16-MONTH HEBREW LIFESTYLE CALENDAR & STUDY GUIDE

A powerful witnessing tool, loaded with teaching, to minister truth and encourage others! This year's calendar is presented in two versions: one teaching on God's Principles and Increasing Honor and the second on our popular Torah in the Womb teaching. Both calendar/study guides include a 90-minute teaching DVD.

16-Month Hebrew Lifestyle Calendar & Study Guide, $20.00/#4146
Torah in the Womb version, $20.00/#4250

HEBREW LIFESTYLE DESK PLANNER

Log your daily obedience from January to December in the fundamental principles and watch God take over your life to bring you abundant blessing! The theme of this year's planner is on God's Principles and Increasing Honor.

Hebrew Lifestyle Desk Planner, $20.00/#4020

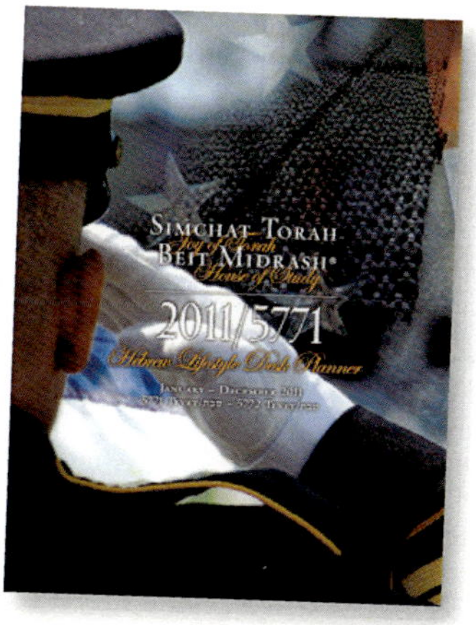

ALSO FROM SIMCHAT TORAH BEIT MIDRASH

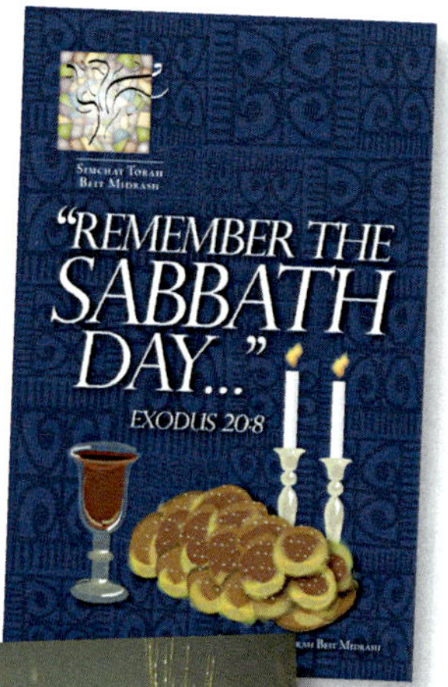

REMEMBER THE SABBATH DAY

Simchat Torah's own step by step guide to help you welcome the Shabbat and then close it with Havdalah.

Remember the Sabbath Day $5.00, #1928

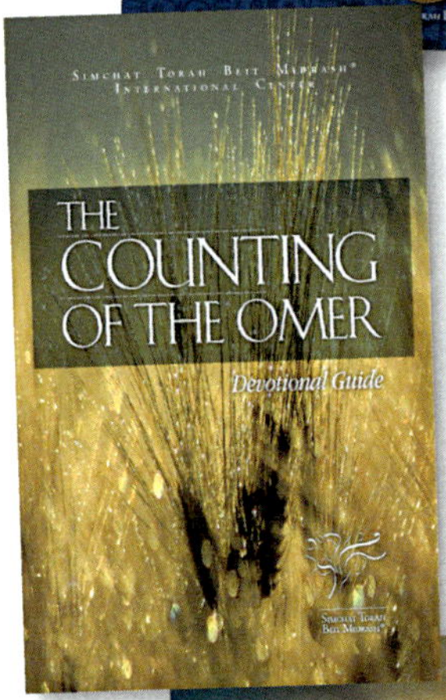

THE COUNTING OF THE OMER

Forty-nine days divide Passover from Shavuot/ Pentecost. This counting, called Sefirat Ha'Omer—"the Counting of the Omer" expresses anticipation of receiving the Torah.This devotional guide will walk you through this time of personal refinement and introspection in preparation for receiving the Torah.

The Counting of the Omer $19.99, #3601

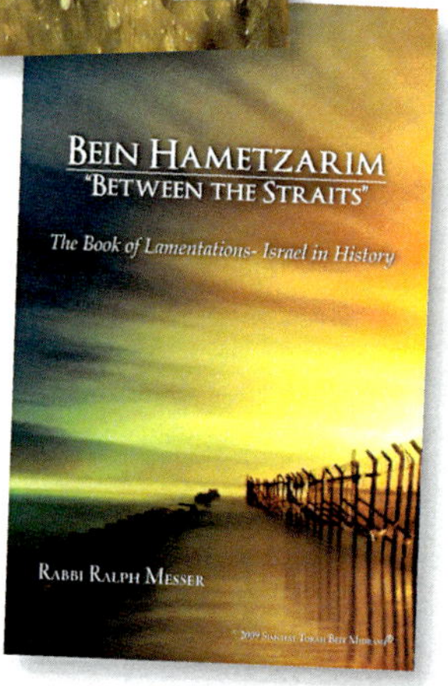

BEIN HAMETZARIM

The three weeks from the 17th of Tammuz until the 9th of Av are known as Bein Hametzarim—"Between the Straits." So called in the Book of Lamentations, this period has seen tragic events occur within the land of Israel and to her people throughout history. In this devotional guide developed for each day of Bein Hametzarim, Rabbi Messer recalls the promises of God—to favor Tzion, to rebuild the fallen Tabernacle of David, and to restore a humbled Nation for the glory of God.

Bein Hametzarim $5.00, #4550

SIMCHAT TORAH BEIT MIDRASH

INTERNATIONAL CENTER FOR TORAH STUDIES

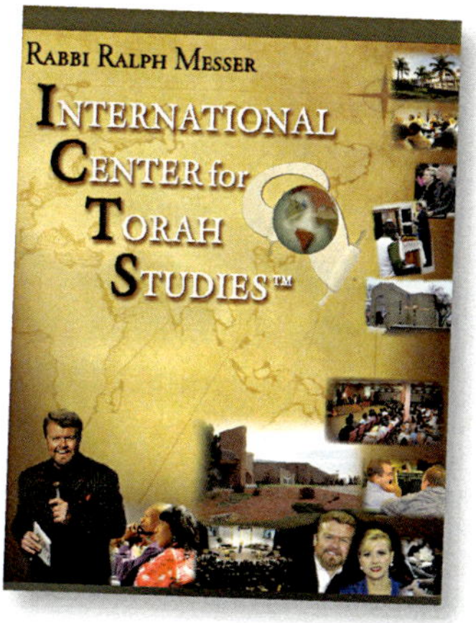

Explore the Hebrew Roots of Your Christian Faith—Torah 101® The International Center for Torah Studies (ICTS) is expanding classes. Learn the essentials about Hebrew Roots and deepen your understanding of the Bible, including the Hebrew life of Jesus Christ, and your identity in Him. ICTS offers multi-media, college-style courses, in an exciting classroom setting. Spring classes are filling up quickly and space is limited!

WALKING WITH YESHUA DISCIPLESHIP PROGRAM

Step 1—Walk with God

Step 2—Walk in the Knowledge of Messiah

Step 3—Walk Redeemed

Step 4—Walk in Covenant

Step 5—Walk in God's Ordained Cycle

Step 6—Walk and Study

Step 7—Walk and Learn

Step 8—Walk and Do

Step 9—Walk with Others

Step 10—Walk as a Nation

For more information, please call 1-866-TORAH-TV or visit www.onlinetorahschool.com

ABOUT THE AUTHOR

RABBI RALPH MESSER

Rabbi Ralph Messer is an internationally-acclaimed motivational speaker, best-selling author, lecturer, educator, business consultant, and teacher. Traveling extensively throughout the world, Rabbi Messer addresses critical issues affecting the spiritual and social development of individuals, families, and communities. The central theme of his message is the transformation of believers into Torah teachers and Sprit-filled leaders. As the President and Founder of Simchat Torah Beit Midrash® (STBM)—a congregation and school based in Colorado, Rabbi Messer, is pioneering a work to bring the "Good News" of Yeshua (Jesus Christ) in the Torah to the ends of the earth, fulfilling the great commission to *"...make disciples of all the nations"* (Matthew 28:19). Rabbi Messer is the executive producer and principal host of numerous radio and television programs aired worldwide.

Translated from Hebrew as 'The Joy of God's Teaching and Instruction/House of Study'—Simchat Torah Beit Midrash is a House of Joy, Worship, and Study. STBM is also a premier Publisher and Resource Center for Hebraic Materials, Bible courses, and curriculum. Rabbi Messer and STBM have received numerous ADDY Awards—the highest award in the graphic design industry—for artistic illustrations and publications. For more than 32 years, Rabbi Messer has facilitated inter-faith discussions between denominations, cultures, and various groups throughout Colorado, across the country, and internationally. Rabbi Messer also conducts leadership training conferences every spring and fall at the STBM International Center. The STBM Yeshiva (Hebrew day school), in support of Rabbi Messer's vision, teaches 'Torah in the Marketplace' to children and youth, teaching them from an early age to be 'deployed' rather than simply 'employed'. Rabbi Messer and STBM founded the International Center for Torah Studies (ICTS)—a multi-level discipleship program facilitating college-style courses in classrooms internationally, including online Biblical studies available exclusively through the STBM website: www.Torah.tv.

Prior to entering the ministry full-time as a Pastor and Teacher—'Rabbi', he was a Regional Vice President for a Fortune 500 company, specializing in Accounting, Business Administration, Finance, Banking, and the Credit Industries. As an entrepreneur, Rabbi Messer was the founder and President of Midwest Technical of Colorado, specializing in Loss Control and Risk Management for Insurance Companies nationwide. Along with his wife Maureen, Rabbi and Mrs. Messer have six children actively serving with them in ministry.